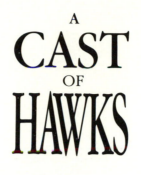

A
CAST
OF
HAWKS

San Francisco—View to the Plaza from northeast, 1850–51

San Francisco at night from Telegraph Hill, 1875

A
CAST
OF
HAWKS

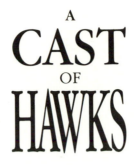

*A Rowdy Tale of Greed, Violence, Scandal, and Corruption
in the Early Days of San Francisco*

By Milton S. Gould

A COPLEY BOOK
COMMISSIONED BY HELEN K. COPLEY

Copley Books, a division of The Copley Press, Inc.
7776 Ivanhoe Avenue, La Jolla, California 92037

Library of Congress Cataloging in Publication Data

Gould, Milton S.
   A cast of hawks.

   Bibliography: p.
   Includes Index.
   1. Frontier and pioneer life—California—San
Francisco. 2. San Francisco (Calif.)—History.
3. California—Gold discoveries. 4. San Francisco
Bay Area (Calif.)—History. I. Title.
F869.S357G68   1985   979.4′6   84-19885
ISBN 0-913938-28-9

Printed in the United States of America

DEDICATION

THIS IS NOT only a book about lawyers and judges and cases, it is about some of the most colorful Californians who peopled the state in its first fifty years. It affords new glimpses of the Vigilante Movement, the fight to bring California into the Confederacy, the fatal duel between Judge Terry and Senator Broderick, and finally, perhaps the most bizarre case in California's legal history—the Sharon-Hill litigation and its terrible aftermath. As the characters and events pass before your eyes, what really emerges is a portrait of that effulgent half-century from the crudities of the Gold Rush days to the rearing of a robust Pacific society. To know and understand the characters in this volume is to know and understand the bedrock on which California of today is built. To those glittering figures whose careers are traced in this book, those exemplars of the state's early years, all of whom left their mark on the new world of the Far West, this book is dedicated.

HELEN K. COPLEY

CONTENTS

FOREWORD

MILTON GOULD'S digging into the legends, political struggles and court records of California and bringing them so vividly to life is a remarkable feat. The quest for power and wealth, the struggle for and against the Union and slavery between settlers from Tennessee and Mississippi, and those from Boston and New York, political, financial and sexual scandals, are played out in the courts and replayed across the nation by telegraph and newspapers. There are dramatic confrontations in which frontier lawyers and harlots, United States senators and state governors, a justice of the United States Supreme Court and his former colleague on California's highest bench, railway moguls and other tycoons go at it with pistols and Bowie knives, bribery and perjury, showmanship and legal scholarship, sex and booze. The scene shifts from statehouse to brothel, from law court to saloon, from mining and railroad project to hotel bedroom and gilded estate. It all winds up in a madhouse. This is a veritable Greek tragedy spun out by a modern Sophocles robed as a lawyer.

The reader will be dazzled by the author's prodigious research, his rich narrative skill, the nuggets of classical, legal and historical allusions he sprinkles as he develops the story. He may also be puzzled about why and how a New York lawyer in great demand for his skills and wisdom resurrected this history and created the fascinating tale. The why is satisfactorily explained as "to cure a persistent itch to tell the entire tale." How he found the time will forever remain a mystery. But don't read any more of my words. Read the first few pages and stay up half the night and the next one to finish it.

WILLIAM J. CASEY
Director,
Central Intelligence Agency

PREFACE

AS I WROTE THIS BOOK and talked to people about its content, I heard one persistent question: Why should a New York lawyer, fully occupied in his profession, devote himself to events which occurred in San Francisco between 1849 and the end of the century? The answer is simple: I could not resist the story.

There is a reason for the writing of every book. It may be as simple as the author's hope that by enticing and entertaining a multitude of readers, the book will earn bread for the writer and his family, or, as Scott wrote, "for the general amusement." As this book took shape, I was often troubled about its character and content, but I have never doubted my reason for writing it. Samuel Johnson said that no man but a blockhead ever wrote, except for money. If the great man was correct, I am a blockhead. Assuredly, this book was not written to earn money, but to cure a persistent itch to tell the entire tale. For almost fifty years the people and events described in this volume and the mysteries that encrust some of these events have fascinated me. Over the years I have made at least two false starts at writing about them. Always, I was driven off the track by the intrusion of lawyer's work or revulsion to the drudgery of the required research. Recently, encouraged by the friendly reception accorded some of my literary reflections, I have surrendered to the impulse I felt almost fifty years ago. Thus, this chronicle of the bizarre.

My interest in the events that make up this tale of the tragically-entwined lives of Terry, Broderick, Sharon, Sarah Althea Hill and Field was kindled in 1932 when I was a student at the Cornell Law School. For a course in Constitutional Law, I read Mr. Justice Miller's singular opinion in In re *Neagle,* written in 1890. *Neagle* is a "landmark" case in American constitutional law. It defines the liability of federal officers who, in performing their duties, are charged with violating state laws. This area of constitutional law has become so important that the torrent of exegesis that flows from *Neagle* has muffled the story behind the case. I remember standing in the stacks of the Cornell law library, enthralled by the abnormally extensive exposition of the facts in the majority opinion, so patently irrelevant to the decision. What swam into my ken was shattering. Too much! Incredible! What a yarn! Strange events must lie behind this departure from judicial norms. I resolved to ferret out the full story behind the opinion and write it all down. The task was put off for decades, but the story has lain heavy in my breast, and for almost five decades I have reached eagerly for the bits and pieces that I occasionally encountered.

Why do it now? Has not the story been told? Indeed it has, over and over again. There is almost no part of this tale which has not been recited somewhere. Nor am I the first lawyer to be enticed by the saga of Terry and Broderick, of Sharon and Sarah Althea, of Field and Neagle. Others have succumbed to the fascination of the tale. My readers are referred to the Bibliographical Sketch which appears on page 339 and describes the books and articles which have been written on this subject. Of course, I have borrowed from many of these books; I hope that I have applied what I found in them with some wit and invention. The greatest writer in our tongue has been charged with his debts to other authors. Hopefully, I am entitled to a small measure of Landor's defense of the Bard: "He breathed upon dead bodies and brought them to life."

I concluded that none of the prior works adequately portrayed the full tapestry, the bizarre intertwining of careers that make up the tale. That judges and senators should consort with whores and brothel-keepers is hardly unique; that generals and admirals should contend with miners and embattled citizens is not novel; that governors, filibusters, pistoleros, rascals and heroes meet up in statehouse and saloon is not news. The novelty and interest of this book are to be found, I think, in the procession of characters, notable and notorious, that march across the tableau of California in the first half-century after the American conquest. Great and familiar names appear: Lincoln, Sherman, Farragut, Frémont, Buchanan, Stephen A. Douglas, Leland Stanford, Huntington, Mark Hopkins, the teacher, and his namesake, the great railroad builder, the members of the versatile Field family and many others are seen in the background. But in the foreground there is a compelling story in a strange assortment of star-crossed adventurers, ranging from a justice of the United States Supreme Court who aspired to the presidency of the Republic, to a voodoo priestess. Their parts are played out against a Bayeux-like spectacle that depicts the rise of San Francisco, the criminal excesses that engendered vigilantism, life in the mining camps, the struggle between secessionists and Unionists to control the West, duels, murders, chicanery, the emergence of the Bonanza Kings and their comic pretensions to grandeur, the depredations of the Railroad Trust, the persecution of Orientals. Finally, there is the story of the Sharon-Hill litigation which brought death to Terry and drove Sarah Althea to madness.

I have tried to compress the tale, with its richness, its folly, and its glory into a single volume that will satisfy and entertain the tastes of a "general" reader, without sacrificing accuracy for effect. The temptation to fictionalize was strong, but I have rejected it in favor of "history." I have denied myself the trick of Thucydides who put into the mouths of his historical characters words he invented appropriate to their thoughts and the events. Nor have I imitated Herodotus, who improvised facts to suit the characters. Where I have set out dialogue, it is usually authentic, taken verbatim from words reported with comparative reliability in sworn testimony of witnesses or in contemporary newspaper reports.

There are three mysteries in this tale: Was Senator Broderick the victim of a deliberate murder plot in which Judge Terry planned to kill? Was

Terry, in his turn, the target of a murder planned by Field, a justice of the United States Supreme Court, abetted by some of the highest federal officials in the land? The third mystery, and perhaps the most intriguing, is in the personality of Sarah Althea Hill Sharon Terry. Was she a maid abused? Was she a whore? Certainly, she combined with great beauty a flair for attracting men to her murky purposes. By the standards of her time and ours, she emerges as a greedy courtesan and a clumsy cheat.

Three times in his life, Terry became the central character in "murder": first, when he stabbed Hopkins, the vigilante sergeant at arms; next in the Broderick duel, which most historians accept as a deliberate homicide; finally in his own slaying at Neagle's hands, recorded as justifiable homicide, but perceived by many as the climax of a carefully-designed assassination plot. I have tried to maintain a balanced judgment on all three events, recognizing that history has been over-generous to Broderick and Field and over-harsh to Terry.

This book is a study of men and women whose excesses and aberrations invest them with heroic, villainous, picaresque, diverting and amusing qualities. Hilaire Belloc has written that "readable history is melodrama." As I wrote this book, the melodrama leaped out of the tale, and the background became as important as the story. The events which make up the tale could only have happened in that special world of the West that grew up in the second half of the last century. Its people are the children of that world and the story is of a confluence of characters and careers nurtured in their own milieu, shaped by their standards, and punished in the end, by their own peculiar codes.

M. S. G.

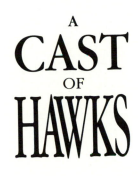

A
CAST
OF
HAWKS

*An 1847 lithograph depicting San Francisco, then called Yerba Buena,
prior to the Gold Rush*

I

SAN FRANCISCO: 1849

They swam the wide rivers and crossed the tall peaks,
And camped on the prairies for weeks upon weeks,
Starvation and cholera and hard work and slaughter,
They reached California spite of hell and high water.
Contemporary California Song, circa 1849

This story happened in San Francisco and its environs in the years after 1849, when that strange and fascinating city began to grow around the great bay. Perhaps the events described could not have happened in any other place. Surely, the exotic society that grew up in this period was a perfect one for my people and their happenings.

Eighteen forty-nine was an eventful year in American history. Peace with Mexico had brought the vast West into the Union and the discovery of gold in California had excited a migration across continents and oceans that changed the face of America and the world. The Forty-niners came overland across the prairies, deserts and mountains; they sailed around the Horn; they trudged through the pestilential swamps of Panama and Nicaragua. They clawed their way by every route and every means of transportation to the new Golconda. For most the goal was the little fishing village of Yerba Buena on the great bay explored by Drake, where in 1806 the Russian admiral Rezanov had dropped his anchor and dreamed of a new empire for Russia.

Within a few months in 1849, there arose by the side of the Golden Gate a city with more than 25,000 souls, Europeans and Americans, Northerners and Southerners, convicts from Australia (the "Sydney Ducks"), deserting sailors, Kanakas, Chilenos, Chinese, swamping the handful of local Mexicans. It was the only gateway to the gold mines, and by the end of 1849, more than 100,000 people had passed through the city en route to the nearby mining camps. Gamblers and confidence men, prostitutes and criminals joined the vast army. Many of these remained in the city and contributed richly to its legends and its problems.

As the new settlement of tents and shacks arose in 1849, there appeared the first of the organized criminal bands that were to make San Francisco a hell by day and night for the next seven years. They called themselves "Regulators" or the "Hounds" — gangs of young toughs who committed murder, robbery and arson, unchecked by any effective police or authority. By summer, 1849, the few respectable citizens rose in protest, formed their own private constabulary and arrested most of the "Hounds." By 1850, the

"Hounds" had been broken up and exiled; no one was hanged, nor did the enforcers yet call themselves "vigilantes."

Emerson writes of America in the mid-nineteenth century as "a country of young men." San Francisco and its vicinage in the early 1850's would have seemed to him a city of children. In 1850 the average age of San Franciscans was twenty-five. Their pursuits and pleasures were those of the young. The air was filled with foolish prattle; political actions and reactions were impelled by "the brisk intemperance of youth. . . . There was scarcely a gray head to be seen." Out of 26,557 inhabitants of Calaveras and Yuba Counties, there were only 90 over the age of sixty. Social life centered in the gambling halls, saloons and brothels that sprang up everywhere, and the tone of life was raw, juvenile and violent.

In 1850, of our principal characters, David S. Terry was but twenty-six, David C. Broderick, twenty-nine, and Stephen J. Field, thirty-three. When J. Neely Johnson was elected governor in 1856 he was only twenty-seven. Henry Adams once wrote that young men have a passion for regarding their elders as senile. The young men of this story disdained every lesson of experience, of accumulated wisdom. We see these young men strutting about emitting their highfalutin platitudes about justice, patriotism, honor, virtue, in orotund phrases that mimic the high-flown prose of their elders in that time. But they deported themselves with the mindless violence of children in schoolyard brawls. They were boys released from all discipline and supervision. In the faded photographs that come down to us, they look like men, their eyes peer out from above beards and chin whiskers that to us signify maturity, but behind the foliage are the smooth cheeks of youth. Their very clothes, their clawhammer coats, boiled shirts, silk top hats and stiff cravats suggest maturity, but their words and deeds are those of adolescents — quick to take offense, sensitive of "honor," rash, imperious, and violent. Of the chief actors in our drama, only Field was ever subjected to serious mental discipline. Under his courtly veneer, Terry was a border ruffian, Broderick an urban hoodlum. As we shall see, not even the tutelary ministrations of Mark Hopkins, that quintessential pedagogue, preserved Field from acting like a spoiled brat in his feuds with Judge Turner. Even in that early time, his manner was arrogant; it was regarded as "lordly," and he was "sublimely confident of his own rectitude."

Untrammeled by normal civilizing influences, traditions, respect for law, family ties, these early Californians were primitives compared to their brothers in Boston or Charleston. The frantic scrambling of the early vigilantes, of such men as Sam Brannan and William T. Coleman for "law and order," for public quiet, was a beginning of normal and even noble aspiration toward shaping a civilized community, and within a few decades there would flower on the Pacific Coast a society that rivaled the East in culture and propriety. But for Terry and Broderick and many of their contemporaries, this came too late. Their lives were formed by the social pressures and peer standards of their time, and that made them eternal adolescents. Even Field, surely one of the most cultivated blooms to come out of the intellectual hothouse of mid-nineteenth century New England, had his life punched into ugliness and brutality by the then prevailing *kinderspiel* of California in the 1850's, when bluster, riot and passion were almost unchecked.

Upper: This is believed to be the first photograph ever taken of San Francisco, circa 1850

Lower: The women of San Francisco, early 1850's

View of San Francisco fire from California Street, June 22, 1851

The only decent women in the community were in the few homes, mostly Mexican, that existed before the Gold Rush. Almost all the women in the city after the discovery of gold were whores or washerwomen. A contemporary journalist describes the crowd of men "making way for the passage of a richly dressed woman, sweeping along, apparently proud of being recognized as one of frail character." The first newspapers lamented the constant influx of women of "indifferent morality," and soon well-furnished brothels sprang up beside the saloons and gambling halls.

Some perspicacious critic has noted that in the saga of the American West, the most prevalent principle was contempt for the law. Novels and motion pictures of the twentieth century have distorted this calamitous lawlessness into something heroic. Bret Harte treated it as picturesque, Mark Twain as humorous. Ambrose Bierce was not deceived. He described the era with characteristic forthrightness for what it was: "murder, armed robbery, assault with intent to kill." For Bierce there were "no chivalrous gamblers, just card sharks; no courtly gunfighters, just homicidal psychopaths; no golden-hearted dance-hall girls, just pathetic whores; no gallant soldiers or stout-hearted pioneers, just men on the government payroll bored by routine or farmers looking for a better piece of land."

Neither statehood in 1850 nor the establishment of regular courts brought law and order. Murder could be committed with impunity; there were "over 1000 men in California who make horse-stealing a regular business." While homicide was widely condoned, there was concern for property and possessions. In 1852 a man was hanged in Grass Valley for stealing a silver watch. There was "wholesale blood-letting and wholesale pardoning. To mention even a small proportion of the outrages perpetrated upon the industrious by the profligate class would convert history into a police report."

Another danger menaced the city. In December 1849 a general conflagration destroyed more than half the jerry-built houses, tents and lean-tos. In May 1850, fire destroyed more than $4,000,000 of property. On May 14, 1851, most of the business section was consumed, with damage exceeding $12,000,000. This fire, believed to be of incendiary origin, set in motion the first "vigilante" movement, which temporarily brought law and order to San Francisco and an imperishable new word to the English language. After the conflagration, came an outbreak of unbridled looting and murder which threatened the property and lives of the respectable citizenry. Criminals virtually took over the city. Among the most notorious of the desperados were the "Sydney Ducks," many of them ticket-of-leave men and convicts released from penal servitude in Australia. These came in such numbers that, by 1850, they formed their own district known as "Sydney Town." Needless to say, it became a sink of vice and iniquity. The "Sydney Ducks" spurned the hard labor of the mines, and remained in San Francisco to prey upon the industrious or lucky men who brought their gold dust to the city to be exchanged for specie.

Not all the trouble was caused by "foreigners." In 1847, Colonel Jonathan D. Stevenson, a prominent politician in New York, had recruited a volunteer regiment in his home state to fight the Mexicans in California. He stated that he would accept "only young men of good character and that

San Francisco Harbor, circa 1851. Note the washerwoman in the shanty door.
This photo is from one of a series of 360° panoramas taken by unknown
photographers during the Gold Rush.

The ''Hounds'' at work

they must be willing to remain in California after their term of military service had expired, and help settle the country.'' Despite these stated qualifications most of his men came from the Manhattan slums, the Bowery and the Five Points; they were trained chiefly in street-brawling and larceny. They fought no Mexicans in California, but under the leadership of a New York tough named Sam Roberts, they formed the ''Hounds'' who became the terror of the city's streets.

Most active in the civic revulsion to the thugs was Sam Brannan, a Mormon who arrived in San Francisco in 1846 with a shipload of co-religionists. They came under Brigham Young's orders to rear in the Far West a tabernacle secure from the fierce religious and social persecutions of their former neighbors in Illinois and Missouri. Their original plan was to trek eastward from California to meet up with Brigham Young and the main body of Mormons headed for the Great Salt Lake. But the missionary zeal of Brannan and his co-religionists was diverted by the commercial opportunities of their new home. Brannan tried to convince Young to bring the Mormons to California; it was a ''delightful country,'' he wrote to the Mormon leader. But Young would not settle his flock among ''new persecutors.'' He preferred the wilderness of Deseret. Brannan's little company of Mormons stayed in the San Francisco area where, through industry and sacrifice, they flourished. By 1851, Brannan owned the largest flour mill in the city, and a prosperous general store at Sutter's Mill. By 1850, the goons and the hoodlums

So many ships were abandoned by gold-hungry crews that some were hauled up on land to serve as hotels and stores.

who infested San Francisco were a plain threat to him and his fellow merchants, and he determined to put an end to the reign of terror they imposed on the community.

Brannan was tough, opinionated and resourceful. He even refused to pay the Mormon tithe to the Mother Church in Utah. Several times he was excommunicated by Brigham Young for heresy and insubordination. There is a legend that more than once Brigham Young dispatched his holy gunmen, his "Destroying Angels," to San Francisco to deal with Brannan and collect the money by force. "But the Angels were invariably met in the desert, and their wings clipped, by Brannan's 'exterminators,' fighting men whom he is said to have employed as a bodyguard for half a dozen years." In his history of California, Josiah Royce writes of Brannan as "lionhearted, always in love with shedding the blood of the wicked."

Sam Brannan has a memorable place in California history. He was at Sutter's Mill on January 24, 1848, when the first gold flecks were found in the creek. The legend is that he rode into San Francisco with the news, displayed a bottle of yellow dust to the citizens and published the happy tidings in the *California Star,* from which the gospel was picked up by eastern newspapers and became the starting gun of the Gold Rush. Brannan did not surrender to the attraction of the mines. He stayed in San Francisco, tended his flock and his shop, and prospered.

It was Brannan who supplied the enterprise to organize the first

The St. Francis Hotel, San Francisco, 1849

Vigilance Committee in 1851. The duly-elected law enforcement authorities were unable to restrain the criminal forces. In the minds of Brannan and the respectable merchants of the city, they were too frightened or themselves too corrupt to be effective. So, under the Mormon's leadership, the merchants formed San Francisco's first Vigilance Committee. The committee held some drumhead trials, hanged a few of the worst reprobates, sent many more into flight, and for the moment restored law and order. One of the early vigilantes coined a happy euphemism for this brand of rough justice: "civic regulation by popular initiative." Brannan was more brusque; he appealed to the outraged citizenry to "hang 'em first, and try 'em later." He composed a manifesto which concluded with this invocation:

> *The series of murders and robberies that have been committed in this city seems to leave us entirely in a state of anarchy.... Law, it appears, is but a nonentity to be scoffed at; redress can be had for aggression but only through the never-failing remedy laid down in the code of Judge Lynch.*

The first formal Vigilance Committee was disbanded in 1852 and local government, including law enforcement, was turned back to the duly-elected officials of the city and state.

Into the turbulent society of San Francisco, in 1849, came the four men whose careers furnish most of this history: Terry, Broderick, Field and William Sharon, the Bonanza King.

Each rose to great power and eminence. Terry became chief judge of the California Supreme Court, and was killed by Field's bodyguard. Broderick, one of the first senators the new state would send to Washington, was slain by Terry's hand. Field became a justice of the United States Supreme Court, a chronic aspirant to the White House. Sharon became one of the Bonanza Kings, his last days poisoned by a specious, fraudulent lawsuit, invented by a black brothel-keeper and prosecuted by a demented doxy who became successively his own mistress and Terry's wife. This book is the tale of these men and women, played out against the background of Old San Francisco. It is perhaps true that only in the strange, exotic and violent world erected on the site of Yerba Buena could these roles have been enacted. O. Henry, who knew something about urban society, once delivered a "Municipal Report" on the city which concluded that "East is East, and West is San Francisco. According to Californians, San Franciscans are not merely the inhabitants of a city. They are a race of people." Our chief characters belonged to that race.

Young Terry—at about the time of his arrival in California in 1849

II

TERRY

Nemo me impune lacessit
(No one provokes me with impunity)
Motto of the Crown of Scotland

D avid S. Terry is the central character in this book. He is our Ulysses, our anti-hero. Like Homer's wanderer, he had a proclivity for blundering into dangerous situations. He is also a pathetic loser; his life is marked throughout by zeal in promoting lost causes. He fights and fails — and even kills — to make California a slave state. He risks and loses everything for the Confederacy; he gambles on the success of Louis Napoleon's Mexican adventure — and loses again. Next, he becomes a trumpet for Denis Kearney's "Chinese-Must-Go!" movement which brings him into collision with California's powerful establishment and, in the opinion of many, marks him for destruction. Finally, he is ground into dusty death when he champions — and marries — a soiled damsel in distress.

Terry's career began in Texas. His birthplace in 1823 was a cotton farm in what is now Todd County, Kentucky. His grandfather, Nathaniel Terry, came to Virginia from Northern Ireland, rose to be a colonel in Washington's army, and was present at the Yorktown surrender. His father, Joseph R. Terry, was a slave-holding cotton planter, who moved to Mississippi after failing as a farmer in Kentucky. Terry's mother was Sarah Smith of Virginia, a celebrated beauty, daughter of David Smith, a Scot who fled the bloody field of Culloden in 1745 to settle in the South. Smith avenged himself on the House of Hanover by serving in the Continental army as a colonel under Washington.

David Terry's father "contracted habits" (the standard antebellum euphemism for alcoholism and exogamous wenching) which led to a separation from his wife in 1834. That sturdy lady gathered up her four sons, packed the furniture and other movables in a wagon and set off for Texas, where they settled on a cotton plantation already established by Mrs. Terry's mother, Obedience Smith, just west of what is now Houston.

When the Alamo fell in 1836, the thirteen-year-old Terry rushed to join Sam Houston's banner at Gonzales. In later life he was fond of relating that he fought with gallantry at San Jacinto; he would tell how a Mexican officer struck him a sabre blow on the head and "was rewarded with a Bowie knife which pierced his heart." A prodigious exploit for a thirteen-year-old!

If true, the unfortunate Mexican is historically notable as the first victim of Terry's knife. Terry's admiring biographer, A. E. Wagstaff, records this yarn and others. A more responsible researcher records that Terry "was too young to have had an actual military role" in the struggle for Texan independence. In 1856, Terry himself wrote only that he "played a man's part" in the Texas War of Independence. He gave no details.

When Texas became independent, Terry returned to the plantation and the quiet study of books. He had no formal education, but became literate and well-informed. In 1841, Terry had grown to his full height of almost six and a half feet. All who speak of him at this time mention his powerful physique and his unusual height. As yet no one was reminded of Bacon's apothegm: "Wise nature did never put her precious jewels into a garret four stories high; and therefor exceeding tall men had ever very empty heads." He was accepted as a pupil in the office of his uncle, Colonel Hadley, a Houston lawyer. That preceptor recorded that the youthful law student "was not bright, but deep and possessed a remarkable memory"; that he "seldom studied, but gained his knowledge by absorption." Terry made such speedy progress in the study of law that he was admitted to practice within two years.

Among Terry's favorite anecdotes was an account of the display of legal erudition which gained him quick admission to the bar of Texas. If true, it is an insight into the fastidious concerns with which candidates for the bar were screened in the frontier community. Terry recounted that three local attorneys were assigned to examine the neophyte. Only one question was put to him. "Young man, do you know the price of a dish of oysters?" "I do indeed," said Terry. "In order, therefore, to test the correctness of your judgment and your legal acumen," said the chairman of the inquiring committee, "I move we adjourn." Whereupon committee and candidate betook themselves to a nearby tavern, where Terry established his legal credentials by paying for oysters and a round of drinks. The young lawyer opened an office in Galveston, the principal seaport of the Lone Star Republic. It is doubtful that he learned much law, but he acquired enough practical experience to qualify him later as a competent lawyer and judge in California.

There is nothing noteworthy in Terry's life until 1846, when the United States and Mexico went to war. At twenty-three, he was among the first to join the Texas Rangers (officially, the "First Regiment of Texas Mounted Volunteers"); mere literacy sufficed to earn him the rank of lieutenant. The Rangers fought under Zachary Taylor in at least one of the decisive battles around Monterrey. After the battle, Terry returned to law practice in Galveston. He made at least one trip to his childhood home in Tennessee, where his reputation as a brave soldier had preceded him, and where he regaled the local belles with tales of heroism at San Jacinto and Monterrey. One of the fair listeners later moved to Texas and became his wife.

In the 1840's Texas was a rough and brawling frontier; fist-fights, duels and assaults with deadly weapons were everyday occurrences. Planters, politicans, lawyers, even merchants observed a puerile Code of Personal Honor, derived from the "Code Duello," which with drink and miscegenation was the curse of young manhood in the antebellum South. Men killed each other for fancied slights, for careless or drunken slurs, for misplaced jokes. They killed each other with pistols, swords and knives. The survivors of these inane contests were usually protected from the law by public opinion. The victims were mourned with "respect" as men of honor. In the Texas of Terry's young manhood, in the 1830's and 1840's, the Bowie knife had become more than a weapon. It was the traditional side arm of every virile young man. To them, it was Mercutio's rapier and Wyatt Earp's Colt!

There is no evidence that Terry ever bloodied his Bowie knife in Texas, but it became part of his normal dress and professional equipment. It has been observed that his lifelong preference for the Bowie knife as a "personal weapon" became part of Terry's personality. "Terry clung to an antiquated weapon as he adhered to outmoded customs of satisfying insults to personal honor." The tradition of the Code was burned deeply into the youthful Terry; he would honor it for the rest of his life.

Terry's reason for leaving Galveston in 1847 is unclear. One story is that he was jilted by a distant cousin with whom he had a romantic relationship. We know that the citizens of Galveston rejected him as a candidate for district attorney in 1847 and he seems to have been at odds with some of his close associates in the Texas port. So, off he went to California, the new Golconda, bearing his fierce personal pride, his faithful Bowie knife, an inordinate reverence for womanhood (Caucasian), and an almost religious belief in the rectitude of Negro slavery. One day these qualities would combine to destroy him in his new life, but in 1847, he was the gayest of caballeros. Hiram G. Runnels, uncle of Terry's wife-to-be and governor of Texas, wrote of Terry in 1847: "If high-toned chivalry and unquestionable integrity serve as a recommendation, he has them."

In 1849, he joined a party led by his brother, Frank, to make the overland trip to California. We know little about the personality of the youth who set out on this grand adventure. We do know that he was "a physical giant," tall, burly and "tetchy as a b'ar." He seems to have been a fine specimen of *Ursus Americanus,* a frontier roughneck cast in the mold of Kit Carson and Jim Bowie, very different from the mincing gallants of Charleston and New Orleans. Terry joined an expedition which consisted of about twenty or thirty Texans "and a few slaves." The overland voyage was uneventful. Wagstaff, Terry's ingenuous and gullible biographer, invests the overland voyage with fanciful romance and excitement. He tells us that the sturdy band of "Rangers"

> in crossing the Plains . . . met bands of hostile Indians who disputed their passage. On two occasions they gave battle and the Indians were severely punished. About fifty Indians were killed and wounded, while the Rangers only lost one man.

This is almost certainly a fable invented by one of Terry's companions. The party's route took them first to El Paso and overland through the wilderness of desert and mountain to the area of present-day Stockton, which they reached on September 3, 1849. They traveled on horseback, their baggage on mules. They were called "Rangers" because Terry and some of the other Texans wore the uniform of the Texas Rangers.

Terry had a brief fling at mining, but soon established himself as a practicing lawyer in Stockton, fast becoming the important and relatively populous center of a large mining complex. Events moved at a fast pace in the

The Stockton that became Terry's home in 1850

California of those years. Terry was in Stockton only a few months when he offered himself (unsuccessfully) as the Whig candidate for mayor.

He formed a law partnership with Duncan W. Perley, a lawyer whom he knew from Houston, which lasted until 1855, when Terry became a judge of the state's highest court. Perley remained a lifelong friend and adherent. In that time and place, a law partnership called for more than a sharing of fees and professional responsibilities; it involved support with tongue, fists, Bowie knives and pistols in and out of court. Perley was at Terry's side in several brawls and acted as his second in at least one duel. The *Spirit of the Age,* a local San Francisco newspaper, describes how in 1850

> *Perley and Terry, partners in the law, pursued a Stockton merchant, a Mr. Way, into and through his own store. They had drawn pistols in their hands, and threatened to take his life; but he escaped through a back door and barely eluded his pursuers who, like fiends incarnate were bent on his destruction.*

The reason ascribed was that Terry and Perley had engaged in a "street row" the night before and the unfortunate Way had "thoughtlessly expressed an opinion about it and it was for this that these chivalrous and high-minded gentlemen took umbrage and sought to exterminate him."

It is also recorded that in one of his law cases, Terry quarreled with a litigant and stabbed him with his Bowie knife. Since the wound was only superficial and the judge observed with appreciation that Terry had paid for a physician to dress the victim's wound, he was fined the nominal sum of fifty dollars. Such exploits helped Terry win his local reputation for skill as a brawler as well as for practical advocacy; his fame was enhanced by the "Purdy Affair." Purdy was the editor of a fly-by-night San Francisco journal, the *Pacific Statesman,* whose columns carried some remarks offensive to Terry. This brought the Texan and two of his friends to the editor's office. There was a quarrel during which Terry struck Purdy "with a small rattan intending not to hurt him, but merely to inflict upon him an indignity." When Purdy brought charges, it was pointed out in court that the "rattan" was Terry's Bowie knife. Terry's explanation was artless and simple: "As I never learned the art of using my hands, I struck him twice, I think, on the head with the handle of the knife." Lucky Purdy! Terry was charged with assault and fined three hundred dollars, but many admired his "pluck." In 1853, Terry made a brutal attack on one N. R. Evans, a citizen of Stockton, beating him with a pistol until he was senseless. These events built up the reputation for violence that would soon plague the Texan.

Like many Southern gallants of his time, Terry combined a dainty punctilio with a hair-trigger temper and a proclivity for brawling. One example of these traits is afforded by his friendship with one Roberts, a fellow Southerner, who came to Stockton via Mexico, claiming to be both a lawyer and a physician. In truth, he was expelled from Mexico for stealing horses and armed robbery. Roberts was recognized and denounced as a rogue by a local merchant, one George S. Belt. Terry came to the defense of his new friend's "honor"; he gave the lie to Belt, who promptly challenged him to a duel. As the challenged party, Terry selected pistols at ten feet. Since Belt and Terry were both well over six feet, their pistols would almost be touching, a circumstance which would seem to ensure the death of both combatants. The prospect was so comical and unpromising that the challenge was withdrawn and the two duellists fell into each other's arms, convulsed with the humor of the situation. In some arcane way, this satisfied the contestants' "honor."

When Terry was tried by the vigilantes in 1856 for stabbing one of their officers with his Bowie knife, there was much sworn testimony and some affidavits about these incidents, attesting to Terry's terrible temper and his propensity for violence. There is no doubt that when angered, he reached for the nearest weapon. Of course his reflexive recourse was to the omnipresent Bowie knife, but on at least one occasion he threw an inkstand at an adversary and threatened another with a hatchet. He was disarmed and fined fifty dollars by an indulgent judge. The jurists of that community quickly developed an understanding that boys will be boys.

Within a year of his arrival, Terry was established in Stockton as a lawyer of standing. Now he threw himself enthusiastically into the political adventures that would lead him to high office and jeopardy. But first he had to satisfy that most pressing need of the virile young exiles in California: he wanted a wife. The available local supply of marriageable females was very tight. So Terry returned to Texas to search. Cornelia Runnels ("Neal" to Terry for the rest of their lives together) was one of the girls who had listened to his tales of heroism on a Mississippi veranda; her family moved to Texas, and she was courted by Terry in his Galveston days. She may have been the shadowy lady whose rejection had driven him to California. In 1852, when Terry was twenty-nine, they met again in Galveston, and she returned with him to Stockton as his bride. She remained at his side literally through every vicissitude, until she died in 1884, just as Terry became embroiled in the fateful Sharon-Hill litigation.

From his earliest days in California, Terry was one of the recognized leaders among the many new Californians who came from the Southern states. He was a conspicuous and outspoken member of the social and political set which modestly called themselves the "Cavaliers" or the "Chivalry Democrats." The other citizens derisively called them the "Chivs," and the attitude of the Southerners toward the crude shopkeepers and miners who came from the North was essentially contemptuous. The Southerners felt themselves better-born and better-mannered and they displayed their contempt with a general air of condescension toward the northern "mudsills." In turn, the Northerners despised the Chivs for their extravagant clothes, their elaborate manners, and their loudly-proclaimed airs of social superiority. But, by their very arrogance and solidarity, the Chivs achieved great political power in the wild hurly-burly of California politics in the years before Fort Sumter. They were so firmly united in their fierce partisanship of the Southern cause that in the 1850's their very unity of purpose won for them control of the political machinery of the state and wrested from Broderick political control of the city of San Francisco. While Buchanan ruled in Washington, they enjoyed a stranglehold on federal political appointments, and they took good care of their own. The San Francisco Custom House, the center of federal administration in the state, was so filled with their adherents that many called it the "Virginia Poorhouse."

By 1852, Terry was among the noisiest and most active pro-slavery Democrats in the state. He was among the leaders of the schemes to win California for slavery or, if that failed, to divide the state so that the southern half would be slave territory. By now, there were many hot-blooded Southerners in California who plotted incessantly to bring the state into the slavery column. The Southerners were bitter when California adopted a constitution that banned slavery, and in his own words Terry worked with them "to change the Constitution of the State by striking out that clause prohibiting slavery . . . or failing in that, to divide the state and thus open a portion of California to Southerners and their property."

Terry's views on the institution of Negro slavery were those of the Southern hotheads, the "Ultras." Field would recall later that in 1858 or 1859, when both men were members of the California Supreme Court, he and Terry had a passionate controversy over Terry's expressed conviction that the South should not only secede from the Union, but should revive the slave trade with Africa! Terry argued that the blacks were "better off" in servitude in the South than in their own jungles. His views on the inferiority of colored peoples, and on the superiority of the Anglo-Saxon race were deeply ingrained. They would surface later in his life when he supported Denis Kearney and the other racist demagogues in the "Chinese-Must-Go" movement. Certainly, in the 1850's, Terry's commitment to "The Cause" of the South was deep enough to justify in his mind even transparently treasonable plots against the Republic.

In that time, the Democratic party of the state was split between the "Southern Chivalry" and the "Northern Free-Soilers," anti-slavery forces led by another newcomer to California, David C. Broderick. Schism and sectional conflict were as inevitable in the West as in the East. The antagonists were shaping up. Since a majority of the immigrants in California were of Northern or foreign origin, it was probable that if the conflict were to be decided by votes, Free Soil would win out in the new state. The Southerners knew they

Cornelia Runnels, at about the time of her marriage to Terry in November 1852

could win only by force, terror or trickery, and they unabashedly resorted to all three methods. A contemporary historian writes of the "Southern Chivalry" in the California of the 1850's that they "had by some strange logic of their own come to regard themselves as the proper rulers of the people gathered here." To them, the merchants and businessmen of San Francisco were "the damned pork merchants of Front Street" and were treated with studied contempt. The division over the slavery issue was exacerbated by Southern sneers at Northern "peasants" and by Northern resentment of the "Chivalry's" airs of social superiority. An explosion was inevitable.

In 1855, Terry's natural tendencies made him an adherent of the clandestine Know-Nothing party, one of the extremist political cults that sprang up during the convulsions of the 1850's. The party had a brief hour of dubious glory, and vanished in the clear-cut contest between pro-slavery and Free Soil. Its beginnings were frighteningly simple. In the late 1840's and 1850's, the country was enduring one of its periodic flashes of super-patriotism and xenophobia. The best known Know-Nothing leader was Samuel F. B. Morse, born in Boston to a Congregationalist minister-father. He became a prominent artist, inventor of the telegraph — and an uncompromising anti-Papist. In this time, popular hatred was directed chiefly against Roman Catholics and the German "radicals" who had brought their own brand of socialism from the banks of the Rhine. At first the xenophobes called themselves the "Grand Council of the United States of America." But to most they were the "Know-Nothings." As usual, demagogues recruited native-born Protestants into private armies to protect the sacred Republic from Papists and "radicals." In an 1844 anti-Catholic riot in Philadelphia, the "nativists" burned two churches and murdered thirteen Irishmen.

The feeling against Papists was largely a consequence of the tidal wave of Irish immigrants fleeing famine and British oppression to seek "freedom" in America. The "radicals" were mostly Germans who had rebelled against the tyrannies of Metternich's Europe; they had seen their fellows massacred in windrows in Baden and Bavaria and came to America for "freedom." Before long, that same spirit of Know-Nothingism would flower into the Ku Klux Klan. Like the Klan, the Know-Nothings cultivated secrecy, childish rituals and strict discipline. Indeed, the party's very name derived from the formula of silence imposed on its members when queried by outsiders. "I know nothing" was the prescribed reply.

At first, the membership devoted itself to such relatively harmless cultural pursuits as investigating the mysteries of convents, insulting priests and nuns, and generally expressing contempt for Irishmen and other foreigners. But before long, violence became a commonplace tactic. Then came the inevitable riots, murders, lynchings, barn-burnings and the other deeds that would make the Know-Nothings despised by decent society. There were sanguinary street clashes in New York, in Maine, in Massachusetts. The bloodiest *émeute* was in St. Louis where the military had to quell the rioters after a dozen were killed. Persecution of Irish Catholics reached a level where they were attacked in the most despicable vocabulary of bigotry on the floor of the House of Representatives. Andrew Johnson, then a congressman who would learn some lessons about persecution in the White House, flamed with anger: "Are the bloodhounds of proscription and

An illustration from The Satanic Plot, *a Know-Nothing publication*

persecution to be let loose on the Irish? Is the guillotine to be set up in a republican form of government? . . . Show me a Know-Nothing and I will show you a loathsome reptile on whose neck every honest man should set his foot." In 1855, Abraham Lincoln, disgusted by an outbreak in Louisville, Kentucky, that cost a dozen lives, wrote, "As a nation we began by declaring that 'all men are created equal.' When the Know-Nothings obtain control, it will read: 'All men are created equal except Negroes, foreigners and Catholics.' "

In 1855, the followers of Know-Nothingism presented slates of candidates for office under what they modestly called the "American party." The party dropped its cloak of secrecy in June 1855, and held a national convention, control of which was in the hands of the brashest and most bellicose Southern members. The assemblage proclaimed its contempt not only for the Irish and the Germans, but for abolitionists. It enthusiastically espoused the pro-slavery cause and nominated old Millard Fillmore for president.

In California, the Know-Nothing American party was eagerly embraced by many of the Southerners. It nominated a slate of candidates in opposition to the "regular" Democrats, whose political apparatus was under the transient control of David C. Broderick. It was not a long step from approval of Negro slavery to nativism, xenophobia and every other kind of ethnic bigotry. Terry and many of his fellow Chivs quickly marched to the beat of the Know-Nothing drum. Terry was now thirty-two years old and almost designed by nature for the Know-Nothing cause. He became the party's candidate for judge of the supreme court. The American party had little success in the national elections, but in California it was triumphant; Terry, elected judge of the supreme court, became overnight a man of statewide prominence. The election carried into office Governor J. Neely Johnson, aged twenty-seven, whose contest with the vigilantes would soon furnish California with one of the stormiest and most romantic chapters in its history and bring young Judge Terry to the foot of the gallows.

Terry's ready acceptance of Know-Nothing principles must be seen as consistent with his personality, not only in terms of his dedication to the institution of Negro slavery, but in his rejection of all egalitarian principles. He was a typical antebellum fire-eater, with a fanatical devotion to the cause of Negro slavery and the geographical extension of that peculiar institution bred in him from childhood. Also instilled in him was a profound contempt for Yankee "clerks and mudsills," especially if they were abolitionists. When he came to California in 1849, Terry's intellectual equipment embraced a sparse legal education, a passion for all things Southern, a revulsion against the "mudsills," and an uncontrollable temper. These qualities brought him into inevitable collision with the leader of the anti-slavery forces in the new territory of California, David C. Broderick.

In California's history, Terry is recalled chiefly for two important events in his life: he is the man who slew Broderick, the state's first statesman of national importance, and who was himself slain when he physically attacked Stephen J. Field, the state's leading political figure in the nineteenth century. But before either of those events came to pass, Terry played a role in the vigilante struggle of 1856, which strangely foreshadowed both the duel with Broderick and his final tragedy at Lathrop. As we shall see, in the tumultuous vigilante insurrection of 1856, the decent citizens of San Francisco arrayed themselves into an outlaw army to contend against the lawfully-constituted government to secure law and order for the city. In that quarrel, Terry displayed the same tragic qualities of arrogance and headstrong violence which were to lead to Broderick's destruction, bring the titanic figure of Field to fury and humiliation, and finally inflict on Terry himself a doom that might have been conceived by Sophocles. They were the strains of character that pervaded his life and would in the end bring him down. Foremost among them was that special sensitivity to the conduct of others towards himself that drove him to excessive violence. The sensation that he was a victim of injustice drove him into a frenzy, although he seemed indifferent to the force of his own injustice to others.

Broderick in the early 1850's

III

BRODERICK

So Caesar, when he first went into Gaul, made no scruples to profess "That he would rather be first in a village than second at Rome."

Francis Bacon, *The Advancement of Learning*

I f Terry is the Ulysses of this tale, David C. Broderick is our Hector, although he came from no royal House of Priam. He rose from the humblest of origins to great political power and eminence in the new state, and fell to a death that became an apotheosis. A leading historian of California, writing in 1914, calls him "the ablest man in California's political history and in many respects the most interesting." He was born in Washington, in 1820, the son of a stonecutter brought over from Ireland to carve the ornamental capitals on the columns that supported the portico of the new federal Capitol. Broderick's youth and early manhood were spent in the Irish ghettos of New York, where he became one of the lusty boyos of Tammany Hall. He kept a saloon, became foreman of a volunteer fire company, and generally fell into the pattern of the politically ambitious young Irishmen of his time. Had his life followed a normal pattern he might have become mayor or governor of New York.

When he was only twenty-five, Broderick had enough standing in New York's Democratic organization to be a candidate for Congress. He lost the election, but gained much respect for his tactics and oratory. He felt frustrated and disappointed in New York, and the cry of "Gold!" from Sutter's Mill drew him into the army of adventurers that swarmed to California. The young Irishman hungered for recognition and high office. He was impatient, and he felt that his prospects would be better in the West.

During his activities in Tammany Hall politics in Manhattan, Broderick formed a close personal and political alliance with Daniel E. Sickles, who would win his own fame in war and politics. When the wanderlust seized him in 1849, Broderick consulted his friend Sickles, who urged him to stay in New York and make a career in local politics; he predicted that Broderick would certainly go to Congress from New York. Broderick answered that he was determined to go to California, and that he was sure that if he ever returned to the East, "he would return as a United States senator from the new and untrammelled State of California." The prophecy was fulfilled and

Broderick did indeed find himself in Washington as a United States senator from California at a time when Sickles had become one of the best-known personalities in the country.

In 1858, Washington and the whole country were momentarily diverted from the struggle over slavery and secession when Sickles shot to death Philip Barton Key, son of Francis Scott Key, who wrote "The Star Spangled Banner." Key held the high post of United States attorney for the District of Columbia. Sickles killed him when he learned of Key's adulterous dalliance with Sickles's beautiful young wife. Edwin Stanton, who became Lincoln's secretary of war, defended Sickles on the charge of murder; the jury acquitted him on a defense of "unwritten law." Broderick attended the trial and gave his friendship, support and encouragement to Sickles. When war came, Sickles became a general of volunteers in the Union army; he lost a leg at Gettysburg and was one of the Union's most widely-acclaimed heroes. It was Sickles who said of Broderick, after the latter's death, that in his New York years he had learned "Tammany Arithmetic: Addition, Division and Silence!"

When the nomadic urge seized Broderick in 1849, there were three routes to California: across the Plains, around the Horn or over the Isthmus. Broderick chose the Isthmus route, an experience that scarred his memory. There was not even a well-defined wagon track across the jungles and mountains that separated the two oceans. The famous Panama Railroad that would eventually span the Isthmus was begun in 1850 and not completed until 1855. So Broderick clawed his way by canoe, by mule and on foot. Some companions died on the way from cholera, exhaustion or the mysterious "Chagres Fever." Only the toughest, the hardiest, the most determined made it through to the Pacific port, where they boarded overcrowded Pacific Mail steamers for the comparatively comfortable run to the Golden Gate. You had to be tough to make it; Broderick was among the toughest, and he made it.

When he arrived in San Francisco Bay in June 1849, the Mexican fishing village of Yerba Buena had already burgeoned into the sprawling ramshackle city that became San Francisco. Broderick was shrewd enough to escape the general march to the mines; he stayed in San Francisco. An acquaintance from New York lent him $1,000. Later, Broderick would claim that the source of his sudden wealth was his shrewd investment of this money in waterfront lots. The money was quadrupled in a few weeks. Certainly Broderick was a successful land speculator and he became rich in a very short time. His own explanation of his meteoric rise to affluence is disingenuous. In truth, his quick prosperity came from a shady alliance he formed with a local assayer. Broderick's borrowed capital and the assayer's technical skills were combined in a useful — if palpably criminal — scheme. They bought gold dust from the miners and minted it into coins or "shags." Four dollars' worth of gold went into a five-dollar coin. In the East, Broderick and his nimble-fingered friend could have gone to prison for "coining" or counterfeiting. In the mad new world of the West, there was such an avid demand for the coins that such legalities were ignored, and both men became very rich, very fast. When a friend questioned the propriety of the scheme Broderick cynically pointed out that "only the last holders could suffer." By 1851 Broderick was rich enough to be included in a list of local plutocrats entitled

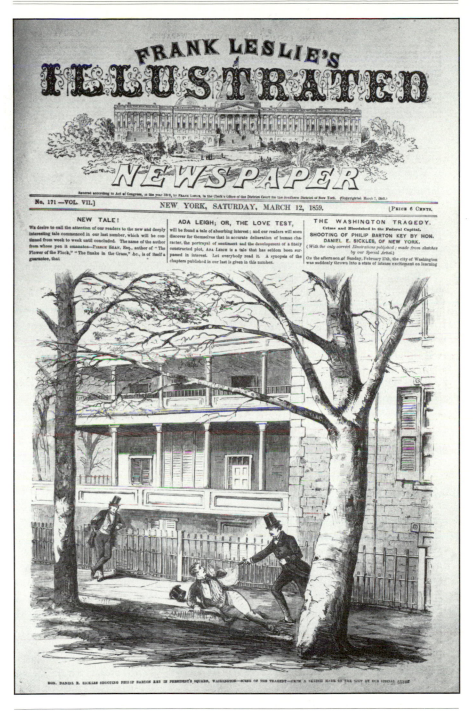

Sickles shooting Key

"A Pile — or a Glance at the Wealth of the Monied Men of San Francisco and Sacramento City and an Accurate List of the Lawyers."

The Broderick of 1850 was thirty years old, "with superb physique and strength." His photograph shows a long, flaring nose, piercing eyes and prominent chin whiskers which make him look almost a stage Irishman of the time. He was over six feet in height, stocky and strong. In manner, he was aloof and domineering. Contemporary descriptions make him out to be "large, robust and very powerful . . . with a face rugged and determined." He was a man of "physical magnificence [together with] ability, ambition and character." His only real interest was politics and in politics it was helpful to own a newspaper. So Broderick used some of his quick profits to have a printing press carried around the Horn in a sailing ship. When it arrived, he established one of San Francisco's earliest newspapers, the *Herald*. His choice of an editor was less than ideal; it was William Walker, a young man of twenty-eight whose volatile temperament was calculated to generate trouble in a frontier community of roughnecks and rascals, many of them already heating up for the explosion between the pro-slavery and anti-slavery factions.

His brief employment by Broderick was a relatively peaceful interlude in Walker's stormy life. He was a native of Tennessee, with a degree in medicine from the University of Pennsylvania. Somehow, he was admitted to the bar in New Orleans. But the young Walker was made for adventure, not the lamp or the scalpel. In 1853, he led a party of restless San Franciscans into Baja California and proclaimed that peninsula and the neighboring province of Sonora as an independent republic. Routed by Mexican forces, he came back to San Francisco and his brief fling at journalism. By 1855 Walker would be famous; the American press would dub him the "Gray-eyed Man of Destiny." That destiny would lead him to a harebrained invasion of Nicaragua and death before a firing squad in 1860. His exploits helped to popularize a new word in the English language: "filibuster."

Broderick hired Walker to make friends, not fights. When he understood that Walker was a dangerous troublemaker, Broderick dismissed him from the editorship of the *Herald,* but not before the editor's vigorous prose had drawn Broderick himself into a duel with a local judge, an émigré from Virginia, "Extra Billy" Smith, who earned this sobriquet by his susceptibility to the blandishments of the lawyers. The *Herald* published some judgments on "Extra Billy's" judicial obliquity, and the judge bypassed the editor to challenge the proprietor to a duel. Broderick and Smith exchanged fire with Mr. Colt's new Navy revolvers, but none of the shots struck home, and the "honor" of the duellists was apparently satisfied. Broderick later claimed that his life was saved when the ball from Smith's pistol struck his watch and failed to penetrate the flesh.

Broderick had no real interest in journalism. His full devotion was given to the bitter wrangling between Southern zealots and Yankee settlers which flamed through the years 1850 to 1855. It is plain now that it was through Broderick's indomitable efforts that California came into the Union as a Free State in 1850. But the struggle continued, with the Southern partisans breathing fiery vengeance against the "nigger lovers" and fomenting plots to divide the state, with slavery in the southern half. The battle was fought with votes, money and fire-breathing journalism.

CHAPTER THREE

William Walker—the "Gray-eyed Man of Destiny"

When murder, arson, and every other kind of crime rocked San Francisco in 1851, and the law enforcement authorities proved either powerless or indifferent, the respectable elements of the city formed the first Committee of Vigilance, hanged a few reprobates, exiled others, and restored law and order. Terry and Broderick buried their own personal and political antagonisms long enough to support the committee's efforts at reestablishing law and order. By 1852, the first Vigilance Committee was disbanded. It would be resurrected in 1856, when the hoodlums and thugs were again rampant, and for almost a year the civic revulsion to lawlessness and municipal corruption would overshadow even the contention over the slavery issue.

After he arrived in San Francisco, Broderick put to immediate and effective use the lessons he had learned in Tammany's school of political pragmatism. Things happened fast in the tumescent city and within a year or two of his arrival on the scene, Broderick had fixed his hold on municipal affairs in a way that would have earned him the admiration of his most cynical mentors back in New York. Even his indulgent biographer, Jeremiah Lynch, blandly concedes that Broderick's methods were high-handed and corrupt:

> His political lessons and observations in New York were priceless. He introduced a modification of the same organization in San Francisco with which Tammany has controlled New York for lo! these many years.
>
> It was briefly this. At a forthcoming election a number of offices were to be filled; those of sheriff, district attorney, alderman, and places in the legislature. Several of these positions were very lucrative, notably that of the sheriff, tax collector and assessor. The incumbents received no specified salaries, but were entitled to all, or to a certain proportion of the fees. These fees occasionally exceeded $50,000 per annum. Broderick would say to the most popular or the most desirable aspirant: "This office is worth $50,000 a year. Keep half and give me the other half, which I require to keep up our organization in the city and the state."

As Artemus Ward put it, Broderick's politics were "of a exceedin' accommodatin' character." No wonder the young Irishman became so rich so fast and made so many enemies. To his great cost Broderick never learned one lesson taught by another Irishman: "A man cannot be too careful in the choice of his enemies." Study of Broderick's career must excite curiosity about the high literary quality of his public speeches. His prose and expression display care, precision and power. How did one of his meager education attain this quality? The answer is probably found in the quiet, but significant, influence of George Wilkes.

Wilkes was a New York journalist, with a gift for trenchant expression, who befriended and admired the young Broderick in New York and schooled him not only in the intricacies of local politics, but in language and demeanor. When he heard of his protégé's success in California, Wilkes took the next boat to San Francisco. He arrived in 1851 and remained Mentor to his Telemachus until Broderick died. Wilkes was well educated and highly literate and in California he continued his tutelage of Broderick. He wrote his speeches, edited his writing and advised on policy. The process by which a rough-tongued, unmannered Tammany ward heeler was transformed into a statesman who could associate with such men as William H. Seward, E. D. Baker and Horace Greeley, and earn their respect and admiration was, in great part, the result of Wilkes's devotion and skill.

Broderick used his new wealth to feed his single passion: political power. Money talked him into being a state senator within a year after he landed in San Francisco. By January 1851, the state Senate elected him lieutenant governor of the new state. During this time Broderick came to know Terry well and he became intimate with the young New Englander, Stephen J. Field, who represented the Marysville area in the state legislature. When Field was attacked in the Assembly by a fellow legislator, Broderick offered to act as his "second" in arranging a duel. His adroitness exacted an apology and retraction. The duel never came off and Field remained an admiring friend. Their relationship was intensified when Broderick and his supporters protected Field from being ambushed in a saloon. In later years Field wrote, "I could never forget his generous conduct to me; and for his sad death there was no more sincere mourner in the state."

Broderick's position as one of California's earliest and most renowned heroes is based on his battles with the Southern Hotspurs against slavery and his assumed martyrdom to the Free Soil cause in his duel with Terry. But much of the extensive literature about him has been well described as "a worthless mass of fulsome panegyric." A reputable California historian writes of him: "the truth of history demands the statement that for a long period his methods were utterly vicious, and that he shrank from no infamy that would promote his objects."

There was no substantial challenge to Broderick's political hegemony until 1854. He devoted every waking hour to the profession of politics; he did not frequent saloons, gambling halls or brothels. He had no family, and his only associates were his fellow politicians. If we are to judge Broderick on his behavior between his arrival in San Francisco and the beginning of his final struggle with Terry, Gwin, the Secessionist leader, and the other Southerners, he would earn little praise. He would stand forth merely as a tough, resourceful scamp who sold debased coins and public office with cool indifference. But by 1855, when there began to be apparent rifts in his own party which led to the final battle with Gwin, Terry and the pro-slavery forces, there emerges a politician-statesman of vision and character. Even on the point of Broderick's leadership of the anti-slavery movement in the state there is historical disagreement. But his contemporaries saw him as the foremost champion of the Free Soil movement in the state. As eminent an historian as Royce thought that, as a "leader in the struggle against the extension of slavery . . . to the Pacific Coast," Broderick's role was more apparent than real. At this distance Royce's judgment seems unfair; no other leader of the Free Soil forces had Broderick's force or prestige. Without Broderick, the Southern hotheads might have carried the day in California.

While the Tammany-like structure that Broderick erected was wrecked by the Know-Nothing victory of 1855, and by the austere clamp that the Committee of Vigilance imposed on local political activities in 1856, his personal stature as a statesman was preserved. As the struggle over slavery wound down to the final climax, Broderick was justly regarded as the clearest and loudest voice of the anti-slavery Unionist forces in California. He would discharge his role with distinction and bravery, and it would cost him his life.

James King of Wm. at about the time of his assassination by Casey in 1856

IV

THE RISE OF THE VIGILANTES

In all forms of Government, the People is the true Legislature.

Edmund Burke, *Tracts on the Popery Laws*

By 1855, both Broderick and Terry were embroiled in political battles, most of which were fought over the slavery issue. For the moment, they confined their polemics to vitriolic speeches and malicious screeds in the journals of the time. Broderick and his Free Soil adherents had their organ in the *Herald;* the pro-slavery faction found its voice in the *Bulletin,* edited by the flamboyant "James King of Wm.," an early muckraker with a fanatical devotion to two institutions: slavery and civil tranquillity. King was born in William County, Maryland, and appended "of Wm." to his name to distinguish him from other James Kings in San Francisco. King spent his first years in San Francisco trying to be a banker, but his methods of business were as reckless as they were honest, and in 1854, his banking firm, Adams and Co., crashed in ruins. He found the means of supporting his young family in the patronage and support of Terry, Gwin, Edmond Randolph and the other pro-slavery politicians. They helped him establish the *Bulletin,* a newspaper fiercely partisan in the cause of slavery.

In 1855, the city had shaken off the chastening effect of the vigilante purge of 1851; lawlessness and violence were again rampant. In 1855, by actual count there were 537 saloons in the city — one for every fifteen men, women and children. A contemporary diarist records: "No place in the world contains anything like the number of drinking-houses in proportion to the population as San Francisco. This, perhaps, is the worst feature of the city. The quantity of ardent spirits consumed is almost frightful." No equivalent statistics are available for gambling halls and brothels, but they abounded.

In November 1855, James King of Wm. was temporarily diverted from his daily diatribes in the *Bulletin* against Broderick and the abolitionists to concentrate his journalistic fire on professional gamblers in general, and on one Charlie Cora in particular. Cora was the most successful and flamboyant of San Francisco's gambling house proprietors.

Before he took aim on Cora, King's chief target was Broderick. In his vitriolic attacks, King justifiably charged that the New Yorker's corrupt political minions protected gamblers and other criminals. He assailed Broderick

The banking house of James King of Wm. before his business failed

Charles Cora, from a contemporary lithograph, May 1856

for corruption in sales of land to the city, for buying votes and selling political offices, and in return for the political contributions, shielding the gamblers and criminals from the law. "David *Catiline* Broderick" was his favorite epithet. "If we can only escape David C. Broderick's hired bullies a little longer," King wrote, "we will turn this city inside out, but we will expose the corruption and malfeasance of her officiary." Many of King's charges were true: Broderick's methods were indeed those he had learned in New York's Tammany Hall, and his application of Tammany's sordid techniques was undoubtedly responsible for the municipal corruption that finally drove a tormented citizenry into the uprising known to California history as the Second Vigilance Movement. There is some controversy over King's sincerity. Royce says he was not altogether "free from selfishness in the conduct of his mission" and often expressed his "personal spite" against the sinners he assailed. A contemporary, George D. Lymon, speaks of him as a citizen "with a spotless reputation . . . with iron in his soul." When reprisal came to King for his vitriol and fire, it came from one who had served as one of Broderick's "hired bullies," although at the moment he was in Broderick's political doghouse. The climax of the controversy between King and Broderick's local minions was touched off when Charlie Cora murdered General William H. Richardson.

In attacking Cora, King was performing the traditional role of the muckraking journalist. Cora was the personification of everything that King abhorred. He was flashy and arrogant; his bribes bought him the protection of the local authorities; he had political clout and he flaunted it. He coupled his insolent airs with the brazen parading of his beautiful mistress, Arabella Ryan. Arabella was known to be Cora's mistress and the proprietress of one of the city's most luxurious bordellos, but her beauty and charm made her

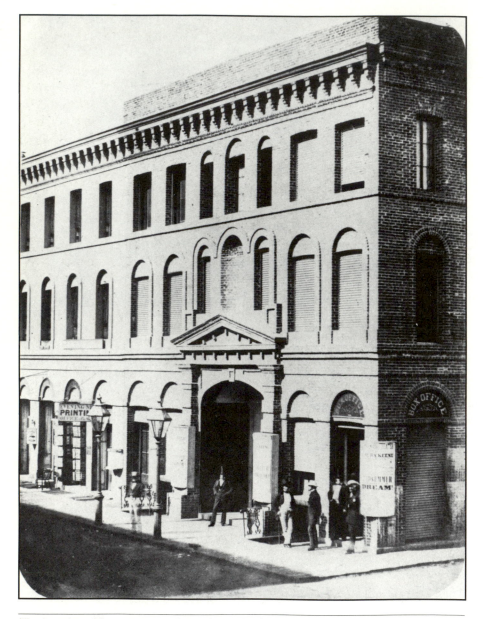

The American Theatre, scene of the altercation between Richardson and Cora

William A. Richardson. This, the only extant photograph of Richardson, was lost for over a century and rediscovered only in 1972.

welcome even in some respectable social circles. Cora was an Italian who came to San Francisco via New Orleans. To the local press he was "a member of the sporting fraternity"; to the Chivs, he was a contemptible "greaser," a foreigner. Of course, he earned the hostility of the city's more respectable elements, but his chief enemies were the "Southern Chivalry," among them Terry and James King. In that age of blustery Know-Nothingism, it was bad enough to be a foreigner; to be a "greaser" with power, money and the most pulchritudinous girl in town was insufferable to the respectable merchants as well as King's Chivs. Cora's enemies concealed neither envy nor hatred.

Cora offered his enemies a rich excuse for revenge when he shot and killed General William H. Richardson, a thirty-three-year-old hero of the Mexican War, recently appointed United States marshal for Northern California, and highly-esteemed at all levels of local society. While Cora knew that his enemies would not wait on the slow and dubious processes of San Francisco's justice, he could not have known that the killing of Richardson would not only cost him his own life, but would ignite the spark that touched off the Second Vigilance Movement. Like all such sparks, from Jenkins' Ear to Sarajevo, it started with what, in retrospect, is a piece of silliness.

On the night of November 15, 1855, Cora and his delectable Arabella attended the American Theatre where a visiting eastern troupe was performing *Nicodemus, or the Unfortunate Fisherman*. Richardson observed Arabella seated with Cora in front of his wife and young daughter. He expressed to the theatre manager his outrage that his own chaste ladies should be exposed to a woman of loose character. He demanded her expulsion; the manager refused and there was an altercation in which Cora made some unhappy remarks about the Richardson ladies. On the following evening, Cora and Richardson encountered each other in the Blue Wing Saloon, "where further explanations were made, in conformity with which [bystanders] understood that all unkind feelings on the part of either were dropped." The two men left the saloon and "walked off together arm-in-arm." But after a short promenade, Cora made some careless comparison between his mistress and Mrs. Richardson. Richardson slapped Cora, who then shot the marshal dead with a derringer.

Cora took no chances. He betook himself to the local jail where his political friends offered him protective custody. When news of the shooting circulated, a lynch mob assembled. A bloodthirsty crowd surrounded the local jail chanting, "Lynch Charlie Cora! Lynch him!" Armed deputies kept the mob at bay. To the respectable elements of the city, the killing of Richardson presented an issue far more deadly than whether Cora lived or died. They saw in Richardson's murder a frightening portent, a sign that the lawlessness and disorder which had activated the Vigilante Committee of 1851 had returned. As it had in 1851, the bell on the California Engine House tolled to call the city fathers to caucus, even as the lynch mob surrounded the local jail.

Some members of the old Vigilance Committee and their sympathizers assembled at the Oriental Hotel "where Mr. Samuel Brannan delivered an exciting speech upon the inefficiency of the law and the propriety in this instance of lynch law." Now, Broderick's hand-picked sheriff and his city marshal made a false move. While Brannan was urging the crowd at the Oriental to lynch Cora, these two officials entered the hotel and arrested Brannan. They took him off to the station house, where Brannan promptly furnished bail. He returned to the Oriental in a wild fury, where he renewed his invocation to Judge Lynch. Next, he and his friends joined the mob in front of the jail all "gesticulating violently" and calling for the lynching of Charlie Cora.

While the mob screamed and the former vigilantes pondered their course of action, James King thundered in his *Bulletin* against Cora, the sheriff and Broderick's other minions. He charged they were not only protecting Cora from the fury of the mob, but would rig his trial so that he would be acquitted by hand-picked and well-bribed jurors. King expected an acquittal. His paper trumpeted: "What we propose is this: If the jury which tries Cora is packed, either HANG THE SHERIFF or drive him out of town!"

The fiery editor had good cause for expressions of concern over the working of local justice. Richardson was only one victim of a recent outbreak of homicide. The collector of the Port of Monterey had recently been shot and killed. Four hundred and eighty-nine murders had been committed in San Francisco in just the ten months before the murder of Richardson. The law had punished only six of the killers. Nor was King the only journalist to express his misgivings over the purity of San Francisco justice in that day. On the Monday after Richardson's slaying the *Daily Alta California* first abjured any belief in "mob law" but predicted that "Cora's friends have money . . . his paramour and others will furnish thousands of dollars to fee lawyers, and to procure such a jury as will release him." The cynical editor even predicted that "if, in the end, a corrupt jury does not release Cora, application will be made to some prosecuting attorney who is easy in his conscience as to quashing indictments." Public anger was stimulated when it became known in the city that while the gambler languished in jail, he was being supplied with fine food and wines by his friends and enjoyed daily visits from his lovely mistress. When King was furnished with details of the Lucullan fare supplied to the murderer and of the consolations he received from the luscious Arabella, he was driven to new heights of fury.

Cora was brought to trial, defended by the city's most respected and formidable lawyer, Colonel E. D. Baker. Baker was an intimate of Broderick, and there was some muttering that the Irishman had induced his friend to defend the sleazy gambler. Baker understood both the depth of the popular feeling against the little Italian and the strength of the evidence against him. He knew that an acquittal of Cora would touch off a storm of public indignation, perhaps a lynching. The local press reported that "one hundred thousand dollars [raised by Arabella] will be used to screen Cora from punishment if necessary. It will be proffered to jurymen — it will be proffered to attorneys — it will be proffered to witnesses. The question is, will money avail?" After some reflection, Baker tried to pull out of the case. But he had been well paid; Arabella had indeed raised a fat purse from the gamblers and the brothel keepers, and the redoubtable barrister found it expedient to stay in place as Cora's lawyer. He "was eloquent and effective in Cora's defense." He was somewhat disturbed when "Cora appeared before the Court in a gorgeous waistcoat, light gloves, a new pale suit, and a jaunty overcoat, and lolled with insolent indifference as the trial went on." But Cora's arrogance did him no harm. There was apparent cause for the concern of King and the *Alta* editor about

Colonel E. D. Baker, lawyer, senator, and close friend of Abraham Lincoln, killed at the Battle of Ball's Bluff, 1861

"the fix." For after twenty-four hours of deliberation the jury failed to agree on a verdict, and Cora was returned to custody to await another trial. Again, he was well fed and well treated; he was allowed his daily compassionate visits by Arabella. King went berserk. His paper screeched:

> *The money of the gambler and the prostitute has succeeded and Cora has another respite! . . . Rejoice ye gamblers and harlots, . . . your money can accomplish anything in San Francisco!*

He stridently demanded a new Vigilance Committee to deal summary justice to the villain. But the men who had organized the vigilantes in 1851 were reluctant to revive that deadly instrument. They had been hoping for a conviction that would assuage public anger. Even the lionhearted Brannan held back, fearing a confrontation with the state and city authorities. The respectable citizens clung to the hope that Cora would be punished by the lawfully-constituted authorities and that there would be no need for a revival of vigilantism. They were disappointed!

Months passed, and the local authorities did nothing to bring Cora to trial. Meanwhile the miscreant enjoyed the hospitality of his friendly jailers. Each day Arabella was seen to enter the jail, carrying a basket of culinary comforts. Each day she returned to Cora's friends with accounts that he was prospering. The honest citizenry seethed with suspicion and anger. By May, the city was ripe for explosion. It needed only a spark — and that was furnished by the murder of King.

Cora's friends were the politicians and municipal officeholders, who owed their places to the patronage of Broderick. Any friend of Broderick was an enemy of the Southern faction. Urged on by Gwin, Terry and the Chivs, King attacked Broderick's appointment of a minor henchman, a creature named Bagley, to a position in the customhouse. Bagley's appointment was also opposed by San Francisco's Supervisor, James P. Casey, who wanted Bagley's job for himself. Casey was another refugee from New York who had become one of Broderick's stalwarts. He had fallen into the great man's disfavor by some breach of party discipline.

When Broderick preferred Bagley over Casey, the New Yorker tried to enlist in the ranks of Broderick's enemies, the "Chivalry." They spurned him on social as well as political grounds, and King sneered in his newspaper that the rejected Casey was an ex-convict who had served a term in New York's Sing Sing Prison, and had furnished to the Broderick forces his raffish talents and experience in political corruption and in rigging local elections.

Casey's *amour-propre* was equal to that of the "Southern Chivalry." When he read in the *Bulletin* that he had been "an inmate of Sing Sing Prison in New York" and that he deserved "to have his neck stretched for his fraud on the people," Casey was outraged. Then King added an especially revolting detail: he disclosed that Casey's prison term in New York was for the heinous offense of robbing his own mistress, a lady of dubious virtue. That was too much for the sensitive Casey, who marched into the *Bulletin*'s office and confronted King. "What do you mean," demanded Casey, "by saying that I was a former inmate of Sing Sing?" "And were you not?" asked King. "That's not the point. I don't want my past raked up. On that point I am sensitive," said Casey. King menaced Casey with a hammer and threw him out. A number of witnesses heard Casey threaten the Virginian with retribution;

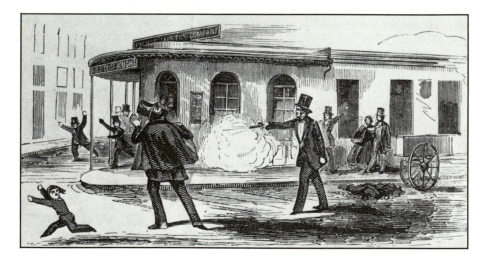

Upper: James P. Casey, from a contemporary lithograph, May 1856

Lower: The shooting of James King of Wm., as portrayed in the July 19, 1856 issue of Frank Leslie's Illustrated Newspaper

they heard him vow in explicit terms to castrate the editor.

Since everybody in San Francisco knew Casey's shady history, King's charges could hardly have impaired his social standing, especially in a milieu inured to shady pasts. For some reason, Casey persisted in his demands that King tender him a retraction and apology. Of course, King met his demands with sneers and new onslaughts. Casey went from saloon to saloon, breathing threats of Gaelic vengeance against King; had he been a man of any social standing there would have been a duel. Casey may not have been a Chiv, eligible to invoke the "Code Duello," but he had his own code of vendetta, even older than the Southerners', one that stretched back to the stark hills of Connemara. Casey hectored from barroom to bagnio, snarling maledictions against King. There was no retraction, no apology. Casey resorted to personal revenge and thereby touched off a civil revolution.

As King walked from his office to his home, one evening, "to join his loving wife and adoring children," Casey suddenly appeared "from behind an express wagon in front of Phil's Oyster Saloon" at the corner of Washington and Montgomery streets. In his hand was a Navy Colt revolver aimed at the editor. Without a warning word, Casey fired two shots into King's breast. King fell, mortally wounded, and the assassin fled to a nearby police station where, like Cora, he could count on the protection of his political friends. Even by local standards, the murder of King was outrageous; it was wanting in those qualities of contemporary *machismo* which in that world could elevate assassination into chivalric jousting. Here there was no preliminary gasconade, no confrontation of two armed men, no invitation to "draw!" Eyewitnesses testified that this was plain murder, from pusilanimous ambush. As the city learned of King's martyrdom in the cause of civic justice, the press and all respectable elements gathered around Casey's refuge. When it was learned that Casey had been spirited out of the local station house, his first asylum, by a ruse, and was now being sheltered in the same fortress-jail that already protected Cora, the mob became uncontrollable. There were "cries of 'hang the son of a bitch . . . take him out.'" Soon the mob screamed for the lives of *both* Casey and Cora. But King was not yet dead. As he lingered, the mob's fury increased, and Brannan and other former vigilantes came to reluctant realization that only a new vigilance committee could avoid chaos in the troubled city.

Committee of Vigilance Membership Certificate, 1856

V

THE VIGILANTES OF 1856

Oh, what was your name in the States?
Was it Thompson or Johnson or Bates?
Did you murder your wife, and fly for your life?
Say what was your name in the States?
Contemporary California Song, circa 1850

When Casey ambushed King, it was unavoidable that the Committee of Vigilance should be revived. The merchants and honest citizenry who had been reluctant to act after Cora's first trial, now gathered in secret and made plans for a new vigilance movement on a grand scale. They arranged for the collection of arms, the selection of "officers," and the formulation of disciplinary standards. They did not flinch from the power struggle they knew would follow. On one side, bent on bringing Casey and Cora to justice and restoring order to the city, were the vigilantes, in whose ranks were the most respectable elements in the city. Arrayed on the other side were the local authorities, the sheriff, the police and their temporary allies, the gamblers, saloonkeepers, pimps, prostitutes and all the other riffraff of the town, miraculously transformed into champions of law and order. The vigilantes agreed with the local press that "it seems almost like a mockery to talk to the people of this city about the law 'taking its course.' "

The vigilantes did not anticipate that they would also be bitterly opposed by the state authorities; since the Know-Nothing election, almost all derived from the "Southern Chivalry." It was reasonable to expect that Governor Johnson, Judge Terry, Senator Gwin and the other Chivs would side with the vigilante movement, especially since King was of their own blood. But other forces were at work which produced the paradox of the Southerners supporting the local riffraff under a banner of "law and order." The state authorities were headed by the callow Governor Neely Johnson, elected as a pro-slavery Know-Nothing, distinguished neither for vigor nor strength of character, and, of course, a tool of the "Chivalry," and especially susceptible to Terry's influence. A council of the newly-elected Know-Nothing officials led by Johnson and Terry determined that despite their fury over the murder of King, they should resist with all their power the formation and activities of the new Committee of Vigilance. Any other course would have been inconsistent with their deep and secret purpose: to establish slavery on California's soil, even if it meant division of the state or secession from the Union.

Eng⁺ by A.H. Ritchie.

MAJ GEN. W. T. SHERMAN

William T. Sherman, as he appeared after attaining the rank of major general,
six years after he was a commercial failure in San Francisco

Revenge for King was a small price to pay for this objective. The vigilante leaders were surprised by the official attitude; they had anticipated that at worst, the state officials would keep their hands off a local situation. It took some time to understand the deeper motive.

The pro-slavery faction had successfully wrested control of the state government from Broderick and his predominantly Northern anti-slavery friends in the 1855 election; they could not afford to risk that hegemony, all-important to realizing their hopes of keeping California out of the anti-slavery ranks. They were indeed the duly-elected lawful authority in the state, and if the city was in a state of lawless chaos, it was the plain duty of state government — their own state government — to take over and restore order. If they needed armed help, there were United States Navy ships in the bay, commanded by Captain David Glasgow Farragut; and a small but well-armed detachment of federal troops under General J. E. Wool was at the nearby army post of Benicia. If the duly-elected, lawfully-constituted authorities of the State of California called on these federal forces to avoid anarchy, the Secesh believed there was every sound reason to assume it would be forthcoming. And, of course, once military force was concentrated in the hands of the Secesh, it could be used for the higher cause. The state militia, under the governor's direct control, seemed to furnish an answer to their needs. Considering their real purpose, their selection of a military leader was historically ironical. They turned command of the state militia over to a newly-appointed major general, William Tecumseh Sherman. But the rank and file of the state militia in San Francisco refused to protect the sheriff and his prisoners from the angry mob of the vigilantes. The rank and file sympathized with the vigilantes. They shed their militia uniforms, turned in their arms and refused to play any role in protecting the jail from the mob. Most of them were awaiting only the actual formation of the Vigilance Committee to join its armed force.

Sherman was then thirty-five; he was not yet the man of Shiloh and Atlanta, the iron-hearted leader of decisive action and martial slogans. He had enjoyed a previous sojourn in San Francisco. On July 4, 1846, three transports filled with American troops landed at what was still called Yerba Buena, among them young Lieutenant Sherman. His stay in the Bay area was a round of balls and fetes to celebrate the American takeover. Soon he went back East, and left the Army for the banking business. But his self-confidence was shattered by a series of reverses. He tried being a lawyer in Kansas, but quit after one disastrous case; he tried to get back into the Army, where he found he was not wanted. Some friends in St. Louis sent him to San Francisco to establish a branch bank. Things went so badly that he termed himself "the Jonah of banking." Now, as commander in chief of the state militia, he found himself in command of a force which existed more in name than in power. The militia had virtually no arms; almost all its officers were committed to Brannan and the other vigilante leaders. The privates of the militia in San Francisco would overnight become the soldiers of the Vigilance Committee.

The murder of King, the use of the city jail as a luxurious refuge for Cora and Casey, the shameful indifference of the municipal authorities, was too much for the honest merchants of the city. By nightfall, after the shooting of King, they were in a secret meeting to reconstitute a formal Committee

This document is the actual Vigilance Committee subscription form, 1856, with William T. Coleman's name heading the list. The original can be found in the Bancroft Library.

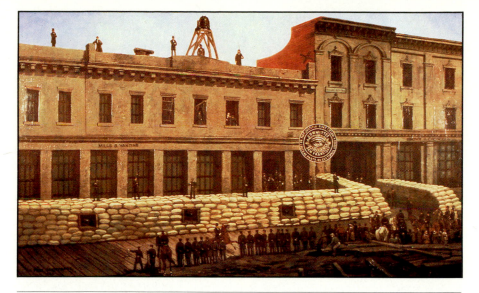

Fort Gunnybags, 1856

of Vigilance. A new leader emerged from the deliberations of the Committee of Vigilance, William T. Coleman, who had Brannan's zeal but excelled him in organizing talent. By early morning on May 17, 1856, the Vigilance Committee rooms were opened and a long line of applicants for membership was waiting to be enrolled. By noon, a cordon of armed vigilantes was stationed around the jail.

The San Francisco vigilantes of 1856 were no such ragtag posse as we now see in the western movies. They had a deep concern for observing both the form and substance of "legal" procedures. There was none of that cavalier indifference to personal rights and human life epitomized by Mark Twain's celebrated line: "Hang him now, and try him later!" They were well organized, disciplined, well armed, even uniformed; they constituted a superbly-led private army of several thousand sturdy men. The California historian, H. H. Bancroft, calls "the second Vigilance Movement . . . the greatest of popular demonstrations in the cause of civic righteousness, without subversion of the law or of the government that the world has ever seen."

Over a single night, the Committee of Vigilance was organized with swiftness and skill. It took control of the city through its private army which operated from a fortified headquarters first called "The Committee's Rooms," then "Fort Vigilance," and finally "Fort Gunnybags," from the sand-filled gunnysacks protecting the structure. Armed sentries patrolled the stronghold and cannon defended it from attack. The building contained a well-equipped command post, detention cells with steel bars and an arsenal of weapons. On the roof was a firehouse bell which clanged to summon the committee's cohorts to arms when danger threatened. The Committee of Vigilance was the organ of all the respectable elements in the community. One local newspaper announced: "All business men have yielded to it, and have regarded those who favored the cause of Law and Order [i.e., Governor

Johnson, Terry, the "Southern Chivalry," et al.] as enemies of the people, and withdrawn their patronage from newspapers and all other interests controlled by Law and Order men." Aside from the vigilantes of 1851 in San Francisco, there had been vigilance committees in many of the mining camps, but these held no formal courts, and in the early days such offenses as claim-jumping, horse stealing and cheating at cards were all punished by impromptu barroom trials and quick executions. The Vigilance Committee of 1856, by its dignified procedures and its adherence to "lawful standards," invested civil insurrecton with a strange and impressive decorum. But the vigilantes were immediately in conflict with the forces of Law and Order.

When Governor Johnson and his advisers (among whom Terry was the most vociferous) learned that the new Committee of Vigilance had been formed and was ready to take action, he ordered Sherman and his militia forcibly to disband the committee. The majesty of the State of California and the summons to its arms were expressed in newspaper proclamations sandwiched between advertisements for "Holloway's Pills for the Blood" and notice of a meeting of the "Ladies' Aid and Protective Association for the Benefit of Seamen." But Sherman found that newspaper proclamations were no substitute for armed men; he was a one-man army. He valiantly presented to Coleman and his associates Governor Johnson's demand that the vigilantes disband and leave matters in the hands of the elected officials and the courts. His demand was met with polite scorn. By the afternoon of Sunday, May 18, the vigilantes were fully organized, armed and ready for action. They had no ears for Sherman, Johnson or Terry.

Once it was known that the vigilantes had been reconstituted, there was a general exodus of criminal types. The steamer *Sea Bird* left the harbor for San Diego with a passenger list that was compared by the local press with a police blotter. When the firehouse bell tolled at noon on Sunday, May 18, the armed host assembled, and led by officers on horseback marched up Sacramento Street in well-ordered ranks to the city jail.

The vigilantes announced their intention to storm the jail if Cora and Casey were not delivered forthwith into their hands. At first the sheriff and the jailers laughed at the ultimatum. They expected the vigilantes to be driven off by the state militia led by General Sherman and the governor. But no rescuers appeared. The vigilantes then produced their artillery. Contemporary newspaper engravings show a loaded cannon aimed at the jail entrance, the chief artillerist beside it, smoking match in hand, while the minutes were counted off. The sheriff had taken office to earn fees and bribes, not to face cannonballs and grapeshot. He promptly capitulated. The two murderers were turned over to the vigilantes who transported them to the committee's "Rooms," where they were locked up under strong guard. To the city the failure of Sherman and his absent militia to prevent the collapse of "duly-constituted authority," meant that the vigilantes were in complete control. In a letter from Sherman to his banking partner in St. Louis, the chagrined West Pointer wrote:

> *San Francisco is now governed by an irresponsible organization claiming to be armed with absolute power by the people. The Government is powerless and at an end. I don't care if they take the jail, the courts and what they please.*

The capture of Casey and Cora by the Vigilance Committee. Note the cannon aimed at the jail door.

Like Othello, his occupation gone, Sherman resigned as major general in command of Johnson's state militia.

For the moment, the vigilantes were unopposed. They made arrests, summoned witnesses and conducted secret "trials" of Casey and Cora. At noon on May 21, the news came that King was dead, and the vigilante "tribunal" promptly condemned both Casey and Cora to hang. The San Francisco newspapers all exhibited a deep concern that "the people in the Atlantic States" should not get the impression that the city was in the grip of "mob law," and that "whatever has been done, has been done by the people in their might, and done coolly and deliberately without any haste or heated action." On May 22, 1856, throngs of San Francisco's more respectable citizens followed King's cortege to his grave. While the public's attention centered on the King obsequies, the committee carried out its plan for a quick execution.

But first there was enacted a little comedy that might have been devised in the Hollywood-to-come. A priest was brought into Fort Gunnybags by a secret entrance; he united Charlie Cora and Arabella in hurried but holy matrimony; then he administered the last rites of his church to Cora and Casey. Now for the hangings, carefully stage-managed by the Committee of Vigilance to make a deep and lasting impression on the lawless! An engraving of the scene survives; it shows at least three thousand vigilantes, armed with muskets and bayonets, forming a hollow square around two platforms extending out from Fort Gunnybags. Above the platforms are two projecting beams from which ropes dangle. As the bells of the churches tolled for King, Casey and Cora were led to these improvised gibbets, nooses were placed

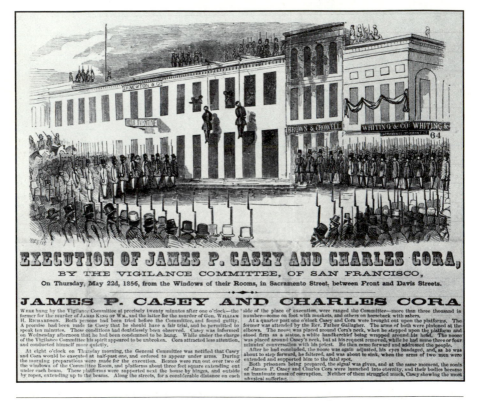

Execution of James P. Casey and Charles Cora, May 22, 1856

round their necks, and the vigilante sergeant at arms, Sterling Hopkins, severed the ropes that held the platforms horizontal. The platforms collapsed, and the two murderers were left writhing in death, a frightening example for the crowd to savor! The committee hoped and expected that the lesson would serve its purpose and that no more hangings would be needed. The local press could not stifle its jubilation: "The reign of terror [by the criminals] is ended!" "The battle has been fought and the victory is ours!" "We have met the enemy and they are vanquished!"

The Law and Order party (Governor Johnson, Terry, Gwin) did not share the general exultation, but they did believe that with the hanging of Cora and Casey the "insurrection" would end. Alas! The committee refused to disband; it felt it was not yet at the end of its Augean labors. There were other Coras and Caseys, although the ships leaving the San Francisco wharves were crowded with miscreants seeking healthier climates. Now it remained for Terry, a judge of the Supreme Court of California, to provide the vigilantes with an experience that ranged from comedy to tragedy to opera bouffe.

Before Terry's contribution to the history of vigilantism in the San Francisco of 1856 is described, let us take a brief glance at the fate of the delectable Arabella "Belle" Ryan, now by benefit of clergy, Arabella Cora. The *Bulletin,* under the leadership of King's successor, printed a letter signed "Many Women of San Francisco." It announced:

> *Every virtuous woman asks that her influence and example be removed from us. The truly virtuous of our sex will not feel that the Vigilance Committee have done their duty till they comply with this request.*

"Too cruel!" wrote another lady, in the *Bulletin.* She signed herself only "Adelia":

> *Belle Cora has suffered enough. . . . She has shown herself a true-hearted woman to him [Cora] and such a heart covers a multitude of sins.*

"Adelia" carried the day. Belle was not sentenced to banishment. She elected to remove herself to Los Angeles, where it was hoped she would lead a life of undiluted virtue as the lawful widow of the lamented Charlie Cora. But the legend is that she founded the first of that city's deluxe brothels.

Now the spotlight shifts to that champion exemplar of the tragic blunderer, David A. Terry. The youthful judge of the state's highest court provided the vigilantes with their moment of high drama, an extravaganza that would echo across America and would bring the state to the edge of civil war.

William T. Coleman

VI

TERRY AND THE VIGILANTES

They jest want this Californy
So's to lug new slave-states in
To abuse ye, an' to scorn ye,
An' to plunder ye like sin.

James Russell Lowell through his Yankee character,
Hosea Biglow, in *The Biglow Papers*

I must remind the reader that to Senator Gwin, to Governor Johnson, to Judge Terry, and to the other Southerners now in control of the state government, the Vigilance Committee was a menace, not because it was anarchic, but because it was an armed threat to their objectives: control of the political processes of California to transform it into a slave state, or when the inevitable showdown came, to lead the state by armed force into the secessionist parade. The devotion of these men to the Southern cause, now within a few years of its desperate contest with the Union, far outweighed their pretended concern about local lawlessness and criminality. In the opportunity to exploit the differences between the legally-constituted authorities of the state and the Committee of Vigilance, they saw the chance to strengthen their hand in the coming struggle. They recognized that the Committee of Vigilance controlled a private army of almost five thousand men, well armed and well led, the most formidable military force in the West. They recognized that this host, overwhelmingly Unionist and anti-slavery in sentiment, presented a mighty obstacle to their secret plans. Of first importance to them was that the "insurrection" should be quelled, the private army disarmed, its weapons neatly stacked in state arsenals for use on "the day," and the police power of the state restored to their hands. To this end, as the vigilantes were considering their action against Cora and Casey in May 1857, Governor Neely Johnson came personally to San Francisco, accompanied by Terry and some of the other Southerners in the state government. From the beginning, Terry was the dominant personality in the official party. Terry's plan was first to make an effort to persuade the vigilantes to disband; if they refused, the governor would call for federal help. If it brought the state authorities into direct collision with the vigilante leadership, federal arms, troops and ships would be arrayed on the side of Law and Order.

But Law and Order had to contend with the elected chief of the vigilantes and the dynamic mainspring of the movement, William T. Coleman. He had come to California from Kentucky, and was thought to be generally

Coleman's office, California Street, San Francisco, from a photograph taken by Fardon in 1856

friendly to the Southern interest. But Coleman was typical of the better class of émigrés who came to California for gold, and stayed for commerce. By 1856, he owned William T. Coleman & Co., contractors and builders, with a splendid office at the corner of Sansome and Jackson streets. In the unprecedented demand for new construction, he quickly became a millionaire. With other prosperous merchants and professionals, he wanted peace, true law and order above everything else. He had no confidence in the elected officials or the local courts filled with corrupt timeservers whether installed by Broderick's machine or by the Secesh. Coleman and his principal associates shrewdly understood the motives of Johnson, Terry and the newly-elected Know-Nothing officials. They knew that the pro-slavery hotheads led by Terry were already deep in plans for secession. About June 10, Terry and Johnson approached Coleman with a daring proposal; they would support him in a coup to lead California out of the Union, form a new "Bear Flag Republic" — of course, with Negro slavery as a legal institution — which would later join with the Southern Confederacy already envisioned by these zealots. Despite his Southern sympathies, Coleman spurned this fantastic proposal.

The Southerners failed to seduce Coleman into treason, but they persisted in their assault on the Committee of Vigilance. The "Chivalry" knew that their own political success was ephemeral, that they were outnumbered more than two to one among the citizenry of the state, and that the continued vitality of the vigilantes could in the end defeat their plans to dominate the state and lead it into secession. They rightly perceived that the vigilantes' private army would in the end fight for the Union against secession and slavery with the same power and efficiency they had shown in their fight against violence and crime. The governor's Law and Order party proceeded with Terry's plan to destroy the committee. The next step was the appeal to the federal authorities for aid in their dramatic need to terminate "armed rebellion against constitutional authority." Terry spurred Johnson to demand of General Wool, commander of the federal military garrison at Benicia, that he release the arms stored in the federal arsenal to the state-controlled militia, even though there was no substantial body of militia to wield these arms. Officers and men of the militia were already enrolled in the vigilante army. But to men whose daily conversation was filled with bombast about seceding from the Union and gasconades about setting up a pro-slavery republic on the West Coast, possession of a cache of arms was invaluable to the future, even if the men to use them were not yet at hand. The Southern Hotspurs, who called themselves the Law and Order party, saw themselves as knights-errant in the Southern cause. Mark Twain wrote, after the Civil War, that Sir Walter Scott had so large a hand in making Southern character as it existed before the war, that the Scottish novelist was in great part responsible for the rebellion. Now the Southerners behaved like characters in one of Scott's romances. But Terry was no Campbell or Claverhouse.

When it became clear that the vigilantes would not disband after hanging Cora and Casey, the Law and Order group opened its counteraction in earnest. At a meeting on May 27, 1857, three of Terry's closest friends were designated by Johnson, at Terry's behest, as a subcommittee to cooperate with the governor in suppressing the "insurrection." The committee included two of the noisiest Southern Hotspurs, Calhoun Benham and Volney E. Howard. The committee called formally on the governor to declare martial law. An official proclamation ensued placing the City of San Francisco in a state of insurrection and establishing martial law. Now Terry and Johnson persuaded Sherman to accompany them to Benicia to renew their request for federal arms. Johnson also sent an emissary to Farragut at Mare Island to request naval aid. Farragut made it plain he would act only on direct orders from Washington; Wool did some waffling. According to Sherman, Wool first promised him that if the governor should declare martial law, Wool would supply arms. That condition was now obtained, but Wool still dragged his feet.

Judge Terry's plan was going awry, and he took personal command of the tactical situation; he issued a writ of *habeas corpus* to the Vigilance Committee for the production of one Mulligan, a prisoner in their hands. Of course, the committee disdained to respond. Next, following Terry's plan, the governor asked the local sheriff in San Francisco if he needed military assistance to execute Terry's writ. The sheriff responded that indeed he did need such assistance. On June 2, the governor issued orders to "General" Sherman (temporarily restored to state service) to call out the militia. But the governor's orders were obeyed by only a few militiamen; seventy-five

Southern sympathizers answered the call, and they were without arms. Again, a demand was made on Wool for arms. Again, Wool refused.

The Law and Order forces emphasized that they did not ask Wool to send his troops into San Francisco. They wanted only arms and ammunition. It is an amusing fact that not long before Johnson's emissaries came to Benicia, one of the officers at the Benicia garrison was Captain Ulysses S. Grant. He had commanded a detachment of infantry sent to garrison California in 1852. But shortly before the vigilante movement, he had been transferred to Oregon, and had resigned his commission in disgust. It would have been a supreme historical irony to see Grant, along with Sherman and Farragut, as actors on the Secesh side in the vigilante drama.

John Ellis Wool was no easy mark to be tricked or dragooned into furnishing arms to men whose designs against the federal government were notorious. He was one of the Army's senior generals, much admired by Winfield Scott. During the Mexican War, he had led the invasion into Chihuahua, and was cheated of success and glory when he had to march to the relief of Zachary Taylor, hard-pressed at Buena Vista. Wool was "an excellent officer, cold, a martinet." When Wool again refused to arm the militia, the governor again appealed to Sherman for help. He reappointed the West Pointer as "Major General of Militia."

Between May 22 and the middle of June, the city was comparatively quiet. The governor issued proclamations and threats — "paper bullets" sneered the pro-vigilante press; another trumpet-call to arms produced a handful of "law and order advocates" who "wrote their names with a trembling hand, and left the room instanter." These patriots were almost all petty officeholders in Broderick's municipal machine or the keepers of grogshops and gambling halls. On June 6, at Terry's prompting, the governor again issued a thundering proclamation that the city was in a "State of Insurrection," and that the majesty of the law required "ACTION!" This brought contemptuous silence from the committee and challenges from the pro-vigilante press for Neely Johnson to "come down here and take the field in person." The only important impression Johnson made was on Queen Victoria's consul in San Francisco. He published a "Notice to all British Subjects resident in the State of California" in which he adjured his countrymen "to abstain from any act which would give offense to the government."

The Vigilance Committee was not idle. By June 10, it had sentenced twenty-two miscreants "to remove themselves from hence" — i.e., banishment from the state. On June 21, the Committee of Vigilance issued a "catalogue" of the "results of the Committee's labors to date as far as the expulsion of notorious persons is concerned." In addition to the execution of Cora and Casey, there was another fatality — the suicide of one "Yankee" Sullivan, a hoodlum and convict released from long imprisonment in Australia. Sullivan was terrified of sharing the fate of Cora and Casey; he stabbed himself to death with a table knife while awaiting "deportation." Besides the three dead, twenty-three notorious troublemakers were shipped off to Mexico, South America and the Sandwich Islands. In July 1856, after two more murderers were hanged, it seemed that the Vigilance Committee's work was almost finished and they could begin to wind down their efforts.

But the governor and his advisors were impatient; egged on by Terry,

Benham and General Howard, Johnson persisted in his efforts to destroy the committee by force. At Terry's prompting, Sherman agreed to participate in a meeting at Benicia where he joined Governor Johnson and Terry in trying to persuade Wool to provide arms. There was a bitter scene in which Terry's voice was the loudest. He charged Wool with being in collusion with the Vigilance Committee whom he denounced as a "set of damned pork merchants." The immediate effect of Terry's outburst was finally to alienate Sherman from the cause of Law and Order. Sherman recalled:

> Seeing that we were powerless for good, and that violent counsels would prevail under the influence of Terry and others, I sat down and wrote my resignation, which Johnson accepted in a complimentary note on the spot.

In this meeting with Wool, Sherman seems finally to have understood that the governor was a tool of Terry and the "Southern Chivalry," and that the true target of the Law and Order partisans was not vigilantism but the Union. Sherman later wrote: "All of these men were known to be of the most ultra kind, men of violent feelings, determined to bring about a collision of arms." Indeed, from the time of the meeting with Wool, Sherman made it clear he had no interest in leading a phantom militia against the vigilantes. Appalled as he was by insurrection, he understood that he was being used as a pawn in the game that the Secesh were manipulating.

With Wool seemingly adamant in his refusal to supply arms to the Law and Order men, and Sherman out of command, Terry's plan seemed frustrated. He went on the offensive and took personal charge of the counterattack on the vigilantes. By the middle of June, Terry was established as the chief of the Law and Order forces; Johnson was merely following the Texan's lead. In desperation, and at Terry's direct prompting, the governor wrote to President Franklin Pierce in Washington for help from the federal government in putting down the "rebellion." But letters to Washington needed weeks for transmittal and events would not wait. In the end, Pierce replied months later, rejecting the demands on grounds that he termed "constitutional." By the time the presidential answer came, events had divested it of all but academic import.

Faced with Wool's refusal to supply arms to the clandestine secessionists, Sherman's refusal to act as the head of a militia melting away before the power of the vigilantes, and the reality that help from Washington, if it ever came, was months away, Terry came up with a plan to rescue Neely Johnson and the Law and Order cohorts from frustration. Acting formally in his judicial capacity, Terry provided the governor with a long and outwardly impressive "legal opinion" that, under existing federal law the state was entitled to a share of federal arms stored on its territory whenever they were requested by a state government faced with a local emergency. The doctrine had a special appeal to the people of the Deep South, who lived with the daily spectre of a slave insurrection; the doctrine would be heard again in a few years, as federal officers with Southern sympathies turned over guns, ships and forts on the demands of Southern governors. Armed now with Terry's legal opinion, the governor again approached General Wool. That veteran was accustomed to dealing with Mexicans and Indians, not with lawyers and judges. He was "impressed," he said, with the legal force of

This is the letter which tipped off the Vigilance Committee that the Law and Order party in San Francisco was expecting a shipment of guns from Benicia arsenal.

*The troops of the Vigilance Committee capturing the vessel carrying arms from
Benicia to the Law and Order party*

Terry's opinion. After all, Terry was a judge of California's highest court. But he was not sufficiently impressed to empty the arsenal. Reluctantly, he agreed to release some muskets and ammunition to the state militia: 100 muskets, one sabre and two bullet molds. (In the summer of 1863, Wool would be confronted with another, far more sanguinary insurrection. He was the military commander in New York when the draft riots occurred. His feeble response to that emergency cost him his command.)

The few guns Wool delivered were useless without the hands to wield them, and the Chivs were better at plotting and talking than at organizing. It would not be surprising if Wool's concession to Terry and the governor was attended with less than the highest degree of military security. Certainly, the vigilantes were forewarned. In character, they moved too swiftly for the governor and his friends. The small barque loaded with arms for the militia was intercepted in the Bay by vigilantes who were waiting for the barque before it arrived at the wharf in San Francisco. Wool had provided no military guard, and the vigilantes had no trouble seizing the little boat. The muskets were seized by the vigilantes and added to their own private arsenal at Fort Gunnybags. The vigilantes also arrested the governor's appointed "agents" for the distribution of the arms, including one Reuben Maloney, also known as "Rube." After questioning, Maloney was released.

He celebrated his escape with a tour of the waterfront saloons, in the course of which he announced to impromptu audiences his intention to avenge his brief detention by removing the gizzards of the vigilante leaders. As he made these pronouncements, he brandished a Bowie knife, describing it as the instrument with which he would perform his surgery. His alcoholic threats reached the ears of the vigilante executive committee. They decided it had been a mistake to release Maloney, and sent the redoubtable Sterling A. Hopkins (the sergeant at arms who had pulled the cords on Cora and Casey) with a small detachment of vigilantes to bring Maloney to a safe place, Fort Gunnybags.

Hopkins was regarded as a tough character. A New Englander, aged thirty-three, he had toiled briefly in the gold fields, and he was now a professional well-digger in San Francisco. His courage and devotion to the vigilante cause had been proved in the Cora-Casey affair. When Maloney learned that Hopkins and his squad were searching for him, he fled to the protection of a temporary headquarters that the anti-vigilante forces had set up in the naval office of Dr. Richard P. Ashe in a building at Washington and Kearny streets. The vigilante patrol found the braggart Maloney drying out under the protection of a knot of Southerners, led by Judge Terry. Of course, Terry took charge of Maloney's defense. Hopkins announced his intention to arrest Maloney; Terry "drew a knife and would have used it upon Hopkins had not Dr. Ashe intervened." Next, Terry threatened Hopkins with a pistol. The patrol leader was under Coleman's orders to avoid a clash of arms, to avoid a shoot-out, especially with a judge of the California Supreme Court. He promptly retired from the scene of action. Hopkins was also deterred from violence by the presence of Dr. Ashe, the local "representative of the United States Navy," as he styled himself.

Ashe had served in the Texas Rangers with Terry, and their friendship was renewed when Ashe became sheriff in Stockton. In 1853, by Gwin's

JUDGE DAVID S. TERRY, STABBING S. A. HOPKINS, OF THE VIGILANCE COMMITTEE, SAN FRANCISCO, CAL.

A contemporary portrayal of the street melee in which Terry stabbed "Sergeant at Arms" Hopkins. This engraving appeared on the front page of the August 16, 1856 issue of Frank Leslie's Illustrated Newspaper.

influence, he was appointed as "local agent" for the United States Navy. His only duty was to purchase needed supplies for the small squadron in the Bay, but Ashe comported himself as if he were a four-striper in command of an armada. Hopkins showed restraint and good sense in avoiding a gun battle with the judge and the *soi-disant* admiral. He made a wise retreat to vigilante headquarters, for new orders and reinforcements. Now, he was told to return to the Law and Order "headquarters" with an augmented patrol, keep Maloney under watch, but at all costs to avoid armed conflict. That was a prudent assignment, but one not easy of execution when it included dealing with Judge Terry.

As Hopkins and his men returned to Ashe's office, they encountered Terry and Ashe leading the group of Southerners (including Maloney) out of the office building on Jackson Street, headed for the state armory, a strong stone building with iron doors, at the corner of Dupont and Kearny. Here the Southerners believed they could withstand the vigilantes until they were relieved (by whom?). Terry assumed command of the small force, heavily armed with shotguns, rifles and knives, all of which were brandished ominously. The fracas that followed opened with an exchange of virile rodomontades, as to which there are varying accounts. Plainly, Hopkins tried to arrest Maloney, and Terry threatened Hopkins with a shotgun; there was some pushing and jostling during which one of the Southerners fired a pistol. Hopkins jostled Terry, whereupon Terry, "in a towering rage, stabbed Hopkins

An actual informer's note to the Vigilance Committee, alerting them
to witnesses ready to testify against Terry

in the neck with his Bowie knife." Hopkins fell to the ground, bleeding profusely, and Terry, Ashe and their cohorts stormed into the armory, slamming the iron doors in the faces of the pursuing vigilantes. Hopkins was carried to a nearby firehouse, where he received the medical attention of four doctors. A fifth surgeon arrived to "take up the artery," and Hopkins was tenderly transported to his nearby home. A committee of doctors pronounced him to be *in extremis.*

Members of the patrol rushed to Fort Gunnybags to inform the executive committee that armed conflict had finally broken out between the vigilantes and the governor's forces, and that the committee's emissary had been stabbed, probably mortally, by Justice Terry of the California Supreme Court, abetted by a high federal officer. From that moment the name of Terry was on the lips of every man in San Francisco; it was the beginning of an odium, a notoriety that would persist for almost four decades. Coleman and his lieutenants had tried in every way to avoid a clash of arms with the governor's people. Terry's knife had forced the issue, and the vigilantes were enraged, but they reacted with disciplined restraint. Within minutes, the firehouse bell was clanging for the vigilantes to assemble. As the troops poured in from all parts of the city, a Council of War resolved to take the armory by storm. Led by its "chief marshal" mounted on a white charger, a strong wellarmed war party of vigilantes marched to the doors of the armory. Like a medieval herald, a "sergeant" advanced to the door under a white flag and demanded the surrender of the occupants; the demand was coupled with the threat to launch a general assault on the building and put its inmates to the sword.

As the news of Hopkins's "murder" by Terry spread through the city, rank-and-file vigilantes gathered in unprecedented force. While Terry and Ashe pondered the committee's ultimatum, the force besieging the armory grew to more than a thousand heavily-armed men. Behind the besieging force of uniformed vigilantes was an angry lynch mob screaming for the blood of Hopkins's "murderers." "Hang Terry! Hang Terry!" was the refrain chanted from thousands of throats. In the armory, the fugitives held their own desperate council; they were less frightened by the vigilantes than by the mob. Plainly, if the armed and disciplined vigilantes did not protect them, Terry, Ashe, Maloney and their companions would soon be swinging from lampposts. When the vigilantes wheeled a loaded cannon into position facing the armory doors, it was plain that there was no hope of rescue. A successful sortie was out of the question; it would have led the Southerners into the arms of a lynch mob.

In the manner of besiegers and besieged, there was a parley, a "negotiation." First, Ashe appeared at a second-story window and pleaded for "terms of surrender." The crowd shouted him down. Then, the Southerners sent out a note: "If the Executive Committee will give us protection from violence we will agree to surrender." It was signed by Ashe not in his naval capacity, but as "Capt. Co. A." and by one of his companions, Reese, as "1st Lieut. Co. B." Ashe had in fact received a "commission" as a captain in the militia. The vigilantes replied that if Terry, Maloney and one Philips were to surrender and the arms in the building were turned over to the committee, they would protect the inmates from the mob. They demanded an answer

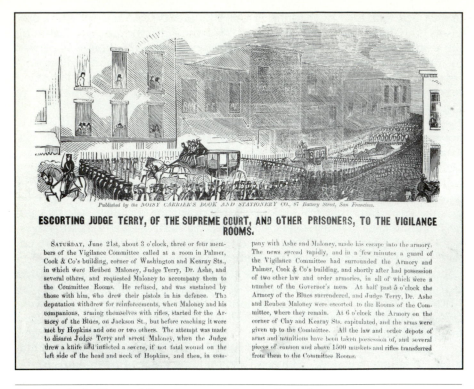

ESCORTING JUDGE TERRY, OF THE SUPREME COURT, AND OTHER PRISONERS, TO THE VIGILANCE ROOMS.

SATURDAY, June 21st, about 3 o'clock, three or four members of the Vigilance Committee called at a room in Palmer, Cook & Co's building, corner of Washington and Kearny Sts., in which were Reuben Maloney, Judge Terry, Dr. Ashe, and several others, and requested Maloney to accompany them to the Committee Rooms. He refused, and was sustained by those with him, who drew their pistols in his defence. The deputation withdrew for reinforcements, when Maloney and his companions, arming themselves with rifles, started for the Armory of the Blues, on Jackson St., but before reaching it were met by Hopkins and one or two others. The attempt was made to disarm Judge Terry and arrest Maloney, when the Judge drew a knife and inflicted a severe, if not fatal wound on the left side of the head and neck of Hopkins, and then, in company with Ashe and Maloney, made his escape into the armory. The news spread rapidly, and in a few minutes a guard of the Vigilance Committee had surrounded the Armory and Palmer, Cook & Co's building, and shortly after had possession of two other law and order armories, in all of which were a number of the Governor's men. At half past 5 o'clock the Armory of the Blues surrendered, and Judge Terry, Dr. Ashe and Reuben Maloney were escorted to the Rooms of the Committee, where they remain. At 6 o'clock the Armory on the corner of Clay and Kearny Sts. capitulated, and the arms were given up to the Committee. All the law and order depots of arms and munitions have been taken possession of, and several pieces of cannon and above 1500 muskets and rifles transferred from them to the Committee Rooms.

Escorting Judge Terry, of the supreme court, and other prisoners, to the Vigilance rooms

in fifteen minutes; their note was signed "Nos. 12, 13, 50, 645, 332." The beleaguered band answered promptly:

> *If you will agree to see that Judge Terry and Mr. Maloney will also be protected, while in your hands, from violence from persons outside your organization, then we will agree to surrender on the terms of your note just received.*
>
> *Respectfully*
> *R.P. Ashe Capt. Co. A*
> *J. Martin Reese, 1st Lieut. Co. B*
>
> *P.S. Lieutenant Philips is not with us.*

The whereabouts of Philips remained unknown. The committee signified its acceptance, the iron doors swung open and the "Southern Chivalry," somehow swollen to a force of sixteen, marched out with hands raised in surrender, led by the two Texans, Terry and Ashe. The terrified Maloney, whose drunken braggadocio had caused the ruckus, made up the rear. The prisoners were marched under heavy guard to Fort Gunnybags. The vigilante escort had to use musket-barrels, butts, and even bayonets to protect the prisoners as they ran the gauntlet through the streets. The mob knew that Terry had knifed Hopkins, and the popular well-digger was thought to be dead. The judge was known by sight to many in the mob, and the vigilantes engaged in a running battle to fight off a determined effort to seize him and lynch him. At length, the convoy reached Fort Gunnybags, where Terry and the others were securely locked in cells. Outside, the mob howled for their blood.

The legendary "Fort Gunnybags," headquarters of the Vigilance Committee, from a photograph taken by Fardon in 1856. Terry was imprisoned in one of the second-floor rooms. The famous fire bell is seen on the roof.

VII

"TERRY WILL AND MUST BE HUNG!"

The liberty of the individual must be thus far limited;
he must not make himself a nuisance to other people.

John Stuart Mill, *On Liberty*

On the day after the surrender of the armory, the *Daily Alta California* could report that "a very general quiet prevailed throughout the city yesterday considering the unparalleled excitement of Saturday." But the vigilantes had some very embarrassing guests on their hands, a California Supreme Court judge who, as soon as he was safe from the lynch mob, breathed fire against his captors, and the "resident agent" of the United States Navy, who threatened that if he and his friends were not released immediately with an appropriate apology, he would order the warships in the Bay to level Fort Gunnybags. Terry was the noisier of the two. He shouted that his detention was not only illegal, it was *lèse-majesté* — a man of his importance arrested "merely for sticking a knife into a damn little Yankee well-borer." While the troubled executive committee pondered the fate of their eminent judicial detainee ("thrust upon us with all the weight of his office," lamented the chief of his captors), Terry and Ashe composed a letter to E. B. Boutwell, commanding officer of the U.S.S. *John Adams,* anchored in the harbor. Couched in Terry's most sententious prose, Boutwell was besought to afford the eminent captive "the protection of the flag of my country."

Before many years passed, Terry, Ashe and Boutwell would all be in arms against that flag, but for the moment the judge saw himself and his fellow Southerners as patriotic Americans engaged in resisting an armed insurrection. Everybody knew that Terry's fate depended on the life of Hopkins. If the New Englander died of Terry's knife wound, the vigilantes had to hang Terry, judge or no judge, or forfeit their hard-won authority over the city. The reality was that if news of Hopkins's death should reach the city, Terry would be hanged — either by a vigilante squad or a lynch mob.

But what of Hopkins, who had been carried first to the firehouse of Pennsylvania Engine Company No. 12, and then to his home by the tender hands of fellow vigilantes? A vigil was mounted at his door. He became the cynosure of the city; bulletins on his condition were issued every hour. The vigilantes competed with the firemen in their "unremitting attention and kindness to the sufferer." There was no question that if he died, Terry would follow Cora and Casey to the gallows, and there were thousands who could hardly wait for the well-digger to die so they could hang Terry. As Hopkins teetered between life and death, the town's physicians vied with each other to treat the hero of the day; gifts poured in upon him from the admiring citizenry. His sickroom was likened to a royal levee at Versailles. The principal topic of conversation among those in attendance was the retribution to be exacted from Terry — if Hopkins died, the noose; if he miraculously survived, banishment from the state and a cash indemnity.

The committee hesitated over "indicting" and "trying" Terry; it hoped that Hopkins would survive and avert the need to hang a judge of the state's highest court. But they were under pressure to act; popular sentiment against Terry was noisy and violent. The press, too, clamored for an immediate "trial." One editor wrote:

> D. S. Terry, Judge of the Supreme Court, has proved himself a rowdy, having been not only engaged in numerous brawls and street fights, but on more than one occasion spilt the blood of his fellow men; and on one occasion, in the presence of a court, he cut with a knife a witness on the stand.

It was clear that the general sentiment was so strong against Terry that, if Hopkins died, his high office would not save him from the gallows. "Murderers must be punished, regardless of station," trumpeted the press. The San Francisco *Bulletin* appointed itself the official organ of the vigilantes. On June 23, it announced:

> If Hopkins dies, Terry will and must be hung. Should Hopkins live, which is extremely doubtful, Terry must be banished. His doom is unalterable; justice requires it.

The June 24 issue of *Daily Alta California* left little doubt about Terry's fate if Hopkins died:

> At [Hopkins's] death, capital punishment must be meted out to the destroyer. . . . There is but one sentiment in respect to the fate of Terry in case his victim dies, and that is he deserves death.

On the night of June 24, to allay popular unrest, the executive committee announced that it had only one concern with the homicidal jurist: if Hopkins died, Terry would hang! Terry was hardly established in his cell when the committee received a letter from Volney E. Howard, "Major General 4th Div. Commanding, S. F.," and co-signed "B. W. Leigh, Acting Aide-de-Camp." The "General" had succeeded Sherman in command of the anemic militia. It recited that:

> A person named Hopkins, claiming to be under your authority, a short time since visited the room of Hon. David S. Terry, in this City, rushed upon him and attempted to disarm him, and otherwise assaulted him. Judge Terry, in self-defense, was compelled to use a knife with which he inflicted a severe, and perhaps a mortal wound.

"Why," said the "General," "if Hopkins died it would be a clear case of justifiable homicide! Give us back our friend, Judge Terry!" The committee did not reply.

The three days that passed after Terry's capture on June 21 were indeed comparatively quiet. During these three days it was assumed that the

Crowd gathering outside Vigilance Committee headquarters

wound inflicted on Hopkins would be fatal. The angry throng that waited outside Hopkins's house and surrounded Fort Gunnybags made no secret of its attitude: when the well-digger died, the judge would hang. The committee had shown that it could deal with the little criminals, the Coras and the Caseys. The real test of their courage was in dealing with a man of Terry's stature. The members of the executive committee alternated between prayers that Hopkins's rugged constitution would prevail and somber reflections on what would happen if he died and they had to deal with Terry as they had with Cora and Casey. Saturnine bulletins about Hopkins's condition reached Terry in his cell. On the 24th, he addressed a missive to the committee, an unmistakable *cri de coeur* from one who feels the noose tightening around his neck. He pleaded that the charges against him be referred to "a legal tribunal in this city," under a local judge. He agreed that the committee could supervise the jury selection, that he would make no bail application, no motion for a change of venue. He asked only "to submit my cause to a jury composed of honest men, though all may be members of the Vigilance Committee." He further agreed that "if death should ensue from the wound inflicted by me, I will at once resign my position, and, if acquitted will at once leave the state, should you require." The fire-eater was obviously very frightened. He heard the mob howling for his blood; every time his jailers approached to bring him news of Hopkins, he trembled that he would hear the worst.

The accounts of Terry's ordeal at the hands of the Vigilance Committee are enriched by their descriptions of the part played by his loyal and pugnacious wife, Cornelia. That formidable Southern lady was summoned to San Francisco from her home in Sacramento on the night of June 22, the day following the attack on Hopkins. Of course, she tried to see her husband in Fort Gunnybags, but permission was refused by the committee. On June 30, Terry composed a letter to his wife, unmistakably meant for publication. First, he described his preoccupation with taking the testimony of witnesses to be used in his forthcoming trial. During his days of imprisonment in Fort Gunnybags, the fire-eater had that opportunity for reflection and self-examination that so often alters a man's character for the better. Old Samuel Johnson said it well: "Depend on it, Sir, when a man knows he is to be hanged in a fortnight, it concentrates his mind wonderfully!"

Terry's mind may have been concentrated, but it was not humbled or conciliatory. He justified his attack on Hopkins as an act

> [s]olely from regard to a sacred principle, from the desire to prevent the consummation in my presence of an act which (though it may have been attempted from good motives would certainly have worked an injury to the community, as the man sought to be removed was a bad man) was a violation of the Constitution of this state which I had sworn to support as well as the Constitution of the United States to secure the blessings of which to their posterity both my grandfathers "fought and bled and suffered."

More references to the sacred Constitution, the military exploits of his ancestors (and himself), then: "My Darling, don't fear that I will falter."

This last is a reference to the news that had reached him in his cell that his friends were proposing a "deal": if the committee would release Terry, he would resign his office and leave the state. Now Terry spurned the solution that he had earlier proposed. The letter ends with: "Good bye my only love, May God bless you and my Son." Of course it was meant to be published. It is hardly a farewell letter to his wife; he addresses her as Gladstone his Queen, as if she were a public meeting. Of course, Cornelia published this affecting missive in the *Daily Herald,* the organ of the Chivs. A true daughter of the South, she dismissed with contempt any "deals" to have him resign and leave the state:

> I cannot tempt him to dishonor. I know my husband too well to suppose that any influence would induce him to betray a trust. [He is] confident to his core.

One of her friends attests that when the vigilantes relented and Cornelia was finally admitted to see her husband, as she left his prison, she turned to wave farewell, raised her voice and said,

> Judge Terry, I would rather see you hanged from one of those windows than to recognize that you were compelled to resign your official position.

But while the judge lay in the committee's second-floor dungeon, what of his friends, the cavaliers, the governor, the frock-coated admiral, Senator Gwin? They gnashed their teeth, chagrined that Terry's Bowie knife had ruined any prospect that the cause of Law and Order would prevail over the vigilantes. But the Southern party felt that it must devote itself to saving Terry's life. On June 28, the governor, probably at Ashe's suggestion, again appealed directly to Commander Boutwell to rescue his judge. On the same day, Terry again "invoked the protection of the flag of my country" in still another appeal to Boutwell. It elicited from that unhappy officer a written promise to the executive committee:

> *If Hopkins dies, and the Committee condemns [Terry] to death, I will*
> *make an effort to save his life in such a manner as not to be offensive*
> *to my fellow-citizens.*

Boutwell did not explain by what tactics he planned to carry out that purpose.

Terry's knife had wrought an important change in popular sentiment. Until he stabbed Hopkins, there were many respectable citizens who held back from supporting the vigilantes. Law and Order was not without its intrinsic appeal to law-abiding citizens. But from the moment Terry plunged his Bowie knife into the well-digger, all respectable opposition to the vigilantes dissolved in anger. The committee now felt secure enough to release their other prisoners, including "Admiral" Ashe and to concentrate on preparing its charges against Terry. In Terry's mind, the members of the Vigilance Committee were little more than a lynch mob, a secret society of murderers. Here he was, a high judicial officer of the state, locked up in a cell by a crowd of civilians to await "trial" for homicide, for resisting an armed attack by men who wore no badges and acted under no civic authority other than the orders of their self-appointed murderers-in-chief! It would never occur to Terry to inquire why he should have abandoned his judicial duties in Sacramento and come armed into the streets of San Francisco to engage in bloody brawling with the vigilantes. He demanded his release, his liberty. His friends, his devoted Southern wife, gathered daily in front of Fort Gunnybags to shout for liberty for the Texan. Dr. Ashe, now free, used his naval influence to persuade Commander Boutwell to demand of the committee that Terry, as an important state official, be delivered to his ship.

The committee started taking the testimony of Ashe and other witnesses the day after Terry's arrest on June 21, 1856. It promptly issued an "indictment" against Terry. The charging document revealed that in the minds of his captors Terry was guilty not only as the assailant of Hopkins, he was an habitual brawler and troublemaker; he was precisely the kind of man the vigilantes wanted to expel from their society. The "indictment" charged the prisoner with:

> *Resisting with violence the officers of the Vigilance Committee while*
> *in the discharge of their duties. Committing an assault with a deadly*
> *weapon with intent to kill Sterling A. Hopkins on June 21, 1856.*
> *Various breaches of the peace and attacks upon citizens while in the*
> *discharge of their duties, specified as follows:*
> *1. Resistance in 1853 to a writ of habeas corpus on account of which*
> *one Roach escaped from the custody of the law, and the infant heirs*
> *of the Sanchez family were defrauded of their rights.*
> *2. An attack in 1853 on a citizen of Stockton named Evans.*
> *3. An attack in 1853 on a citizen in San Francisco named Purdy.*
> *4. An attack at a charter election on a citizen of Stockton named*
> *King.*
> *5. An attack in the court house of Stockton on a citizen named*
> *Broadhouse.*

A copy of Terry's pompous letter to his wife was furnished to a group of friends, led by the state treasurer. They applied to the United States Circuit Judge, M. S. McAllister, to issue a writ of *habeas corpus*. The jurist declined on the grounds that he "did not wish to provoke the animosity of the people." A strange reason for a judge, but he too could hear the clamor of the mob coming through the open windows.

When the news of Terry's predicament came to the people of his native state, the legislature of Texas prepared a "memorial" to Congress, to be presented by the venerable hand of Sam Houston himself, imploring that the federal government rescue Terry from "the insurrectionists." Several Southern senators and congressmen supported the Texas "memorial." One of them, overcome by his sympathy for poor Terry, wrote: "Judge Terry is an honorable, high-minded prudent man, who felt bound to use the whole of his moral influence in favor of sustaining the laws." Prudent! Moral influence in the point of a Bowie knife! But what was happening back in the East had no effect on events in San Francisco.

There, things looked pretty bad for the judge. Hopkins teetered between life and death; the crowds were becoming impatient for another *auto-da-fé;* Wool had nothing to offer and Boutwell seemed to be held in check by his superior, Commander Farragut. Terry's Southern supporters decided to play a trump card: the august Senator William M. Gwin. Gwin had carefully removed himself from the dangerous goings-on in San Francisco. He remained safely in Sacramento while the vigilantes took over the port city, hanged Cora and Casey and jailed Terry. He probably took some quiet satisfaction in Terry's troubles, for at the moment there was a personal grudge between the two men. Gwin saw himself as the standard-bearer of the Democratic party in California, and he had dark thoughts about men like Terry, who had bolted to the Know-Nothing American ticket and — worst of all — had won the last election. But Southern blood proved thicker than the watery fluid in the veins of Yankee mudsills, and Southern ties stronger than ephemeral political animosities. The great man was persuaded to take the steamer for San Francisco and use his influence in behalf of the unfortunate judge immured in Fort Gunnybags. Gwin was a happy choice for conciliator. He was highly respected by the principal members of the committee, and he was known to be a close friend to Farragut who — unlike the pusillanimous Wool — may have held the key to the situation in his hands: the guns and marines of the *John Adams* could only be used with Farragut's approval.

A "peace" meeting was arranged in San Francisco attended by Gwin, Farragut, two of Terry's close friends and four representatives of the vigilantes. To nobody's surprise, the vigilante leaders explained that they

> *had organized to hunt down and drive away or kill off a lot of villainous coyotes, but they had unexpectedly trapped a grizzly bear, and they were worst puzzled how to get rid of him than anybody on the outside could possibly imagine.*

They continued:

> *[The] Committee of thirty-six was not its own master; their actions were controlled by 6000 armed men, many of them reckless and hasty, some of them foreigners who did not speak the English language, and all of them clamorous for the execution of Judge Terry if Hopkins should die.*

When the Southerners in the meeting suggested that the committee should permit Terry to "escape" from Fort Gunnybags, the vigilantes said that their own lives and the lives of the executive committee would be in danger if they let Terry go. Farragut joined Gwin in trying to persuade the vigilantes to deliver Terry to the United States Navy for safekeeping. Gwin described the stigma that would forever attach to the fair reputation of California "in the East, in Europe and throughout the world should the lawless organization put to death one of the highest judicial officers of the State."

The meeting ended in frustration as the committee's representatives "sullenly" insisted that if they released Terry he would be lynched — and so might the vigilantes' leaders. Everybody went home to wait for word from Hopkins's sick room. On the afternoon of July 17 the word came that the well-digger was out of danger. Now, the executive committee, breathing more easily, decided to proceed with the "trial" of Terry, without the torturing fear that they would have to hang him. The "trial" had actually begun on June 27, but it was adjourned several times "to afford the defense an opportunity to prepare." Despite Hopkins's recovery, things still looked so bad for Terry that his friends renewed their efforts to make a "deal": resignation and exile from the state. His answer was conveyed to them by Mrs. Terry: "My husband will never leave the Committee fort alive save as a justice of the Supreme Court." While the trial was in progress, and Terry's friends were negotiating for his release, a new force was introduced into the confusion: the United States Navy.

The naval base at Mare Island, commanded by Captain David G. Farragut, 1855

VIII

THE UNITED STATES NAVY
TAKES A HAND

"Would that be justice?" asked the just man.
"It would be success," said the Duchess, "which is much the
better of the two."

Anthony Trollope, *Phineas Redux*

On June 28, the committee received from Commander Boutwell a letter which may have been composed with literary and legal assistance from Ashe and other members of the Law and Order forces. Boutwell had conferred with his superior, Commodore Farragut, at Mare Island when the vigilante "insurrection" first broke out and they had agreed upon a "hands-off" policy. But Terry's arrest on June 21, and the certainty that the committee would hang him if Hopkins died, rattled the young naval officer. Without consulting Farragut, Boutwell wrote:

United States Ship John Adams,
off San Francisco,
June 28, 1856.

To the Executive Committee of Vigilance:

Gentlemen: You are either in open rebellion against the laws of your country, and in a state of war, or you are an association of American citizens combined together for the purpose of redressing an evil, real or imaginary, under a suspension of the laws of California. . . . I, as an officer of the United States, request that you deal with Judge Terry as a prisoner of war and place him on board my ship.

But if you occupy the position of a party of citizens, acting under a suspension of, or against, the law of California, you will, I think, on reflection, and from a desire to conform to the requirements of the Constitution of your country, from a due regard to justice, and, above all, from a desire to avoid the shedding of American blood by American citizens upon American soil, surrender Judge Terry to the lawful authorities of the State.

You, gentlemen, I doubt not, are familiar with the case of Kotza[sic]. If the action of Captain Ingraham in interfering to save the life of Kotza (who was not then an American citizen) met the approbation of his country, how much the more necessary is it for me to use all the power at my command to save the life of a native-born American citizen, whose only offense is believed to be in his efforts to carry out the law, obey the Governor's proclamation, and defend his own life.

The attack of one of the policemen of the Vigilance Committee, who perhaps would have killed the Judge if the Judge had not wounded his adversary, was clearly without the sanction of the law. Gentlemen of the Committee, pause and reflect before you condemn to death, in secret, an American citizen, who is entitled to a public and impartial trial by a judge and jury recognized by the laws of his country.

I trust you will appreciate my motives, and consider my position. I earnestly pray that some arrangement may be effected by which peace and quietude may be restored to this excited community.

I have the honor to be, very respectfully,

Your obedient servant,
E. B. Boutwell, Commander.

The "case of Kotza" referred to an incident in 1853, in which Captain Ingraham, in command of an American naval vessel at Smyrna, became a hero for a day by threatening to fire on an Austrian ship which had forcibly taken on board one Martin Koszta, a Hungarian rebel thought to be an American citizen. Ironically, the Koszta Incident would be exhumed in 1890, in Mr. Justice Lamar's dissenting opinion in In re *Neagle*. Naval commanders in the middle of the nineteenth century were virtually out of touch with any source of political authority. They were expected to, and often did, act with a degree of independence and flexibility that would become unthinkable after the invention of the cable and the wireless. The possibility that Boutwell would use force was not fanciful.

The committee did not want to bring down on its city a bombardment by a man-of-war whose guns were in easy range. Also, it was concerned to preserve the appearances of due process. It decided to send Boutwell's letter to Commodore Farragut, at Mare Island, on the assumption that Farragut, as Boutwell's superior officer, could persuade the hotheaded young Southerner to keep his nose and his ship out of a local quarrel.

A letter of transmittal was carefully composed and entrusted to two vigilantes, Messrs. Farwell and Case, local merchants, who professed an acquaintance with Farragut and felt they could impress him with the committee's lofty purposes. The letter has been preserved, together with Farragut's reply.

Executive Committee Chambers,
Committee of Vigilance,
San Francisco,
June 29, 1856.

To Captain David G. Farragut,
United States Navy,

Sir:
We take the liberty of enclosing herewith a letter received this day
from Commander Boutwell of the U. S. Ship John Adams, *also a copy*
of our reply.
    Owing to the extraordinary logic and menacing tone of Com-
mander Boutwell's communication we deem it advisable to submit
it to his superior's notice, for whom we entertain the highest regard
and esteem.

Under the Seal of the Committee,
33, Secretary.

The signature "33, Secretary" was consistent with the committee's
almost juvenile emphasis on secrecy and anonymity. Everybody in San Francisco knew the identity of the committee's leaders, and that "33" was a local
dry goods merchant named Isaac Bluxome, Jr.

Farragut's response must be admired for the delicacy of his recommendations and for the measured moderation of its prose. Since the committee had sent Boutwell's letter by the hands of Messrs. Farwell and Case (names
not numbers), the naval officer addressed his reply to them, not to "No. 33,
Secretary":

Navy Yard, Mare Island
July 1, 1856.

To Messrs. Farwell and Case,
Of the Committee of Vigilance,
San Francisco, California,

Gentlemen:
I have perused with great attention the correspondence between the
Committee of Vigilance and Commander Boutwell, and although I
concur with the Commander in many important facts of the case, still
I conceive it to be my duty to avert, as far as possible, the evils now
hanging over this highly excited community. And although I believe
Commander Boutwell to be actuated by the same motive, he has
perhaps taken a different mode of attaining this end. I perfectly
agree with him that the release or trial of Judge Terry, in accordance
with the Constitution of the United States, would be the readiest mode
of attaining the great object we all have in view. That instrument, in
Article 5th of the Amended Constitution, says: "No person shall be
held to answer for a capital or otherwise infamous crime, unless on
presentment or indictment of a grand jury, etc." [The letter then
quotes Article 6 of the Amended Constitution and comments on the
secrecy of the Vigilance Committee.]
    Article 4th (Section 4) of the Constitution provides that "the

Farragut as Commander of Mare Island, 1854

United States shall guarantee to each State a republican form of government, and on application of the Legislature, or of the Executive (when the Legislature cannot be convened) shall protect each of them against domestic violence."

The last is a grave and momentous decision which is truly embarrassing to the officers of the general Government, so far removed from the seat of government, and one which every officer must decide for himself, according to his sense of duty to his God and his country. But you may be assured, gentlemen, that I shall always be ready to pour oil on the troubled waters, rather than do aught to fan the flame of human passions, or add to the chances of the horrors of civil war.

You will please inform the Committee that I shall address Commander Boutwell on the subject today, by the same conveyance that carries this communication to you.

I am, gentlemen, very respectfully,

Your obedient servant,
D. G. Farragut, Commandant of Mare Island.

Farragut's reply reflects the quality of the man. He is remembered today by American school children as the hero of Mobile Bay, whose courageous "Damn the Torpedos!" is one of our most stirring patriotic slogans. But Farragut was more than a skilled officer and a felicitous sloganeer: he was one of those self-taught giants of the nineteenth century whose accomplishments enriched his country. A midshipman at the age of ten, in the War of 1812 he accompanied Porter into the Pacific during the famous cruise of the frigate *Essex.* He had enough poise at twelve to command one of Porter's prizes into Valparaiso harbor. Back at his post on the *Essex,* he fought his section bravely in the frigate's historic last battle. During routine service in the Navy in the next three decades, he taught himself French, Spanish, and even Arabic.

When we consider Boutwell's impetuous character and his Southern bias, Farragut's tact and diplomacy may have averted a tragedy. We will never know if, in his zeal to rescue Terry, Boutwell would have turned his ship's guns on the vigilante fort. It would have required a masterpiece of naval artillery practice to level the fort without destroying the surrounding area and perhaps setting the whole town afire. But Farragut's cool head prevailed over Boutwell's bellicosity and the city was spared the threat of selective bombardment.

It is not known whence Farragut derived his knowledge of "Article 4th (section 4)" of the Constitution, but his legal courage was of a piece with the intrepidity he would display in later years at Mobile Bay. There is some evidence that Farragut had the benefit of talking with at least one lawyer. While Terry was languishing in Fort Gunnybags, his supporters again applied to Judge McAllister of the federal court to issue a writ of *habeas corpus.* Gwin arranged a meeting between McAllister and Farragut in which the judge seemed to favor federal action. But no writ issued. The judge could still hear those street voices. Farragut's letter to Boutwell is as wise and temperate as his letter to the committee, which was delivered on the same day:

Navy Yard, Mare Island
July 1, 1856.

To Commander E. B. Boutwell,
United States Ship John Adams,

Sir:
Yesterday I received a communication from the Vigilance Commit-
tee, inclosing a correspondence between yourself and the Committee,
in relation to the release of Judge D. S. Terry, and requesting my
interposition. Although I agree with you in the opinions expressed,
in relation to the constitutional points, I can not agree that you have
any right to interfere in this matter, and I so understood you when
we parted. The Constitution requires, before any interference on the
part of the general Government, that the legislature shall be con-
vened, if possible, and, if it cannot be convened, then the application
of the Executive. I have seen no reason why the Legistature could not
have been convened long since, yet it has not been done, nor has the
Governor taken any steps that I know of, to call it together.

In all cases within my knowledge, the Government of the
United States has been very careful not to interfere with the domestic
troubles of the States, when they were strictly domestic and no colli-
sion was made with the laws of the United States, and has always
been studious of avoiding as much as possible, collision with State
rights principles.

The commentators Kent and Story agree that the fact of the
reference to the President, by the Legislature or Executive of the State,
was the great guarantee of State rights. I feel no disposition to inter-
fere with your command; but, so long as you are within the waters
of my command, it becomes my duty to restrain you from doing
anything to augment the very great excitement in this distracted com-
munity, until we receive instructions from the Government. All the
facts of the case have been freely set forth before the Government by
both parties, and we must patiently await the result.

I am, very respectfully,

Your obedient servant,
D. G. Farragut, Commandant.

The first paragraph of Farragut's letter and the third paragraph of
Boutwell's reply make it clear that the two officers had indeed understood
the delicacy of their position when the Committee of Vigilance had first been
revived, and had wisely concurred in the conclusion that they should take
no action without orders from Washington. But Boutwell's Southern bias
and the importunity of Terry's friends persuaded him to change his mind.
The *John Adams* carried a large crew and a file of marines, all trained in the
use of small arms. Certainly, Boutwell had it in his power to cannonade the

vigilante fort or to put a heavily-armed landing party ashore to try to rescue Terry. It is interesting to speculate what would have happened if he had ordered a bombardment or a rescue attempt by a naval landing party—probably, the carnage of a street-by-street battle. The young officer may well have been supported by his superiors in Washington for taking such drastic action. The administration had proved by many other actions that it was pro-Southern in sentiment, and at a distance of three thousand miles, the vigilantes would have appeared not as a force of law-abiding citizens trying to quell wholesale lawlessness, but as an insurrectionary mob. In Boutwell's phrase, they were "a portion of the people of San Francisco on one side" in arms against the lawfully-constituted authority of state and local government. Any rescue attempt might have had terrible consequences.

Boutwell could hardly have understood that he was toying with the deadliest kind of civil strife when, in a letter to Farragut on July 2, he wrote:

I must inform you that I have been applied to by the Governor of the State, Judge Terry, the prisoner himself, the Collector of the Port, and the United States Marshal of this district, and appealed to by the distressed wife of the Judge, to interfere in this unhappy controversy between a portion of the people of San Francisco on the one side and the State on the other; and what I have done has been dictated by humanity and a conscientious discharge of my duty, and I am prepared to meet the consequences.

How could Boutwell "interfere in this unhappy controversy" except by using his cannon or an armed rescue force? While he was pondering his military options, he received a measured answer from Farragut which included this:

I felt no disposition to interfere with your command, and should not have done so, had you not written a letter to the Committee which induced them to think that it was your intention to fire on the city.

Farragut wrote again to Boutwell on the following day, July 3, giving him some routine orders on other Navy business, but he concluded with this prudent order:

You will not sail until these arrangements are made, nor until further orders from me, as your presence may be necessary in the harbor.

You will receive on board Judge D. S. Terry, for his personal safety, should any arrangement be accomplished to that end.

This letter seems to have been written on the day following the meeting Farragut attended with Gwin and the vigilantes' representatives. He was still hopeful that it could be "arranged" for Terry to be released to the Navy.

In the end, Terry's life was saved not by a landing party from Boutwell's ship, but by the sturdy constitution of "the little Yankee well-borer." Under the ministrations of the local doctors and buoyed by prayers and gifts of countless well-wishers, Hopkins staged a swift recovery. "A prince could not receive greater attention than is bestowed upon Mr. Hopkins in his affliction."

Nature had not cast [Hopkins] for a hero's role. Sudden prominence went to his head. He held daily bedside receptions like an invalid queen; offered to settle with Terry for a considerable cash payment;

*and when able to walk, strutted about town like a Coriolanus in
reverse, eager to display his wounds. He was an embarrassment to
the Committee, and a serious drama was in danger of degenerating
into a farce.*

While the imprisoned judge justified his reputation as a belligerent fire-eater by screaming defiance and threats at his captors from his jail cell, and while his victim recuperated, Terry's friends made a last effort to get military assistance from Farragut. Boutwell's blustering had not been translated into action, so they sent another committee to visit Farragut at Mare Island. The little captain listened to them as he had listened to the emissaries of the committee and to Gwin. Again, he counseled patience and moderation. "No," he said, "I will not order Commander Boutwell to shell the town, and 'exterminate the insurrectionists.' " But he would have another talk with Mr. Coleman, the leader of the vigilantes. During the crisis, while Hopkins hovered between life and death, Farragut came to the city, dined with Coleman in a public place, to "let himself be seen talking to the chief insurrectionist in a friendly way." He then went with Coleman for a carriage drive through the city in Coleman's carriage, and generally did everything possible to allay suspicion and fear. The cool heads of Farragut and Coleman unquestionably did much to avoid any more melodrama and bloodshed.

The sentiment of the public and the attitude of the vigilantes demanded that Terry's "trial" be concluded. So with Coleman presiding, the proceedings went on for three weeks while scores of armed guards stood within and without Fort Gunnybags. Of course, Terry pleaded not guilty to all the charges. A large number of witnesses were examined and cross-examined. On July 22, Terry testified in his own behalf. He maintained stoutly — if factitiously — that he had "merely resented an insult and defended his own life." Terry's written "plea" to the indictment is a masterpiece of self-justification. Says Terry:

*I am aware that at times I have acted hastily. I am naturally of a very
excitable habit, but it cannot be said by any one that I ever sought
difficulties. The specifications speak of my violent and turbulent
habits; and what do they prove? That I will promptly resent a personal affront. . . . I believe if a gentleman should wound the feelings
of any one he should at once make suitable reparation, either by an
ample apology or, if he feels that circumstances prevent this — that
is if he made charges that he still thinks true — should afford him the
satisfaction he desires.*

Since Hopkins was alive, the popular pressure to convict for attempted murder had somewhat abated. But as the trial progressed, at least one newspaper did its best to inflame sentiment and excite a lynching. The *Bulletin* usually referred to the defendant as "the rowdy judge"; it described how he had "bathed his Bowie knife in the blood of an unarmed witness"; how he came to San Francisco

*to gloat on human gore even to satiety . . . with the sworn purpose
of making our streets run with the blood of our innocent citizens.
Blood, blood, blood, seems to be the only substance in nature capable
of slaking the thirst of this man-beast.*

The committee was not impressed by this kind of prose; it was just as anxious to see the trial terminated as were Terry and his supporters. The trial was concluded on July 22, after twenty-five days of hearings, by a verdict hedged about with the deepest secrecy: the committee found Terry guilty of resisting its officers, of the charge of "assaulting" Hopkins and of the attack on Purdy three years earlier. The secret verdict was referred to the vigilantes' Board of Delegates, more than one hundred representatives of the various divisions, Coleman presiding. Both sides were heard.

The result was astonishing; Terry's conviction was affirmed by the larger group, but they concluded:

the usual punishments in their power to inflict not being applicable in the present instance, the said David S. Terry shall be discharged from their custody.

They also decreed that the interests of the state "imperatively demand" that Terry resign his position as a judge of the supreme court. In this part of the sentence, the committee gave expression — probably unconsciously — to that venerable principle of English law that judges should hold office *"quam se bene geserint"* — only as long as they behave themselves. These sensible merchants found it hard to believe that a man could comport himself as Terry had done and still retain the right to judge the conduct of other men.

To appease the populace, the committee informed the local press that they "were fully determined to execute Judge Terry, had Mr. Hopkins died from the effects of the wound received on June 21st last ." But the rapid verdict frustrated and enraged the rank and file. When they learned of the decision to release Terry, most of the vigilantes responded with unconcealed fury. But Coleman and the other leaders had had enough. They had contrived a verdict and release that they hoped would avoid a riot and lynching. It was first thought that Terry should be released "in broad daylight" as befitted the dignity of the committee. But the street crowds made it clear that Terry would not get ten feet from Fort Gunnybags before there would be a rope around his neck. Dignity was subordinated to expediency! Terry was released in the middle of the night through the back door of the vigilantes' fort. He was escorted to the home of his friend, Duncan Perley, where the faithful Cornelia awaited him. On arrival, he was advised that some of the vigilantes, having learned of his release, were gunning for him "still crying for his blood"; that he was in great danger; "a thousand men were looking for the missing judge."

Coleman later explained that nothing that occurred in the Terry episode frightened the vigilantes more than the report that a lynch mob was searching for Terry after his release. If he were lynched, it would be an ineradicable stain on the committee; it would be said that the committee had contrived his death. Therefore, under a carefully-picked escort of the committee's troops, he was spirited aboard the *John Adams,* where Boutwell received him with "a show of respect." Terry and his wife were placed aboard the next steamer for Sacramento. When the steamer passed the *John Adams,* Boutwell ordered the firing of a salute in his honor. Farragut was delighted to hear that the "hot potato" was off everybody's hands, including the Navy's. His report to the secretary of the Navy is somewhat inaccurate in advising that Terry was "acquitted by the Executive Committee," but it does accurately reflect that the judge was "set at liberty."

Once Hopkins's recovery was expected, Farragut met secretly with Gwin and Judge McAllister and told both men that he might be forced to take military action against the committee, if Terry were sentenced to hanging. McAllister agreed to issue a writ for Terry, if Farragut would back him up. As the committee deliberated Terry's fate, Farragut sent two other vessels from Mare Island to support the *John Adams* should action become necessary. The committee's knowledge of Farragut's preparations and plans unquestionably strengthened the hands of Coleman and the other moderates in tempering the "sentence" with expediency.

The "order" of the vigilantes that Terry be banished from the state was never enforced. As soon as he returned to Sacramento, Terry resumed his judicial duties as if nothing had happened. It would have been better if he had returned to Texas, for he would presently emerge from his temporary obscurity to play the role, that in the minds of generations of Californians, has stamped his memory with the mark of Cain.

When Terry resumed his place on the bench of the supreme court, the demands that he resign, that he be banished, were ignored or forgotten. By August 23, even the *Daily Alta* was reconciled to the prospect that Terry would continue as a judge. He should be "closely watched by the people" but "his worst personal enemies have accorded him always the credit due to official honesty." The Vigilance Committee was glad to see the end of Terry — and Terry wanted no more to do with the committee. Years later, he would concede that the vigilantes "had exerted one of the greatest moral and political influences for good in the State."

"Vigilante justice" has become a synonym for something less than ideal law enforcement. When the excitement ended, one wag said that the Vigilance Committee was like the bishop who was detested by all the clergy who served under him. When he died, one priest asked another, "Are you going to the Bishop's funeral?" "No," said the second priest, "I'm not going — but I approve of it!" The motives and conduct of the San Francisco vigilantes were examined by Josiah Royce, who many regard as one of the most luminous and dispassionate historians and philosophers of the age. He concluded that the committee "was absolutely necessary . . . an honest and active company of intelligent and able leaders."

One of the mysteries of the vigilante movement of 1856 is the part played by Broderick — or, more accurately, the part he did not play. After all, many of the vigilantes' targets were men who owed their place to Broderick. He did nothing to protect them. After the danger had passed Broderick would claim an active part in defending Terry. It is part of California history that Terry "was freed through intercession by Senator Broderick, a close friend."

We know that among those who joined with Terry and his wife on his return to express their congratulations on his happy escape from the vigilantes were David C. Broderick and Colonel E. D. Baker — the lawyer who had defended Cora in his trial for murder, and whose funeral oration for Broderick would before long plant the imprint of "murderer" on Terry's name. It must be judged that Broderick's performance during the Second Vigilance Movement was cool and astute. He knew better than anyone the part he had played in creating the conditions of corruption that in turn caused the rising of the vigilantes. But he knew better that he wanted to be a United States senator, and that any overt opposition to the committee would hurt him politically. So he took a middle ground: he did not openly oppose the committee, but pretended to remain studiously aloof from the activities of Johnson, Terry and the other Law and Order adherents. Three years later in the quarrel with Terry that led to their duel, it became known that Broderick had paid the San Francisco *Herald* to publish a defense of Terry. Only one contemporary historian reports that Broderick was in communication with the Vigilance Committee. Elijah R. Kennedy, who as a young man experienced the vigilante days, writes:

> *Senator Broderick argued that the conviction and punishment of a man of such exalted official position would be likely to arouse the national authorities and thus perhaps lead to the dissolution of the committee.*

There is no other evidence that Broderick did much to extricate Terry from Fort Gunnybags. The legend of his aid to the Texan is probably a journalist's invention to brand Terry as an "ingrate" as well as a "murderer."

Stephen J. Field, circa 1863

IX

STEPHEN J. FIELD
HIS EARLY LIFE

*There one entered the land of the Yankees, who were famous for
their schools as well as the stones in their fields and the
stiffness of their necks.*

Van Wyck Brooks, *The World of Washington Irving*

When Terry escaped from the clutches of the vigilantes to resume his place on the California Supreme Court, he renewed his association in Sacramento not only with Broderick, but with Stephen J. Field, one of his two fellow judges on the supreme court. Of the four men whose intertwined careers make up the threads of this book, only Field enjoyed a heritage of learning, culture, travel and security. Terry was typical of the lawyers of the Southwest frontier, grandiloquent and ostentatious in manner, but shallow in thought and learning. Broderick almost literally had to brush off the garbage and ordure of the hideous Irish slums of his New York childhood, but in the process of growth he learned little of the world of the mind. Sharon, the Bonanza Senator, whom we shall shortly meet, was a true son of the Middle Border, dedicated from childhood to commerce, to money-making, to "getting ahead," and, despite a fondness for quoting Shakespeare and Byron, he was schooled mostly in the earthy arts that fed his ambitions.

Field must be seen as one of the showiest blossoms of the New England that flowered in the early nineteenth century. He came into the world at Haddon, Connecticut, on November 4, 1816, the son of the Reverend David Dudley Field, a Congregationalist minister and his wife, Submit. His childhood was passed at Stockbridge, Massachusetts, where his father accepted a call in 1819. He was reared in the sternest Puritan Congregational tradition in a family whose devoutness subjected him to three sermons on Sunday, and prayers twice each day. He studied the Bible from Genesis to Revelation. Sabbath observance was strict: its advent was announced at sunset on Saturday when the Reverend Dr. Field would intone, "My sons, we are on the border of holy time."

Field's family, destined to be among the most famous in American history, was one of the oldest in New England. Zachariah Field came to Massachusetts in 1630. Field's grandfather was a captain in Washington's army; his father was a distinguished graduate of Yale, a respected theologian; his mother, Submit Dickerson, was of old Puritan stock. Young Stephen was reared, in his own words, in "an iron creed; it formed an iron character, a firmness and intrepidity which have produced the greatest effects on both Old and New England." It is germane to our story that this stern and devout family produced three other sons who became famous in their time: David Dudley Field, who led a revolution in Anglo-American law; Cyrus W. Field, the entrepreneur in laying the Atlantic Cable; and Henry Martyn Field, nationally known as a clergyman and editor.

According to the custom of the day, Stephen was educated largely at home, and it was assumed that he would follow his two older brothers, David Dudley and Jonathan, to Williams College, thirty miles from Stockbridge. In 1829, when Field was thirteen, his sister Emelia married Josiah Brewer, a clergyman bound for Greece on a mission to Asia Minor. Field accompanied his sister and her husband. If his ancestry and rearing put iron into Field's soul, his sojourn in Smyrna infused steel. According to an American naval officer who visited Smyrna during an outbreak of plague, the Reverend Brewer and his young brother-in-law were the legendary heroes of the stricken city. "Let history record . . . the benevolence and proud contempt of danger and of deaths evidenced by American strangers within the pestilential walls of Smyrna."

In 1832, the wanderer returned to Stockbridge to enter Williams College. To gain admission, he took examinations in English, geography, algebra, Latin and Greek. Field passed with brilliant scores, and led his class for four years. During this time, the leading scholar at Williams was Mark Hopkins, one of America's great thinkers and educators. Hopkins became part of the folklore of American education when one of his former students (supposedly President James A. Garfield) said, "The ideal college is Mark Hopkins on one end of a log and a student at the other." Hopkins was a native of Stockbridge and an intimate of the Field family. He took a special interest in young Stephen and instilled in him a blend of eighteenth century puritanism and nineteenth century progress. Field's chief biographer, Carl Swisher, writes:

> While Stephen may never have admitted that his own system of thinking was founded on that of his teacher, there was indeed a remarkable similarity between the Hopkins system and his own reasoning habits. Clarity, conciseness, and mathematical exactness were characteristics of both, once the major assumptions for particular arguments were chosen. Furthermore, both assumed the existence of fundamental and harmonious principles permeating and explaining all the facts of life, an assumption of no little importance in the world of thought.

Field graduated as valedictorian of his class in September 1837. Now he abandoned all thoughts about a career in medicine, the ministry or education. He turned at once to the mistress he would serve for the rest of his life — the law. He began to "read law" in the Albany, New York, office of John van Buren, who had been attorney general of the state. But Albany was deadly dull, and Field continued his studies in the New York office of his older brother, David Dudley Field. In 1841, he was admitted to the bar and became his brother's junior partner in "D. D. & S. J. Field." The firm's small office overlooked Trinity Church, at Broadway and Wall Street.

David Dudley Field, circa 1861

Field's office on Wall Street. Field had a room in David Dudley's chambers on the second floor of No.8.

For the next seven years, he endured the drudgery of law practice, the routine work brought into the office by David Dudley, already on his way to becoming one of New York's most renowned lawyers. Through his successful law practice and marriage to a rich widow, David Dudley was on the road to affluence. But the two brothers did not enjoy a congenial relationship. David was a legal drillmaster, unsparing in his criticism of the younger man. At one point, they quarreled bitterly and Stephen said New York was not big enough to hold both of them. David Dudley seems to have agreed; in 1846 he tried to persuade Stephen to join a regiment of New York volunteers destined for service in California. But Stephen stayed in New York, impecunious, unhappy, and openly envious of his glittering brother. His father rescued him in 1848 by taking him on a trip to Europe.

Eighteen forty-eight was one of the most exciting and tumultuous years in European history, and the young lawyer was privileged to witness much of the excitement. He watched from the windows of his hotel in Paris as Louis Philippe's regime was overthrown; with brother Cyrus he was in Rome to see French troops occupy the city; he was in Vienna as rebellious students chased Franz Joseph and his Court to Graz; he saw the Russians pour out of the East to reestablish the *ancien régime.* He saw enough to prepare him for future life in one of the most colorful and turbulent communities in the world — California. Certainly, he saw enough to make him unsuitable for the conventional staid life of law practice in New York.

He returned from Europe in October 1849, just as the call of "Gold!" came from the West. By November 13, he was on a steamer bound for Panama, with a ticket supplied by David Dudley. In his *Reminiscences,* Field describes the miseries of the transit across the Isthmus, the fever-ridden voyage from Panama to San Francisco, where he arrived on December 28, 1849, with a trunk and ten dollars in gold. A bundle of newspapers brought from New York saved him from actual poverty: he sold them for a dollar each. He also sold some chamois skins. His biggest asset was a bon voyage present from brother David Dudley, an unpaid note from Colonel Stevenson for legal services. Stephen found the maker of the note and extracted four hundred dollars from him. He tried his hand at law practice in San Francisco, but the competition scared him off. He heard about the new towns growing up around the mining communities, and he took the steamer up the Sacramento River. He disembarked at a tent city called "Yubaville," which, in honor of the wife of one of the first settlers, changed its name to "Marysville," the name it bears to this day.

Field invested the few dollars left from Colonel Stevenson's payment in some lots, which he resold at a good profit. He was also elected to the office of "alcalde," a minor judicial office about equivalent to justice of the peace. He received a commission in his new office from the new governor of the new state at the new capital in Sacramento on January 22, 1850 — less than a month after his arrival in California!

In the next four months the future justice of the Supreme Court swiftly gained his first experiences in the art of judging. He tried criminal and civil cases, jury and non-jury; he imposed fines and even a sentence of "one hundred lashes — well laid on" for theft. He performed administrative duties in a community peopled with "many desperate persons, gamblers, blacklegs, thieves and cut-throats." When Field composed his *Personal Reminiscences of Early Days in California* many years later, he wrote with characteristic modesty that his efforts made Marysville "the model town of the whole country for peacefulness and respect for law." While he was making a reputation for himself, the young lawyer was prospering dramatically. By May of 1850, he believed he was worth $20,000.

The new California Constitution took effect in May, and Field was replaced as "alcalde" by a ferocious Texan named William R. Turner. Turner knew little law, and from the start he resented Field's airs of superior erudition. Turner was one of the pro-slavery fire-eaters; his feelings toward Field were clouded by the conviction that the New Englander was "a black abolitionist." In his first case before Turner, Field was fined five hundred dollars and ordered to serve two days in jail for contempt. When Field obtained a writ of *habeas corpus* from the local district judge, Turner held the district judge in contempt! He also "disbarred" Field, who had to apply to the California Supreme Court for reinstatement. One of the very first actions ever taken by the highest court of the new state, is *People* ex rel. *Stephen J. Field* v. *Turner* recorded in the first volume of *California Reports*. The supreme court reversed Turner and ordered the reinstatement of Field and two other lawyers "disbarred" by the Texan for expressing sympathy with Field. But the controversy did not end there. Field and the other two lawyers attacked Turner in a newspaper story and Turner, in his own words, "redisbarred" the three for "disrespect." Again, the supreme court reversed and ordered the three lawyers reinstated. The record of this action, too, can be found in that first volume of *California Reports*. Apparently, there was not much serious business before the court in that first year.

The ambitious Field had more to do than contend with the hair-trigger temper of the judge from Texas. He ran for the legislature in January 1851, and won against the determined opposition of the pro-slavery Chivs, who circulated the canard that he was an abolitionist. When Field was elected to the legislature, Broderick was the president of the Senate, and the two men formed a friendship that was soon put to the test. In one of Field's bitter speeches about Turner, he had termed him "grossly incompetent! — oppressive and tyrannical in office — guilty of gross indecency in language and conduct — guilty of gross immorality!" B. F. Moore, a Southern legislator friendly to Turner, resented these words and threatened Field with a cocked pistol. Field determined to challenge Moore, but a duel was averted when, with Broderick's aid and influence, Moore retracted his insults to Field.

Thereafter, Field was Broderick's man — in his limited way. He made contributions to Broderick's campaigns, and was one of his most effective political supporters on the hustings. But Field's general attitude toward Broderick, while friendly, was somewhat patronizing. Broderick certainly showed him kindnesses. They were fellow Democrats and were both targets of the Chivs. Yet the discrepancy in background, in education, was such that Field, in his *Reminiscences,* could mention the surprise he felt that he would form a close association with one "whose habits of life and general character had little to attract one like myself." Under the veneer of his frontier camaraderie, Field was a typical New England prig, a snob. He would remain a snob to his dying day. When the legislature chose him for its Judiciary Committee, but named another as chairman, Field said it was "for political reasons," but modestly proclaimed himself "foremost in the Committee."

The Judiciary Committee gave the young lawyer an opportunity to apply lessons he had learned from David Dudley in New York. He adapted to the needs of California the codes for civil and criminal procedure which David Dudley had pushed through the New York legislature and which would be imitated throughout America. In his excellent biography of Field, Dr. Swisher analyzes his contributions to the early law of California, and gives him the highest marks for skill as a legislative draftsman. On the delicate subjects of mining claims, personal property exemptions, homesteading, divorce, and other areas Field made notable contributions.

By spring 1851, when he returned to Marysville from his first legislative session, Field was respected, but broke. Years later, in 1889, Terry would make a bitter attack on Field's character, claiming that the young Field was an habitual gambler who had squandered his money in gambling halls. Undoubtedly, Field patronized these establishments, but the claim that gambling was a serious vice in him is unsupported. He rented an office over a Marysville saloon, and established a prosperous law practice. By 1855, he had paid off his debts and saved enough to make a long visit to his family in the East. Law practice in the little town was varied and stormy. He fought so vigorously with a local judge that they challenged each other to a duel. Bloodshed was avoided when both men backed down. In his later denunciation of Field, Terry used this incident to justify the epithet "coward."

Field was also a participant in the legendary "first hanging of a woman in California" at nearby Downieville, California, on July 4, 1851. In his *Reminiscences* Field recalls that during the bacchic celebration of the Glorious Fourth, Juanita, a dancehall girl, plunged a knife into a drunken miner. A lynch court sentenced her to hanging. Field tried to prevent the execution; he tried to enlist the "magnetic personality" of William Walker (the "Gray-eyed Man of Destiny") who had been attending a political convention in

Downieville. But Walker had left town, and Field was on his own.

With this hope [Walker] gone, young Steve Field tried the persuasive power of his own tongue — and even in his youth Field had gained fame as a pleader and knockabout orator. See this tall, spare, black-bearded youngster in his black surtout and frilled stock mount a barrel in the heart of the mob. He has the face of a knight, all glorified by his high purpose.

"Gentlemen of Downieville, you cannot hang a woman! Think I beg you! Our fair California has been one of the sisterhood of States not ten months. Her fame is world wide. Would you have it rolled off the whole world's tongue that California men are cowards enough to —— "

A voice from the mob — "To Hell with him." Steve Field is knocked off the barrel and rolled in the dust.

The Mexican girl paid dearly to earn a place in California's history. The accuracy of the story is attested by Swisher who derived it from "The Hanging of Juanita," a chapter in *The Hell-Roaring Forty-Niners* by Robert Welles Ritchie. One version is that the girl was certified pregnant by a local physician, who was thrown out of the district for his discouraging diagnosis.

Field continued to move upward in the California bar, in local society, and in politics. In 1857 he was an aspirant for the Senate seat that went to Broderick. Their friendship was subjected to great strain when the Irishman declined to support Field for political office. Later, Field learned that he was one of the chips that Broderick bartered away in a sordid deal with Gwin.

The youthful Field matured into a jurist whose appearance and utterances made observers liken him to an Old Testament prophet. Through his life, he exuded "an air of austere authority." But the man whose demeanor was patriarchal before he was fifty always seemed to be embroiled in quarrels. By his own admission, he became "a great hater" — a quality that would mark him to the end.

Terry on the bench. Terry is the presiding judge in the center.

X

TERRY THE JUDGE

The brain may devise laws for the blood, but a hot temper leaps o'er a cold decree.

William Shakespeare, *The Merchant of Venice*

During the three years from 1856 to 1859, Terry's life was relatively placid. There were no signs of the earlier turbulence. Perhaps he was chastened; more likely, he was deeply occupied with his normal judicial labors and by a deep involvement in the Democratic politics of the state and the ceaseless plotting of his secessionist friends. There were three judges on the supreme court; a vacancy that occurred in 1857 was filled by the appointment of Stephen J. Field of Marysville. For the first time the lives of the two men became closely intertwined. From the beginning, they were polite to each other, but a latent antipathy between them grew out of their contrasting cultural backgrounds and their clashing views on slavery and secession. Years later Terry would say of Field that there was no judge living who could give better reasons for a wrong decision.

Terry failed to win renomination for the supreme court at the Democratic Convention in 1859, probably the price exacted from him for defecting to the Know-Nothing ranks in 1856. There were two Democratic conventions in that year: one "Lecompton," the other "anti-Lecompton"; one for slavery and secession, the other anti-slavery and pro-Union. The "Lecompton Convention" (so-called after the pro-slavery state convention in Kansas) was dominated by Gwin's supporters, Terry's Southern friends. Although his "friends" rejected Terry as a candidate, he remained an active partisan of their cause.

The 1850's was not an easy time for lawyers and judges in California. Of course, among the thousands who came seeking gold there were many lawyers, or at least men who in one way or another had been exposed to the law. Some had learned the rudiments of law in primitive circumstances. "Yet writings of the period give unmistakable evidence of the ubiquity of men who had absorbed the law; even in the rudest circumstances, the frontier impatience with delay and formality is streaked with the trace of a tradition of law and a recollection of its language." In California there were virtually no local precedents on which to rely. Precious law books were still freighted around the Horn. Much of the litigation resulted from Spanish and Mexican grants and the state of law in California in the 1850's was confused and turbulent. It presented "so many legal complications that for a time [California] became the paradise of lawyers." But paradise was slow in developing. In 1849 and 1850 some of San Francisco's lawyers were having such difficult times that "to save themselves from the severe pangs of actual want, [they] have been compelled to fish around the wharves for crabs."

Within a year or two after 1850 the demand for legal help increased greatly, and lawyers and judges realized that the explosive growth of the new state demanded their sedulous devotion to the prompt development of a legal system and a rule of law. To this process, Terry made important and respectable contributions. As in other frontier communities, there was a revulsion against pettifogging lawyers, "harpies of the law," as they were termed in one of the javelins Jeremy Bentham hurled in his guerrilla war against the profession.

Bentham had been dead for more than twenty years when the California lawyers began their task of forging a legal system for the new state, but his ideas were respected and imitated. Bentham's legal thinking had captured the imagination of David Dudley Field, the brother of Terry's colleague, Stephen J. Field. By 1848, the elder Field had persuaded New York to adopt a Bentham-inspired Code of Civil Procedure. Terry learned of this and participated in the work of a committee which adopted California's first Field-influenced procedural code. He joined in the resistance to a movement that urged adopting the law of the "civilians" as a substitute for the traditional common law.

As a judge, Terry seems to have done a creditable job, but he can hardly be regarded as an eminent jurist. It was said of him much later, "He never wrote an opinion or prepared a brief that we ever heard referred to as worth reading a second time." Field, whose legal scholarship would be demonstrated later in many ways in the highest Court of the land and who sat at Terry's side in the California Supreme Court for several years, never questioned Terry's lawyering. On the whole, the general quality of the court during Terry's judicial tenure was not high. One of its three members, Hugh C. Murray, who became a judge at twenty-six, was charged with drunkenness, gambling and brawling. When he died of the effects of dissipation at the age of thirty-two, he was succeeded by Field.

An examination of Terry's opinions in volumes six through twelve of the *California Reports* affords little basis for gauging his professional skills as a lawyer and judge. Of course, judgment must be tempered by an understanding that he was functioning in what Roscoe Pound called the "era of decadence" in the profession of law, an era which tended to reject the concept of a highly-trained profession in favor of a "calling" open to all comers. The law profession was dominated by what has been euphemistically termed the "Lincoln tradition" — the concept that anybody could hang out a shingle and practice "law" without special training. It was one of the phenomena of Jacksonian democracy that, at least in frontier communities, educational requirements for admission to the profession of law were virtually eliminated. Field's legal education was no more academic and just as pragmatic as Terry's; however his exposure to learning and to the substance of human experience was infinitely broader. It was his eclectic New England education, his sharply-developed language skills that made Field a jurist of reknown. Terry had no such advantages.

In one case, *People* v. *Plummer,* Terry the judge got his chance to pour out his bitterness at the vigilantes:

> *A man who could so far forget his duty as a citizen, and his allegiance to the Constitution as to openly advocate the taking of the life of a citizen without the form of law and deprive him of the chance of a jury trial, would not be likely to stop at any means to secure, under the forms of a legal trial, a result which he publicly declared ought to be accomplished by an open violation of the law.*

Clearly, Terry was aiming a judicial shaft at the vigilantes. But he was also expressing his profound feeling about individual rights and fair trials. This strain in him became a passion that would affect his entire life, and thirty years later impel him into the follies of the Sharon-Hill litigation. This passion, in later life, grew into his strong feeling that "the people" had to be protected from "the interests." In time, "the interests" came to mean to him the railroad companies and their ruthless proprietors, constantly growing in economic power and in indifference to the rights of those who opposed them. Deservedly, Terry was deemed a judge who favored the "little man" — a foreshadowing of the strong populist anti-monopoly convictions he showed in years to come.

While Terry gave no sign of violence or intemperate conduct, during the years 1856 to 1859 he kept right on with the conspiratorial activities of the Secesh. The darker forces at work in him would soon break out and overwhelm him, and within three years of his ordeal at the hands of the vigilantes, he plunged into an act which, in the minds of millions, was as foul and brutal as the clubbing of Sumner. He became, at least in popular imagination (and in California history), the assassin of David C. Broderick.

During the 1850's, Terry was among the most prominent and most vociferous of the Southern faction, but he was never its principal leader. That eminence belonged to William M. Gwin, a Tennessean who came to California in 1849 at the age of forty-four to make his political fortune. There is no question of Gwin's talents. He has been called "the most intellectual, brilliant, subtle, suave and unscrupulous leader California has ever had." His abilities were certainly formidable. Within months of his arrival in the West, the Southerners accepted him as their leader, and he became their standard-bearer and mouthpiece in the first state Constitutional Convention in 1850.

By profession, Gwin was a physician; by character and experience, he was a consummate politician. His family was intimate with Andrew and Rachel Jackson, and one of Old Hickory's first acts on reaching the White House had been to appoint his young friend as United States marshal in Mississippi. Next, Gwin was elected to Congress from Mississippi for three terms. In 1847, President Polk named him commissioner to supervise the construction of a new customhouse in New Orleans. For reasons which are now obscure but suggest some financial embarrassment, he resigned in 1849 and went to California.

The all-important statehood convention at Monterey in 1850 was the first formal battleground between the pro-slavery forces and those of the

Gwin in the mid-1850's

Free-Soilers. Gwin and his followers fought to establish slavery in the state, or to divide the state and bring the southern half into the federal Union as a slave state. They failed in both objectives. Their chief antagonist in the contest was David C. Broderick, the acknowledged leader of the anti-slavery forces. Broderick's Free Soil side won out, and on September 19, 1850, when California became the thirty-first state of the Union, its constitution prohibited slavery on its soil.

But the legislature gave Gwin a valuable consolation prize; it named him the first full-term United States senator from California. The other "short-term" seat was awarded to John Charles Frémont, the "Pathfinder," in recognition of his services in winning California for the Americans in the Mexican War. The statehood convention was the beginning of a contest between Gwin and Broderick for control of California's political machinery; it became a duel to the death which lasted to the eve of the Civil War, and did not end even when Broderick was shot to death by Terry. Only civil war and the defeat of the South finally terminated the struggle. While it raged, it was costly and bloody. Broderick, the eastern "mudsill," the fugitive from the Irish slums of New York, became the plumed knight of the Northern cause and the premier obstacle to Southern hopes. When we last heard of him, he was engaged in practicing in state politics the same contemptible arts of spoilsmanship which had won him control of the San Francisco municipal jungle and earned from James King of Wm. the sobriquet, David *Catiline* Broderick. Now, he would be transformed into the champion of Free Soil, and the extirpation of the ignoble institution of Negro slavery. Terry's pistol transformed the earthy Irishman into a legendary martyr — a Roland who gave his life to hold the pass against the forces of evil.

Broderick was "posed" by Matthew B. Brady during his last visit to New York in March 1859. "Brady of Broadway," as he was then known, became famous as the principal photographer of the Civil War: "Mr. Lincoln's Camera Man."

XI

SENATOR BRODERICK

And do not stand on quillets how to slay him:
Be it by gins, by snares, by subtlety,
Sleeping or waking, 'tis no matter how,
So he be dead.

William Shakespeare, *The Second Part of King Henry the Sixth*

Broderick was an exemplar of that ubiquitous American phenomenon, the successful Irish-American political careerist. He never deluded himself or others with the fiction that he was working for the improvement of his fellows. When he came to the West, he was poor, hungry, ambitious, and his eye was fixed on one aim — the advancement of Broderick. Nothing was allowed to interfere with his ambition —and nothing did!

He neither drank nor smoked nor looked upon women. He had warmth and humor, but he rarely allowed these human tendencies to appear, lest they also retard his progress.

He suppressed most normal human qualities; the face he presented to the world was stern and serious. He had little Latin, but he was fond of reciting the maxim *"Ruat caelum, fiat justitia."* To him, *"justitia"* meant no interference with his personal and political objectives and ambitions. His career was always foremost in his plans, and to palter with it was to invite his enmity.

Broderick's very attire proclaimed his hunger for respectability and recognition. When he first came to San Francisco, his garb was the familiar coarse blue shirt and pants tucked into boots. As soon as he had enough money, he sent to New York for the most dignified apparel available, and for the rest of his life he would be seen only in a black frock coat, "boiled" shirt and silk hat. While he cultivated an air of spartan simplicity in his manner of life, he could be offensively imperious to others and fiercely insistent on preserving the prerogatives of his position. Many felt the whip of his tongue, many suffered humiliation at his hands and many remained his enemies. "Loyalty," both personal and political, was a fetish with Broderick. Broderick's political credo was that later attributed to Simon Cameron, Lincoln's first secretary of war: "An honest politician is a fellow who, when you buy him, he stays bought." He never attained the mature quality of submitting to defeat and disappointment. Any setback was an occasion of shame and sorrow, and when reverses came, he reacted with rage. He never had that precious quality of waiting with patience for others to price his worth; he tried always to price himself. Broderick made no secret of his ambition to be a United States senator. When he ran against Frémont, he told one of his listeners: "I tell you sir, by God, that for an hour's seat in the Senate of the United States, I would roast before a slow fire in the Plaza!"

In the vigilance resurgence of 1856 that came close to destroying Terry, Broderick nimbly kept out of trouble. He needed the support of the respectable anti-slavery faction, men like Brannan and Coleman, and he could not risk that support in the vigilante crisis by joining the Law and Order forces. And in the spring and summer of 1856, Broderick was trying to make a political deal with the Southerners, so he dared not risk their enmity. Adroitly, he stayed away from San Francisco during the vigilante crisis, and duped both sides into believing they had his support. But any alliance between Broderick and Gwin was born of the crassest and most ephemeral opportunism. Broderick was personally and ideologically repugnant to Gwin and the Southerners. To them, he was an ill-bred Irish demagogue, whose political views were those of the "new" Americans: the men who favored industry, the dominance of the big cities, and who were bitterly opposed to slavery on both moral and economic grounds. To the fine-mannered protagonists of an agricultural society powered by black slaves, Broderick had to be anathema. Yet, his political tricks worked for Broderick and it was with the temporary help of Gwin and his "Chivalry" that he finally achieved his ambition to be a United States senator.

Early in 1857, when he was only thirty-seven years old, the legislature elected him to a full six-year term in the Senate. His election was bitterly opposed by the "Southern Chivalry," led by Gwin and the Know-Nothing remnant led by Terry, but Broderick overcame their opposition and realized his goal in a series of political maneuvers that left his friends breathless with admiration and his enemies enraged and thirsting for revenge. Gwin conceded that Broderick outwitted and outfought him and his cohorts to become the first important politician in California to withstand the "Southern Chivalry."

Gwin was a formidable rival. When he left Mississippi he, too, had predicted that if he ever returned to the East, it would be as a United States senator. He reached that eminence earlier than his arch-rival, Broderick. It would be pleasant to record that Broderick's own elevation to the Senate of the United States reflected the esteem of his fellow legislators and their undiluted confidence in his integrity. Not so! His success came out of a political deal sordid enough to have earned him the admiration of the sleaziest ward heelers in the New York of his youth.

In 1857, two senators were to be chosen by the legislature, one for the full six-year term, one for the shorter four-year term. Senator John Weller's term was expiring; the seat formerly held by Gwin was unfilled, because of Broderick's opposition. Thus, there were two seats to be filled. The contest for the longer term was not only a personal fight between Broderick and Gwin, it was a battle between North and South, between Free Soil and slavery. It looked to be a bitter standoff, with Broderick's men enjoying a feeble transient advantage. Then, Broderick reached an understanding with Milton S. Latham, a moderate Democrat with Free Soil leanings, who agreed

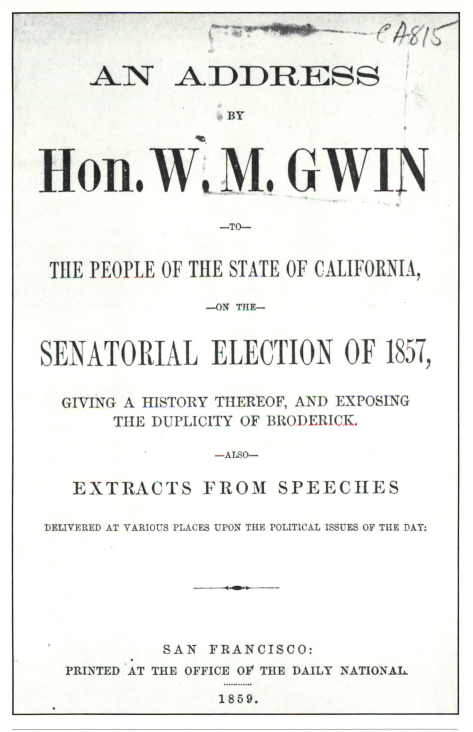

AN ADDRESS

BY

Hon. W. M. GWIN

—TO—

THE PEOPLE OF THE STATE OF CALIFORNIA,

—ON THE—

SENATORIAL ELECTION OF 1857,

GIVING A HISTORY THEREOF, AND EXPOSING THE DUPLICITY OF BRODERICK.

—ALSO—

EXTRACTS FROM SPEECHES

DELIVERED AT VARIOUS PLACES UPON THE POLITICAL ISSUES OF THE DAY:

SAN FRANCISCO:

PRINTED AT THE OFFICE OF THE DAILY NATIONAL.

1859.

Gwin's speech "exposing the duplicity of Broderick"

to support Broderick for the longer seat in return for Broderick's aid in getting him the four-year seat. Latham kept his word scrupulously, and on January 10, 1857, Broderick was named senator for the full six-year term receiving seventy-nine votes against seventeen for the Know-Nothing candidate and fourteen for the Republican. Of course, Latham assumed that Broderick would now back him for the four-year term. But Broderick repudiated his word to Latham and made a deal with Gwin that might have sprung from the mind of a Tweed or a Penrose.

On January 12, 1857, Broderick's henchmen in the legislature surprisingly withdrew their support of Latham and their opposition to Gwin and unanimously voted the second prize to Gwin. Why? How did these enemies reconcile their hatreds? Why did Broderick betray his ally? The answer is found in a letter, dated the day after Broderick's election, a document that became celebrated in California political history as "The Scarlet Letter." When his election was announced on January 13, 1857, Gwin published a high-sounding "Address to the People of California" in which he mystified everybody by acknowledging that he owed "much to the timely assistance accorded to me by Mr. Broderick and his friends." He did not tell the people of California that in a midnight meeting with his mortal enemy on January 11, behind a locked door in Sacramento's Magnolia Hotel, guarded by armed partisans of both men, he had handed Broderick a signed letter wherein, in return for that "timely assistance," he had bartered away his share of federal patronage, the golden rain under which California's federal establishment had bloomed into "The Virginia Poorhouse." Before he signed the letter, Gwin had enjoyed an iron grip on federal patronage in the West. He had named every federal official in California from postmaster to lighthouse-keeper, and almost to a man, his appointees were Southern sympathizers. The letter he delivered to Broderick exchanged those glittering prizes for votes for Gwin as senator. It reads:

While in the Senate, I will not recommend a single individual to appointment to office in the state. Provided I am elected you shall have the exclusive control of this patronage, so far as I am concerned.

With this shameful document in his breast pocket, Broderick opened the door of the meeting room and instructed his minions to vote for Gwin.

The existence of the letter and its contents was concealed from the general public for two and a half years. Latham knew of it, but smothered his rage over the betrayal and kept his counsel. Gwin's Southern retainers knew nothing of the letter, but they soon learned that their sinecures had been sold to Broderick. They reacted like dogs robbed of a bone. But they, too, were under a stern discipline, and they kept their mouths shut. When the letter finally became public, much later, it would be with terrible consequences to Broderick. During the interim, as word about the bargain began to leak, Gwin admitted to his Southern intimates that the document hung over his head "like the blade of an executioner." To those of his own party who knew of it, the letter was an unendurable humiliation. It shamed them that their leader should have had to purchase his Senate seat from the stone-cutter's son, the "mudsill," with such base coin. In the end, despite an outward show of respect the two men despised each other. Gwin agonized over

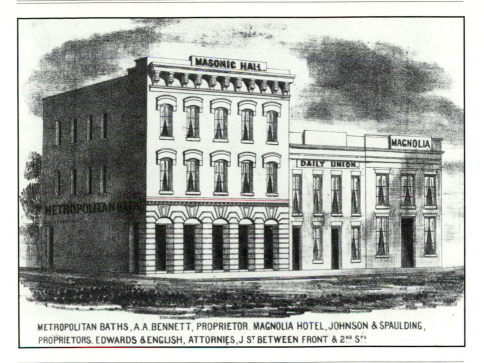

METROPOLITAN BATHS, A.A.BENNETT, PROPRIETOR. MAGNOLIA HOTEL, JOHNSON & SPAULDING, PROPRIETORS. EDWARDS & ENGLISH, ATTORNIES, J ST BETWEEN FRONT & 2ND STS

It was in one of the rooms of the Magnolia Hotel in Sacramento that Gwin gave Broderick "The Scarlet Letter."

his folly in giving the letter, and from the day he signed it, he schemed and plotted to destroy it or suppress it. Broderick would soon learn that the shameful letter was practically worthless.

But the letter did solve the immediate impasse, and California had two senators of antithetical views to represent the state in a Washington that was boiling over with faction and sectionalism. In 1857, the quickest transit from San Francisco to the East was by steamer from San Francisco to Panama, overland across the Isthmus, and by steamer from Colon to New York, a voyage of about thirty days, depending on weather. The two newly-elected senators from California, their hatreds concealed under a thin courtly veneer, embarked on the same steamer for the East. Broderick was in Washington only a few days when he became aware that the promise exacted from Gwin was worthless, that Gwin had tricked him. He learned this when President Buchanan ignored his first recommendations for federal appointments, and it became clear that Gwin's friends in an administration controlled by Southerners could arrange that all appointments Buchanan made in California were just as surely dictated by Gwin as they had been in the past. Broderick could not contain his chagrin and disappointment when friends told him that Gwin was boasting to his intimates that the purchase price he had paid Broderick, "The Scarlet Letter," was "payment in worthless coin."

Gwin was accepted as a charter member of the Southern establishment in Washington. He maintained a luxurious mansion at Nineteenth and I streets, at a reputed cost of more than $75,000 a year, where he lavishly entertained the flower of the "Chivalry." Thanks to the influence his Southern friends enjoyed with the aging Buchanan, Gwin saw himself as a secret Warwick, a kingmaker who kept a sedulous silence on appointments, but whose velvet touch was felt in filling every federal vacancy in California. Broderick's anger over the duplicity of which he was the victim was poured out in private and public. Among those to whom Broderick confided was the celebrated Daniel E. Sickles, congressman from New York. Sickles tried to assist Broderick with the White House, but at the moment he was caught up in his own problems. He was on trial for shooting Philip Barton Key.

Broderick returned to California in the fall, to learn that during his absence in Washington he had totally lost control of the party machinery in his home state. The federal patronage was in the hands of Gwin and the Southerners, and it was a devastating weapon against him. Only one of his party's nominees attained state office: his friend, Stephen J. Field, who was elected a judge of the Supreme Court of California. The incumbent chief judge had died, and as Field ascended the bench, Gwin and the "Chivalry" forced the elevation of David S. Terry to chief judge. It seemed no impediment to that exalted office that Terry's record was spotted with a lack of professional discipline and personal violence, that only a year earlier he had been in peril of his life for stabbing the vigilante, Hopkins. Thus, Field and Terry became colleagues in court for the first time. While the two men were already acquainted, this was the first important conjunction of two careers, a relationship that would fester into bitterness and havoc over three decades. From the beginning the two men were antagonistic; they seemed destined for violent collision. Thus, even this relatively minor victory in 1857, the election of Field to the Supreme Court of California, made its petty contribution to the dark fate that engulfed Broderick within two years, and crept on over the decades to the final tragedy of Terry.

It was an embittered and heavy-hearted Broderick who returned to his duties in Washington in December 1857. The agony of Kansas was the burning issue of the day, and Broderick became active in the struggle. At first Broderick was captivated by the charm and dynamism of Stephen A. Douglas — "The Little Giant," "A Steam-engine in Britches" — but he broke with him over the Kansas-Nebraska Act. Broderick had denounced Douglas's endorsement of squatter sovereignty in Nebraska, but in the new session, only he and Senator Stuart of Michigan had the courage to join with Douglas in condemning Buchanan's attempt to force a pro-slavery constitution, adopted by the illegal Lecompton convention, on the people of Kansas. Broderick went to the limits of parliamentary rhetoric in opposing Buchanan:

> I hope, sir, that in mercy to the boasted intelligence of this age, the historian, when writing of these times, will ascribe this attempt of the Executive to force this Constitution on an unwilling people, to the fading intellect, the petulant passion, and the trembling dotage of an old man on the verge of the grave.

Buchanan was sixty-seven at the time of the speech, and lived for another ten years, so the "historian" would have been somewhat inaccurate.

Broderick's outspoken contempt for the president and his vigorous hostility to the arrogant pro-slavery forces gained him much attention throughout the country. It also brought his conflict with Gwin and the

Southern faction into the open. The warfare soon extended to California, and began to be literally bloody. The issue in Washington became the "Lecompton Constitution" — a deceptive document devised by the pro-slavery forces in Kansas to overcome the numerical superiority of the Free-Soilers. Kansans were required to vote for the constitution either "with slavery" or "with no slavery." The constitution was so tricky that however the vote came out, there would be Negro slavery in Kansas. The California legislature, now owned body and soul by the Southern faction, "instructed" her two senators in Washington to vote favorably on the Lecompton Constitution. Broderick saw through the trumpery and rejected the "instruction."

Let us now return to "The Scarlet Letter," the stake in the squalid bargain in 1857. The meeting in the hotel room between Broderick and Gwin had been arranged by W. I. Ferguson, a Sacramento lawyer, who came from Illinois with strong anti-slavery convictions and became a devoted friend of Broderick. When he left for the East, Broderick entrusted the original letter to Ferguson. In a speech in the California legislature, Ferguson followed Broderick's lead in supporting Douglas in his feud with Buchanan, praised Broderick, and made some allusions to Gwin which suggested to the Southern bravos that he had "The Letter" in his possession. Within weeks, Ferguson was tricked into a quarrel with "a Southern gentleman," was challenged, fought, and was killed. The duel was typical of the political duels of the day. Ferguson had never fired a shot in his life; his opponent was a practiced duellist. When Ferguson's shot missed, his adversary took careful aim at Ferguson's heart, and did not miss. As Ferguson lay dying, his law office was burglarized, his desk ransacked in a feverish search for "The Letter." On his deathbed, Ferguson gave the document to a trusted friend, who returned it to Broderick. Ferguson's death should have been a warning to the pro-Broderick, anti-slavery politicians of California that the Southerners had begun a compaign of exterminating their chief antagonists by duel.

In the spring of 1859, Broderick made his last trip to the East. One of the critical issues to come before Congress was federal aid for the construction of a transcontinental railway. St. Joseph, Missouri, was the westernmost point the railroad had reached; from that place, all overland transit was by stage or horseback. Of the many controversies that raged in Washington, the most exigent to Californians was whether the projected line to the West Coast should follow the "short" route — due west to central California — or the route favored by the Southerners: through Texas to enter California at its most southeasterly point. The dividing line between slave-holding states and free soil had been fixed in 1820 by the Missouri Compromise as parallel 36° 30'. The anti-slavery faction demanded that the proposed line be constructed north of that line. The Southerners espoused a route well to the south. To Californians, the location of the line was vital; most of the development in the state was in the north-central portion, along the line San Francisco-Sacramento. Southern California was sparsely settled. A transcontinental railway entering the state in the south would have to connect with a 500-mile coastwise feeder which would have to be built by private funds.

Before he left for the East, Broderick vowed to fight for the northern route. Gwin fully understood the vital economic reasons for choosing the northern route, but he was committed to all things Southern, and supported the southern line. The battle over the transcontinental railroad became the focal point of tension between North and South; to the Californians of that day it seemed the most important issue for their future. To Broderick and Gwin, it became the most critical personal and political issue. In the end, the clamor over the railway line would be pushed to the rear by more massive events, and when the line was finally built in 1869, the power of the Southerners lay in smoking ruins, and the line followed the northern route.

While Broderick was in Washington fighting for the transcontinental railroad, the few remnants of the political machine he had constructed in California were dismantled. Federal and state patronage, the lifeblood of any political organization, was now entirely in the hands of the enemies; his bitter and vitriolic attacks on President Buchanan offended many whose reverence for the great and powerful dims their judgment. He was stigmatized for his refusal to comply with the "instructions" of the state legislature to support the Lecompton Constitution. In 1859, the legislature of California, firmly in the hands of the anti-Broderick forces, actually adopted a formal vote of condemnation against its *quondam* hero. Broderick knew little of the petty squabbling in California in that spring of 1859. He was still in Washington, contending by the side of Douglas to keep the country from tearing itself apart. The Democratic party was breaking in two, but he was not ready to join the emerging Republicans. Nor were the Republicans yet ready to accept him.

The session of 1859 was Broderick's last. Every debate was acrimonious, and Broderick did his best to support Stephen Douglas's position in the struggle to avert bloody disunion. His efforts won him the admiration of some of the most respected senators. To Seward, Broderick was the "brave young senator." Southerners attacked him on the Senate floor and in the corridors. When Congress adjourned in March 1859, Broderick, heartsick with frustration, left Washington on his last journey to California. Before embarking from New York on the long steamboat trip to Panama, Broderick spent a few days in New York. There, he was singled out and insulted in his hotel by two strangers, obviously Southerners, and just as obviously intent on provoking Broderick into an "honorable encounter." Eyewitnesses record that Broderick reacted with astonishing violence; he attacked the two cavaliers with a heavy walking stick. The incident, together with the verbal battering he had endured in the waning days of the Senate session, seems to have affected Broderick. Before he left Washington, he expressed a foreboding of death. His friend, Colonel John W. Forney, clerk of the House of Representatives, reported after Broderick's death that before leaving Washington, Broderick in a dark and gloomy mood, said to him:

> I feel, my dear friend, I go home to die. I shall be challenged, I shall fight, and I shall be killed.

When he said farewell to friends in New York, after the encounter with the two Southerners, the young senator is reported to have said: "I don't know whether you will ever see me again." The dark prophecy was repeated to others who saw him off on the steamship to Panama.

On his return to California, Broderick found the Democratic party torn apart by the slavery issue. The immediate cause of dissension was the infamous Lecompton Constitution. If adopted, such a measure would have revived slavery in the state. The Southerners, in control of almost every state and federal position, and backed by Buchanan, called a state convention of the "regular" Democratic party and nominated a slate of candidates who favored a "Lecompton" Constitution in particular and the Southern cause in general. The helpless anti-slavery remnants held their own "Democratic" convention, and nominated their own slate. The Republicans obstinately resisted every suggestion for coalition with Broderick and the anti-slavery Democrats, even when that obvious defense against disunion was urged on them by the eminent Horace Greeley.

As the campaign became heated and intense, Broderick attacked Gwin in the bitterest terms, charging him with corruption. Inevitably, there crept into the debates references to the sordid events of the 1857 senatorial election. What rankled most in Broderick's breast was Gwin's violation of the terms of "The Scarlet Letter" of January 11, 1857. In August, at a political meeting in Shasta, Broderick revealed the existence of "The Letter." He said:

I now return to Gwin, and I shall be brief. I will give you the copy of the letter that I believe led to the death of W. I. Ferguson. Do you believe it was for nothing that Ferguson's desk in the senate chamber was broken into immediately after his decease? On his deathbed Ferguson told General Estill where he could find the letter. A curse followed that letter, and I now give it to the public that the curse may return to its author, that its disgrace and shame may burn the brand upon his forehead even as plainly, as palpably as the scarlet letter burned upon the breast of Hester Pryn! Let Dr. Gwin or any of his set deny its authority and I will prove that he wrote it, letter for letter, column for column.

Now "The Letter" was open for all to see. It was published verbatim in the press, and Gwin was exposed as one who had purchased his Senate seat by a meretricious bargain that he had not even honored.

Gwin and his friends reacted with fury. They denounced Broderick as a "cowardly liar" and set in motion a plan to eliminate him from the political scene. Their anger toward Broderick was unmistakable, but their differences were even deeper. The Southerners in California had been plotting for years to plant the institution of slavery on its soil. Balked in this purpose, they were trying again to divide the state, with slavery in the southern half. They knew, too, that they were a minority of the voting population; that they were outnumbered by men from the north. Most of all, they knew that Broderick was the one man who could unite the anti-slavery forces in California and frustrate their schemes. He was not only an enemy, he was a threat to a cause that burned in their hearts. They foresaw the day when Free Soil Democrats would unite with the new Republican party and wrest control of the state from the Southerners. Broderick was the one man, they thought, who could unite their enemies. Broderick had to be destroyed.

The International Hotel in San Francisco, 1856. It was in the dining room of this hotel that Perley overheard Broderick's remarks about Terry, remarks that propelled Broderick to his death.

XII

THE ROAD TO LAKE MERCED

*What is honour? A word. What is in that word, honour? What
is that honour? Air.*

William Shakespeare, *The First Part Of King Henry the Fourth*

The Know-Nothing election of 1856 elevated Terry to the supreme court for a three-year term. As we have seen, when he sought renomination to that post in the 1859 election, Gwin's Lecompton Convention rejected him for another candidate. It galled Terry that his own partisans should deny him renomination to the court, but the Texan had his eye fixed on the goal of secession and slavery, and in spite of his disappointment, he remained an indefatigable participant in the Southerners' struggle to hold their political control of California. He told friends that his devotion to "The Cause" was not diminished by the party's rebuff. He saw himself as an instrument of higher purpose. On June 26, the day after the convention frustrated his ambition to be renominated, Terry made a polemical speech in which he poured his vitriol not only over his fellow cavaliers, who had ended his judicial career, but over Broderick. He denounced the Irishman's adherents as "the personal chattels of a single individual, whom they are ashamed of; they belong heart and soul, body and breeches, to David C. Broderick."

Next morning, June 27, Broderick was breakfasting with friends at the "public" table in the dining room of the International Hotel in San Francisco, when he saw that morning's issue of the San Francisco *Union,* with a full account of Terry's diatribe against him. His companions observed that Broderick's face became ashen as he read the article. He was so enraged that in a raised voice he denounced Terry as an "ingrate" whom he had protected and supported when the vigilantes tried him for murder in 1856. Broderick had always claimed that in that crisis he had paid the local newspapers to portray Terry as a supporter of law and order against anarchy. In a voice clearly audible to all sitting at the table, Broderick shouted: "I have said that I consider Terry the only honest man on the Supreme Bench, but I now take it all back." Angry, unfriendly words, but hardly the kind of personal reflection to be expunged in blood!

By chance or design, at the same "public" table and well within the range of Broderick's angry voice, sat Terry's friend and former law partner,

D. W. Perley. Perley was a Canadian by birth, but by association and conviction he had become an adherent of the Southern party. As Terry's law partner in Stockton, Perley had given many signs of devotion to the Texan, including an appearance before the vigilante tribunal as a character witness for Terry in 1856. Terry was his second in a duel he fought with one Henry Marshall. The two men were close personal friends, who shared an active interest in the Southern project to tear California from the Union. Even Wagstaff, who has a special charity not only for Terry, but for his friends, concedes that Perley "was a hot-headed Southern man, smart, active, able and not a very scrupulous attorney."

When Perley heard Broderick's comment on Terry's speech, he leaped to his feet and confronted Broderick. He said:

I heard you, sir, make some insulting remark about my friend, Judge Terry. You should know that I propose to advise the Judge of your statement.

And Broderick replied:

Do so, by all means. Convey your news as quickly as possible! The miserable wretch, after being kicked out of the Convention, went down there and made a speech abusing me. I paid three newspapers to defend him during the Vigilante Committee days and this is all the gratitude I get from the miserable wretch. I have hitherto spoken of him as an honest man — the only honest man on a corrupt Supreme Court, but now I find I was mistaken; I take it all back. He is just as bad as the others.

This is how Broderick's words were later reported. As to Terry's "honesty," there is no evidence to justify Broderick's imputation. Whatever may have been his failings, there was never any suggestion of venality on Terry's part. Clearly, he was "honest" as a judge, even if his was that "bastard" honesty that Trollope describes as "honesty born out of precept by stupidity." His precepts were those of the South, of the Frontier, of the "Code Duello," of exaggerated punctilio; his stupidity was that of men who personalize every encounter and experience and are almost indifferent to the feelings of others. Surely Broderick was not too fastidious about the integrity of judges!

Field's integrity had been seriously questioned both before and after ascending to the California Supreme Court. Yet Broderick considered him an honest man, and would never have applied to him the slurs he flung at Terry. Before Perley left the hotel dining room, he challenged Broderick on his own account. Broderick treated the challenge with contempt. "Sir," he is supposed to have told Perley, "I fight only with gentlemen of my own position."

Considering the trifling character of Broderick's words, the way in which they were instantly transformed by Perley into a *casus belli*, Broderick's adherents felt that Perley's presence at the table was not an accident, that it was part of a Secesh design to trick Broderick into a duel, to remove from the scene the one man who had the personality and power to unify the anti-slavery forces. Perley's adventitious presence in the hotel dining room coupled with some of the murky circumstances of the duel that ensued from Broderick's outburst, the noisy threats of Gwin, Terry and their friends to eliminate Broderick, the clarity of their motive, all contributed to the conclusion so many reached that Broderick was the victim of a murder plot! A San

Francisco newspaper, the *National,* had the prescience to write:

> *The convictions have been forced on the minds of all men who have read the speeches of Gwin and Broderick that a bloody termination of this controversy is expected by the friends of both senators, that it is one for which one or both are prepared.*

To most Californians of the day, the duel that followed was a put-up job.

Is it unfair to judge that the men of the South, men who prided themselves on the elegance of their manners and the delicacy of their minds, could be roused to insane fury by such paltry words, could be guilty of such brutality, such callous indifference to human life and the law as to contrive a deliberate murder plot? In the decade before Fort Sumter, the passions of Southern "gentlemen" ran so strongly, their contempt for the Northern *canaille* was so deep, their juvenile "honor" so delicate that Northerners felt them quite capable of resorting to murder to eliminate the enemies of their cause. Their excesses were justified by pretended benefits to "The Cause." These Southerners in California may have been three thousand miles from the seat of action, but their sectional fervor was that of the expatriate. They had to "prove their doctrinal orthodoxy by apostolic blows and knocks." An example of these "blows and knocks," of their mad-dog fury, was the brutal beating of Senator Charles Sumner of Massachusetts at the hands of Congressman Preston Brooks of South Carolina.

It was the passion of such fanatics, followed by terrifying words and deeds, that made Broderick's remarks so dangerous. Of course, Broderick's words were immediately reported to Terry, who delivered a challenge to Broderick within hours. But Broderick had time to reflect; now he was sure that he was indeed the target of a Secesh plot and that Perley and Terry were actors in a scenario devised by Gwin. He declined to honor the challenge in a letter to Terry (released, of course, to the general public). He wrote:

> *For many years and up to the time of my elevation to the position I now occupy it was well known that I would not have avoided any issue of the character proposed. If compelled to accept a challenge it could only be with a gentleman holding a position equally elevated and responsible; and there are no circumstances which could induce me even to do this during the pending of the present canvass. When I authorized the announcement that I would address the people of California during the campaign it was suggested that efforts would be made to force me into difficulties, and I determined to take no notice of attacks from any source during the canvass. There are probably many other gentlemen who would seek similar opportunities for hostile meetings for the purpose of accomplishing a political object or to obtain public notoriety.*
>
> *I cannot afford at the present time to descend to a violation of the constitution and the state laws to subserve either their or your purposes.*

In truth, by the law of California, duels were forbidden and participants were subject to severe penalties. At least one of the local newspapers applauded Broderick's moral courage. It wrote:

> *For refusing to fight a duel under the circumstances, the large mass of the people will honor D. C. Broderick. The belief is quite general*

*that there are certain political opponents of his who long for a chance
to shoot him, either in a fair or unfair fight, and that efforts would
be made sooner or later to involve him in a personal difficulty. It is
wisdom on his part to avoid the traps set for him and thus defeat all
the plans of those in whose path he happens to just now stand. His
seat in the Senate would be quite acceptable to a number of gentlemen in the state. The people of California ought to manifest, in a
manner not to be mistaken, their approval of the conduct of a public
man who exhibits courage to refuse upon any ground to accept a
challenge.*

In our time it seems incredible that serious and cultivated men of
affairs, of depth of intellect, should have lent themselves to such juvenile
games. For the next three months, Terry stalked Broderick as a hunter pur-
sues a stag. He publicly advertised his intention to renew his challenge to
Broderick "when the canvass ends, and he has no excuse." And through a
combination of fatalism and mindless acceptance of these childish mores,
Broderick seems to have accepted his fate. Contemporary reports make it
clear that from June 28, the day of the challenge, until September 8, the day
after the state election, one of the principal topics of conversation throughout California was Terry's pursuit of Broderick, the inevitability that they
would fight and that Broderick would be killed! The San Francisco *National*
had no doubt: "The Perley affair . . . was arranged by [Broderick's] enemies
to provoke a hostile collision." A reporter of the time wrote:

*Between the 1st of July and the 7th of September, the political cam-
paign was accompanied by the bitterest personalities, and Broderick
in his speeches did not spare the name of Terry. The latter was ultra-
Southern in his morality as well as his politics.*

The California historian Bancroft would write later: "Broderick was
a novice and no murderer . . . Terry played with blood, not boys." This was
inaccurate; Broderick had fought duels in the past. But Broderick's supporters would charge Terry with the grim and unyielding purpose to bring Broderick into the sights of his pistol and that he plotted with Gwin, Randolph
and other Southerners to eliminate Broderick. Was there really such a plot?

Assuredly there was a reason for such a plot. It was clear to Gwin and
his followers that their triumph in the state election of 1859 was ephemeral
and that their hegemony was threatened by a combination of the Free-Soil
Democratic remnant under Broderick and the new Republican party. Their
greatest danger lay in that combination of the Broderick forces and the Republicans, a coalition that sooner or later had to come. The obvious leader
of that coalition was Broderick, already faltering in his confidence that Douglas's efforts at compromise could save the country from secession and war.
Broderick was certainly an important obstacle to their purpose. If Preston
Brooks could justify his murderous assault on Sumner, these California zealots could justify the elimination of Broderick.

On the morning of September 8, the day after the election, Broderick
sat glumly in his hotel room in San Francisco surveying the wreckage of his
once-prosperous political world. Everywhere in the state his moderate Democrats, their voting power sapped by defections to the new Republican party,
had lost to the Southerners. It was no consolation that the new Republican

party had also gone down in flames. Southerners were in control of every important state office. Telegram after telegram announced defeat. As Broderick counted his bruises, there came a knock at the door. It was Mr. Calhoun Benham, bearing a message from Judge Terry.

Terry remained in Sacramento on September 7, long enough to learn that everywhere the adherents of Gwin and the South were victorious. He wrote out his resignation as chief justice, addressed it to the governor and hastened to Oakland where he composed a note to Broderick:

Oakland, September 8, 1859

Hon. D. C. Broderick:

SIR, — Some two months since, at the public table in the International Hotel in San Francisco, you saw fit to indulge in certain remarks concerning me, which were offensive in their nature. Before I had heard of the circumstance your note of 29th of June, addressed to Mr. D. W. Perley, in which you declared that you would not respond to any call of a personal character during the political canvass just concluded, had been published.

I have, therefore, not been permitted to take any notice of these remarks until the expiration of that limit fixed by yourself. I now take the earliest opportunity to require of you a retraction of those remarks. This note will be handed you by my friend, Calhoun Benham, Esq., who is acquainted with its contents and will receive your reply.

D. S. Terry.

Broderick stood in the doorway of the hotel room, facing Benham and read Terry's demand for a retraction and apology. When Benham pressed him for an immediate response, Broderick sat down at a table and composed a letter which he delivered to Benham:

San Francisco, September 8, 1859

Hon. D. S. Terry:

SIR, — Your note of September 8th reached me through the hands of Mr. Calhoun Benham. The remarks used by me in the conversation referred to may be a subject of future misrepresentation; and for obvious reasons I have to desire you to state what were the remarks that you designate in your note as offensive, and of which you require of me a retraction.

I remain, etc.,
D. C. Broderick.

Perley had done his work well: he had made a careful memorandum of Broderick's remarks in the hotel dining room, for Terry had the words almost verbatim. Next morning Benham delivered another note:

San Francisco, September 9th, 1859

Hon. D. C. Broderick:

SIR, — In reply to your note of this date I have to say that the offensive remarks to which I alluded in my communication of yesterday are as follows: "I have hitherto considered and spoken of him (myself) as the only honest man on the Supreme Court bench; but I now take it all back," thus by implication reflecting on my personal and official integrity. This is the substance of your remarks as reported to me; the precise terms, however, in which such an implication was conveyed are not important to the question.

You yourself can best remember the terms in which you spoke of me on the occasion referred to. What I require is the retraction of any words which were calculated to reflect on my character as an official or a gentleman.

I remain, your obedient servant,
D. S. Terry.

At this point, it would have been better for Broderick, for California, and for the cause of Unionism if he had been mindful of Plato's definition of courage: the virtue of fleeing from an inevitable danger. But once the September election had wrecked his political apparatus, Broderick's associates observed in him what the psychiatrists of a later age would call a "death-wish." He could have "accommodated"; he had done it before. But to friends who urged him to "retract," he argued that if he did so, he would have to acknowledge the Southerners as the political masters of California. This he could not do. He had himself stood on the top rung of the political ladder in the state, and to accept any lower place in his mind involved degradation. He had been Caesar, and he would neither lead a legion nor govern a province under Pompey. Even if there had not lain between him and the Chivs such incandescent issues as Lecompton or Kansas, slavery or secession, Broderick and Terry were fated to be enemies. Terry loomed as the incarnation of his enemies, and neither man could live as second to the other. Both men were designed by nature either to prevail or destroy.

Also, the "Code Duello" had become a way of life for politicians. To refuse a challenge was "cowardice." Like Terry, Broderick was a man of his time. He promptly composed a letter to Terry that could have only one answer:

Friday Evening, September 9th

Hon. D. S. Terry:

Yours of this date has been received. The remarks made by me were occasioned by certain offensive allusions of yours concerning me made in the convention at Sacramento, reported in the Union *of June 25th. Upon the topic alluded to in your note of this date my language, so far as my recollecton serves me, was as follows: "During Judge Terry's incarceration by the Vigilance Committee I paid $200 a week to support a newspaper in his (your) defence. I have also stated heretofore that I considered him (Judge Terry) the only honest man on the supreme bench, but I take it all back." You are the best judge as to whether this language affords good ground for offence.*

I remain, etc.,
D. C. Broderick.

The challenge came back the same day:

San Francisco, September 9th, 1859

Hon. D. C. Broderick:

SIR, — Some months ago you used language concerning me offensive in its nature. I waited the lapse of a period of time fixed by yourself before I asked reparation therefor at your hands. You replied, asking specifications of the language used which I regarded as offensive. In another letter I gave you the specification and reiterated my demand for a retraction. To this last letter you reply, acknowledging the use of the offensive language imputed to you and not making the retraction required. This course on your part leaves me no other alternative but to demand the satisfaction usual among gentlemen, which I accordingly do. Mr. Benham will make the necessary arrangements.

Your obedient servant,
D. S. Terry.

Both men were now fixed on the road of bloody lunacy that would lead to a pasture on the shore of Lake Merced, and to an act that lies like a scarlet stain across the annals of California.

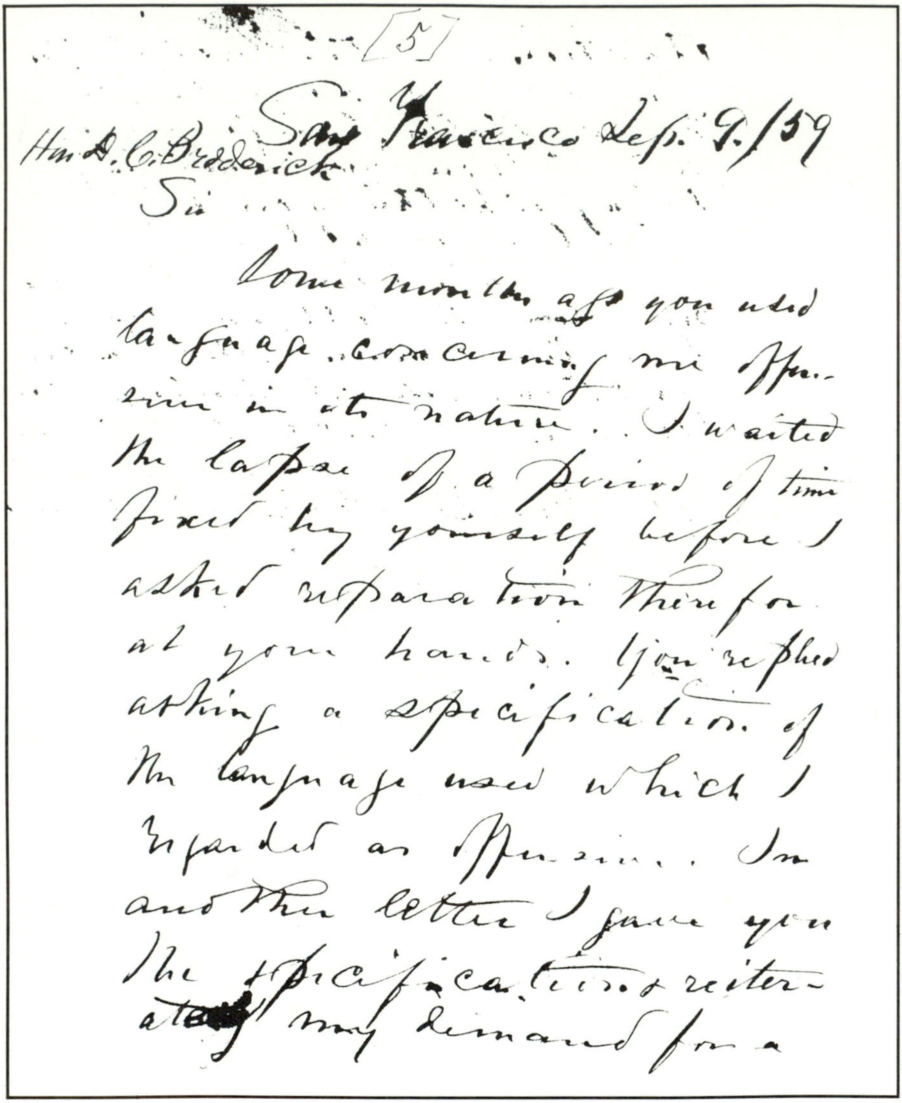

Hon D. C. Broderick
San Francisco Sep. 9./59
Sir

Some months ago you used language concerning me offensive in its nature. I waited the lapse of a period of time fixed by yourself before I asked reparation therefor at your hands. You replied asking a specification of the language used which I regarded as offensive. In another letter I gave you the specification & reiterated my demand for a

Terry's letter challenging Broderick to the fatal duel

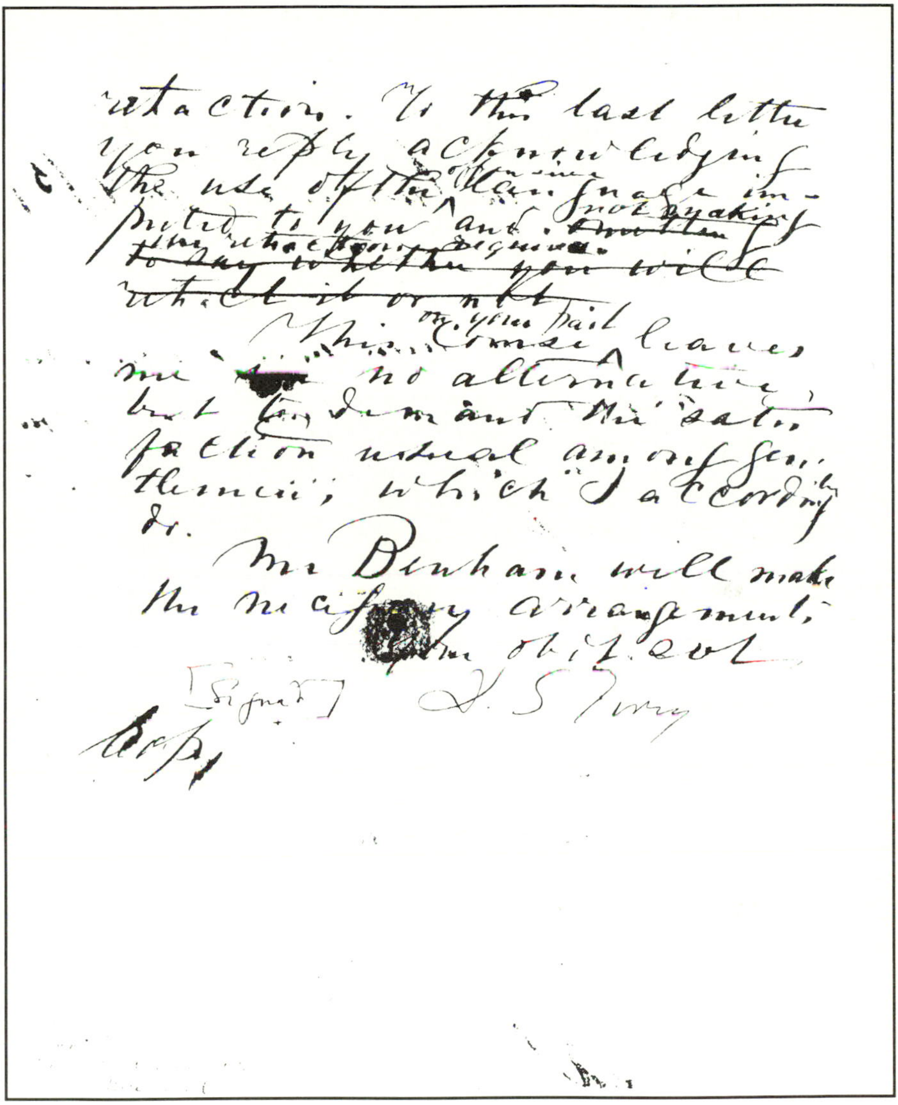

retraction. To the last letter you replied acknowledging the use of the language imputed to you and ~~any other reparation~~ [not making] ~~to say whether you will retract it or not~~

This course on your part leaves me no alternative but to demand the satisfaction usual among gentlemen, which I accordingly do.

Mr Benham will make the necessary arrangements.

Your obt servt

[Signed] B. F. Perry

Copy

The duel, as portrayed in Wagstaff's Life of Terry

XIII

THE DUEL: "WHO NOW SHALL SPEAK FOR CALIFORNIA?"

Th' applause of list'ning senates to command,
The threats of pain and ruin to despise,
To scatter plenty o'er a smiling land,
And read their hist'ry in nation's eyes.
Thomas Gray, "Elegy Written in a Country Church Yard"

As his seconds in the duel, Terry chose his friend Benham and two other Southerners, Thomas Hayes and S. H. Brooks, all men experienced in duelling. Hayes had been a principal in at least two encounters. Broderick entrusted his affairs to three close friends, J. C. McKibben, David D. Colton and Leonidas Haskell, all stout men, but novices in the duelling game. It was arranged that the meeting should take place on a secluded beach nine miles south of San Francisco, near the boundaries of San Mateo and San Francisco Counties, at sunrise on September 12. News of the duel spread through the city, and when the principals arrived, each with his entourage, hundreds of spectators lined the beach. The Chief of Police, Martin J. Burke, promptly arrested the duellists. Burke had been a member of the executive committee of the vigilantes, one of Terry's judges in the "trial" in 1856. He was a no-nonsense character who promptly brought the duelling party before a police justice — who discharged them with a friendly wink, on the ground that no actual misdemeanor had occurred.

Friends of both contestants expressed the hope this would take the steam out of the situation and avoid the duel. But the principals were "adamant" in going ahead. "Honor," they declared, had to be satisfied. It was decided to change the time and place. A San Francisco newspaper carried the story that the duel had in fact taken place and that Terry had been severely wounded in the neck, a yarn that caused some misplaced jubilation among Broderick's friends in the city. In fact, Terry was in excellent health; he spent the day practicing with the very pistols that would be used in the duel. Not that he needed much practice with firearms; guns had been his companions from childhood. While his reputation as a fire-eater was based on frequent recourse to the Bowie knife, he was a practiced hand with the pistol.

Nor was Broderick entirely unfamiliar with firearms, although his skills were not comparable to those of a frontiersman, a former Texas Ranger. But Broderick was under one serious disadvantage. Even casual onlookers thought he was physically unfit to fight a duel. The bitter and acrimonious political campaign he had just endured left him "in an exhausted state." But then,

Terry had also been through the campaign, and had actually lost his job in the election. Friends said that on the day of the duel Broderick was suffering from pneumonia and fever. Under the specious code of "honor" which governed this senseless slaughter, Broderick could have avoided the contest; ill health was normally accepted as good grounds for declining to fight. But Broderick refused to plead illness; his friends observed that he seemed a man in the grip of a fatal impulse, an indifference, almost an acceptance of doom. Those close to him remarked that from the time the congressional session ended in the spring of 1859, Broderick had not been himself. His conversation included many references to the malaise he was experiencing and even more to an apprehension of approaching death.

While his antagonist occupied himself on the eve of the duel with his pistol practice, Broderick drew his last testament and spent his time, like the Socrates of the *Phaedo,* in mournful conversation with his friends discoursing on life and death. His companions were concerned with his seeming insouciance, his inability to understand that he was throwing his life away. Broderick was intelligent enough to understand that, in the words of Colonel Baker, as he wept over Broderick's corpse:

> *The Code of Honor is a delusion and a snare; it palters with the hopes of a true courage and binds it at the feet of crafty, cruel skill. It substitutes cold and deliberate preparation for courageous and manly impulse. It makes the mere truth of the weapon superior to the noblest cause and the truest courage.*

But Broderick firmly rejected every attempt to avoid the duel. He seemed a man eager to rush into the embrace of death. The duel finally took place in a small valley just south of Lake Merced, about ten miles from the center of the city. Today, the scene is marked by a small pyramidal monument.

Ben C. Truman was a San Francisco newspaperman who trailed some of Broderick's friends to the duelling ground. Later he wrote a detailed account of the day's events. From him we learn that the field selected was a dairy farm owned by a Mr. Davis, an admirer of Broderick. Truman describes that there was some wrangling over the selection of the weapons, a point that became important in the days following the duel. Terry won the choice of weapons and he selected the duelling pistols owned by a close personal friend, Dr. Aylette, of Stockton. Whatever basis there is for the belief embedded in California history that Broderick was murdered must be found in the weapons selected by Terry.

The pistols were of Belgian manufacture, identical in appearance, with twelve-inch barrels. They had been used in several duels and were known as the "Aylette pistols." Actually, the weapons had belonged to one Jo Beard of Stockton, a former clerk of the supreme court and an intimate of Terry, who had given the pistols to Dr. Dan Aylette, a Stockton physician who was one of Terry's neighbors and a close friend. Terry borrowed them from Dr. Aylette and practiced with them. Senator Ben Langford, a Terry intimate, confirmed that he accompanied Terry when "they all went out to the doctor's barn to practice." The practicing continued for almost two months, and Terry had the opportunity to observe that both pistols had extremely sensitive triggers.

It was later said that one of them was known to have a hair trigger "so light and delicate that [it] would be discharged on a sudden jar or motion, without touching the trigger." This was the judgment of one Ryer, who had himself used the pistols two years before in a political duel. Perhaps one familiar with both weapons could distinguish between them. In his biography of Broderick, Lynch refers to a letter from ex-Lieutenant Governor Ben Daggett which throws some light on Terry's familiarity with the two pistols:

I had a talk with Senator Langford some years ago, who was a life-long friend of Terry's and, as I believe you know, a reliable and truthful man. Ben, much to my surprise related to me the fact that when the duel was decided upon, Terry came to his house in Lodi for advice, and together they went to Dr. Aylette in Stockton, who had pistols and was an authority upon such matters.

They all went out to the doctor's barn to practice.

Apparently, Terry practiced with these pistols many times while he was waiting for two months for Broderick to finish his election activities, so he could be challenged. From firing the two pistols, he may well have known that one of them had a tricky defect, and he may have learned to distinguish one weapon from another.

In one generally reliable account of the duel, we are told:

Choice of weapons was left to lot. Terry won. He had, therefore, the advantage of a weapon with which he was thoroughly familiar, its trigger so delicately sprung that a breath would move it. He had fought more than once before and had the deliberate purpose to kill his man. Broderick, by evil chance, got a pistol even more sensitive than that held by Terry. The distance was set at ten paces. Broderick was weak from illness, unnerved and in no condition to fight for his life.

Present at the duel was a French gunsmith from San Francisco, one Bernard Lagoardo, called "Natchez." He was asked to examine both weapons. He pronounced them in good order, "except they were light and delicate on the triggers." He also pointed out to one of Terry's seconds that the pistol intended for Broderick was "lighter on the trigger than the other." Why he did not call this to the attention of Broderick's seconds is a mystery, especially since he testified at the inquest that Broderick's pistol "was so delicate it would explode by a sudden jar or movement"; that he had "detected the defect in Broderick's weapon and pointed it out to his seconds." Indeed, Broderick himself, as he lay dying, averred that he had never even touched the trigger of his pistol, but that the mere act of elevating the weapon to the horizontal position had caused it to fire prematurely.

It is ironic that the original duelling ground had been abandoned as "too public," for now there were more than sixty spectators at the scene, in addition to the duelling party. After some preliminary hanky-panky in which friends urged both parties to be reconciled, and some peace officers vainly tried to prevent the duel, the parties reached the ground. The "commissioners" of the two sides had met and drawn "articles." It was agreed that the "word" would be "fire — one, two," that the contestants could fire when the word "fire" was uttered, but not after "two"; that the choice of weapons and position should be determined by chance on the ground. The distance between the two men was to be the traditional ten paces. Now, the seconds engaged in the preliminaries of tossing a silver dollar for "points of advantage." Broderick won "the position and the giving of the words." Terry won the choice of weapons; he drew one of the Aylette pistols from its case. Then, the two enemies faced each other, the pistols at their sides pointing downward. At the word "one," Broderick's pistol fired, the bullet entering the ground halfway between the two adversaries. At the word "two," Terry took careful aim and shot Broderick through the chest, his bullet piercing a lung. It is reported that when he saw his shot take effect, Terry turned to his second, Benham, and remarked: "The wound is not mortal. I have hit two inches too far out." Another version: "Ah! I have struck him a little too high." These words were widely quoted and of course were given the sinister imputation that he intended to kill.

The sound of the pistol shots was still echoing when the first cry of "murder!" was raised. Davis, the dairy farmer who owned the duelling site, was a witness to the duel. As Broderick fell, Davis leaped to his feet shouting: "That's murder, by God!" He made a menacing move toward Terry, but some of the bystanders checked him, saying there had been enough bloodshed for the day. Davis persisted, screaming at Terry and shaking his fist:

> I am Broderick's friend; I am not going to see him killed in that way! If you are men, you will join me in avenging his death!

These are the words attributed to "the milkman" by Truman, who was there. Truman adds that some of Broderick's level-headed friends pacified Davis by pointing out that many of Terry's friends were present and were armed. They told him:

> We know you are Mr. Broderick's friend, but we know as well that if you attack Terry there will be a general fight, and but few will get off this ground alive. Think a moment before you do this thing.

Whereupon, we are told, "the milkman was quieted and sat himself down, breathing threatenings of slaughter."

But the cry of murder first raised by the "milkman" persisted. To this day, Terry is remembered in California history as the "murderer" of Broderick. Was it murder, or merely the tragic outcome of an archaic, barbarous custom of life in that time? Of course, when the news of the duel and Broderick's death came to the super-heated politicians and journalists of the East, there was the expected reaction. In the North, press and politicians treated it as a cold-blooded murder; to the editorial writers and legislative orators of the South, Terry was a hero from the same mold as Preston Brooks. What the Northern press thought is reflected in an article by George William Curtis in *Harper's Weekly*. He wrote:

> Most of the papers here characterized the event as a murder. It seems certain that many politicians, among whom Dr. Gwin occupied a conspicuous place, had determined to fight Broderick; had he escaped Terry, other duels awaited him, and in a country of marksmen he could hardly have escaped in the end. . . . There are parts of the United States where a politician must necessarily be prepared to fight duels. . . . Yet, it is undoubted, that in many states of the Union, a politician who will not fight must stand aside, and cannot command the popular suffrage.

HARPER'S WEEKLY.

SATURDAY, OCTOBER 22, 1859.

THE DEATH OF BRODERICK.

SOCIETY has been shocked by the announcement that Senator Broderick, of California, was killed in duel, on 13th September, by Chief Justice Terry. Most of the papers here characterize the event as a murder. It seems certain that many politicians, among whom Dr. Gwin occupied a conspicuous place, had determined to fight Broderick; had he escaped Terry, other duels awaited him, and in a country of marksmen he could hardly have escaped in the end. What note the California courts will take of the event remains to be seen. A conviction of the successful duelist can hardly be expected, perhaps; but we may look for some legislation on the subject which may enure to the advantage of Californian society.

There are parts of the United States where a politician must necessarily be prepared to fight duels. In the origin, the practice is said to have arisen from the want of some potent corrective of the prevailing rudeness of social customs among the early settlers. Men got into the way of fighting duels in order to anticipate insult; just as Texans carry bowie-knives so as to insure peace and order. Whether the method was sound, and whether it answered its purpose; whether duelists are more tender of each other's feelings than members of the Peace Society; whether turbulence is peculiar to the unarmed, and rare among the General Chollops, it is not now worth while to inquire. However this may be, it is clear that at the present day, as well in California as in every other State of the Union, society could get on very

"*. . . the event as a murder.*"—*a* Harper's Weekly *editorial*

The verdict of San Francisco's citizenry and of almost every California historian is that Broderick was murdered, and that Terry was his murderer. He was branded as a murderer in terms so extravagant that his reputation never recovered. He was "the destroyer with the mark of Cain on his brow." Broderick was "the hunted lion" sacrificed by a "hungry pack of jackals." Whatever the truth, for the next thirty years the shadow of Broderick's killing hovered over Terry's life. References to him in the press were usually accompanied by a reminder that he had gunned down one of California's brightest stars. It may be that in this senseless duel are found the seeds of the paranoiac pride that three decades later drew Terry into the Sharon-Hill tragicomedy. The terrible scenes in San Francisco's federal court and in the depot restaurant at Lathrop may well have had their roots in the tragedy at the Lake Merced picnic ground.

Broderick did not die quickly or easily. The stricken man was placed on a mattress in a spring wagon and carried to the nearby house of his friend, Haskell. He lingered in agony for three days. As he lay dying, one of his friends was reported to have solemnly intoned a paraphrase of the line from *Julius Caesar:* "He loved the name of honor more than he feared death." In his delirium, he is reported to have said: "They have killed me because I was opposed to a corrupt administration and the extension of slavery." These "last words" were widely reported and had great effect upon his sympathizers. They sound like those felicitous deathbed pronouncements usually composed by admirers who were not there.

When the news of Broderick's death reached San Francisco, the city sank into grief. Angry citizens gathered in groups and talked of lynching Terry. Many spoke of reviving the Committee of Vigilance. Before the legions of Broderick's admirers could devote themselves to vengeance, they organized a funeral that would be remembered for years. Broderick's body was brought to the Union Hotel at the corner of Kearny and Merchant streets. There he lay in state until his coffin was placed on a high, black-draped catafalque in what was then the main plaza of the city, Portsmouth Square. A crowd of between ten thousand and twenty thousand mourners ("the entire adult population of the city" according to one newspaper) heard a funeral oration in the most lachrymose Mark Antony tradition, delivered by Colonel Edward D. Baker, the lawyer who had defended the murderer, Cora, in 1856. He had been, with Broderick, among those who had joined Terry in Sacramento to celebrate his escape from the vigilantes.

Baker was more than a silver-tongued orator. He was born and educated in England; somehow he found his way to Illinois, where he became a successful lawyer and formed a friendship with Abraham Lincoln so close that Lincoln named his second son after him. This intimacy is ironically relevant to our story because Baker was one of those who brought Stephen J. Field to Lincoln's notice, and contributed — posthumously — to Field's appointment to the Supreme Court, thus contributing to the events that years later destroyed Terry. Baker had earned his colonelcy by gallantry in the field in the Mexican War. In 1860, the year after Broderick's death, Baker moved from San Francisco to Oregon at the invitation of the citizens of that new state, whose legislature promptly elected him to the United States Senate. To the Lincoln family and the administration he was a close friend. He rode with

Broderick lying in state, San Francisco, 1859

Lincoln in the inaugural parade and had the honor to introduce the president for the inaugural address.

In the Senate, he was an administration stalwart. After Fort Sumter, Lincoln offered to make him a major general of volunteers, but Baker declined because this would have required resignation from the Senate. Instead, he personally raised a Philadelphia regiment. When he died in the disaster at Ball's Bluff in October 1861, Lincoln was seated in the telegraph room at Army Headquarters in Washington. As the news of Ned Baker's death came over the wire, "Lincoln sat for five minutes, stunned, then made his way unaccompanied through the anteroom, breast heaving, tears streaming down his cheeks. As he stepped out into the street, he stumbled groping blindly and almost fell. Orderlies and newspapermen jumped to help him, but he recovered his balance and went on alone, leaving them the memory of a weeping President."

Baker's regard and affection for Broderick were as sincere as his grief. The light was beginning to penetrate the minds of anti-slavery, pro-Union Democrats in the year 1859 that it was imperative to identify and encourage new leaders. Lincoln was, of course, the greatest of these. But in the remote, isolated West Coast, Baker and other men of vision saw in Broderick a new leader who could guide and inspire them in resisting slavery and secession. They saw his death as a tragedy to the state and to the nation.

Baker's eulogy over Broderick's body comes down through the years as one of the longest and most florid funerary orations on record. He compared the martyred Broderick with John Hampden, Tiberius, Gracchus,

Henry II and William of Nassau. He left no doubt in the minds of his listeners that "the slaying of Broderick was anything but a political murder."

> [*His death*] *has long been foreshadowed — it was predicted by his friends — it was threatened by his enemies; it was the consequence of intense political hatred. His death was a political necessity, poorly veiled beneath the guise of a private quarrel.*

He reminded his audience of the killing of Ferguson; the duel he said was "a shield emblazoned with the name of Chivalry to cover the malignity of murder." Baker raised his arms above his head, stared at the hushed thousands and asked the question that was in the minds of those listeners whose deepest concern was for the threatened breakup of the American Republic: "Who now shall speak for California?"

Baker's was but one of many voices that cried "Murder!" An angry crowd thrust into the face of Dr. Gwin as he left San Francisco for the East a portrait of Broderick bearing a sign reading: "It is the will of the people that the murderers of Broderick do not return again to California." The San Francisco *Times* demanded that "the extremity of the law" be visited upon Terry. The *News* trumpeted a demand that Terry be indicted for murder. Bancroft, California's leading historian, had no doubt that "certain gentlemen of that school [the Southern Chivalry] had determined on [Broderick's death]. It was arranged that one after another should challenge him to mortal combat until he should fall." Another historian records that:

> *When the duel was decided upon, Terry went to the owner of these pistols and together they practiced with them until the chivalrous judge doubtless became aware of the tricky fault in one of them.*

Then the writer adds a footnote:

> *These pistols subsequently came into the possession of a friend of mine in New York City who corroborates the statement of the defect in one.*

Public indignation over Broderick's killing was so intense that not even the state political machine controlled by Gwin and Terry's Southern friends could protect him from indictment for manslaughter in San Francisco.

When the duel ended, Terry had left the field in the belief that the wound he had dealt Broderick was not fatal. Whether this was a cause for jubilation or regret is not recorded. I suspect that in the clearer light of anticlimax, even the most fiery of Broderick's enemies would have been happy to hear that the Irishman would recover. When the news came that Broderick was dead, and that angry mobs were clamoring for vengeance, Terry met with friends in council at his house in Stockton. They weighed the advisability of flight to Nevada. The decision was to brazen it out and on September 24 Terry appeared at the courthouse in San Francisco with three of his friends, pleaded not guilty to a charge of manslaughter, and was released on bail of $10,000. Before long his friends in the legislature helped him somewhat by changing the law to provide that persons charged with duelling were to be tried in the District Court, filled with Southern partisans.

The screams for revenge in the local press justifiably forced a change of venue from San Francisco to the District Court in Marin County. All observers agreed that Terry could not get a fair trial in San Francisco. No objective lawyer can complain of this move, but it played right into the hands of

Terry's sympathizers. He was "tried" before Judge James H. Hardy, a Southerner, and a close friend of Terry. Just how close they were was demonstrated by Hardy at the "trial." No evidence was offered by the prosecution, because the witnesses were becalmed on the Bay "by a trick." Hardy's Secesh bias is best measured by the fact that he was later impeached for disloyalty to the Union. "The difficulty in bringing a case to trial where the parties charged were of Southern antecedents, and especially if they occupied official positions, was illustrated by the ease with which Terry eluded the law for the killing of Broderick. A change of venue to a district where the judge was also a Southerner and a sympathizer, a trick to delay witnesses, a dismissal of the case, and all was settled." One of the charges in Judge Hardy's later impeachment trial was that he had "fixed" Terry's trial. At any rate, the judge would not wait for the becalmed witnesses, and the indictment was dismissed "on the merits." A new indictment for murder was found by a grand jury in San Mateo County, where it probably should have been found in the first place, since the duel had occurred in that jurisdiction. When the case was called for trial, Terry's counsel presented a transcript showing that Terry had already been tried and acquitted in Marin County. "Double jeopardy!" said the presiding jurist (quite properly) and the new charges were dismissed. So ended the legal proceeding against Terry. He was safe from the law, but it was only the beginning of his penance.

Today, Broderick is forgotten by all save historians, but for decades he was regarded by his fellow Californians as a venerated martyr, a victim of a Southern plot to destroy him. Gwin denied it; Terry denied it; there is no clear-cut evidence, but the myth of Terry the Murderer persists. The "inquest of history" has rendered its verdict.

If Gwin, Terry and the Chivs thought to advance the pro-slavery cause in California by eliminating Broderick, they must have been bitterly disappointed. His death shocked Californians into a better understanding of the threat posed by the Southerners. Broderick was hardly in his grave before Gwin and his servile legislature made their play. They adopted a resolution which would split the state in two: they authorized the residents of the part of California south of the thirty-sixth parallel to hold a plebiscite on forming a separate state. But the plebiscite was never held; Douglas Democrats and Republicans finally joined together, and Gwin's prediction in the Senate that if the Southern states seceded, "California will be found with the South," never came to pass.

In death, Broderick's faults were forgotten; his tragic end expunged his many delinquencies. In every society, there is a large number of gaping fools who, because they are themselves excluded from large affairs by incapacity, are always eager to trample upon those who are famous and successful. Encouraged by the lowest breed of journalists, these sensation-mongers delude themselves that public virtue consists of sneering at the highly-placed, the successful and the fortunate. But let one of their targets be visited with misfortune, and these vulgar crows change their chant, and transform their targets into idols. Let a governor lose his young wife — who only yesterday was defamed as a *demi-mondaine* — to the cholera, and she becomes a tragic saint and the great man, who yesterday was a byword and a hissing becomes a figure majestic and noble in his tragedy. So it was with Broderick after the

The obelisk honoring Broderick in Pioneer Memorial Cemetery, San Francisco.
The memorial no longer exists, having been torn down when all cemeteries were
removed from the city limits of San Francisco in the early part of this century.

duel. Even in that rugged live-and-let-live society of the young and unlettered, Broderick alive was despised by many for his corruption, his cool indifference to all interests but his own. The people of California were slow to perceive in the Irishman the one man who could coalesce the anti-slavery forces in the West and prevent secession and sectional strife. Terry's bullet changed all that. The feet of clay became pillars of stone; the arrogance became dignity and the selfishness was transformed into zeal for the public good. Within days after his death, Broderick became one of California's most revered heroes, and his "murderer" an object of public revulsion. Broderick's elevation to political sainthood was almost instantaneous. When the Republicans met at Sacramento to designate electors for the 1860 presidential election, one of them said: "A more noble, manly, open glorious statesman never lived than David C. Broderick. . . . I would rather live in retirement all my life than vote for Stephen A. Douglas, the professed friend, who vilely betrayed him, and the man who voted for the confirmation of the appointment of Calhoun Benham, one of the seconds in that fatal duel as United States District Attorney for California."

Neither portrait of Broderick, the saint or the spoilsman, is entirely accurate or fair, but the legends persist. To this day, Broderick is one of the saintliest figures in California's history, foully done to death by a brutal assassin. Terry's memory is still stained by his blood, by the belief that the duel was rigged to kill Broderick. "The verdict of the world is conclusive," St. Augustine tells us — and the world's verdict was that Terry murdered Broderick.

The great Seward, who had admired and supported Broderick, concluded a eulogy on the Senate floor with the words:

> *I leave him, therefore in his early grave, content to confine my expressions of grief within the bounds of sorrow for the loss of a friend, than whom none more truthful and honest survive us; a senator, than whom none more incorruptible ever entered these halls; and a statesman who, though he fell too soon for a nation's hopes, yet like Hamilton, left behind him a noble monument well and completely finished.*

This tribute from Seward! Not bad for the young son of a stone-cutter from Killarney!

Federal fort, Fort Point, built to guard the Golden Gate against invasion, circa 1860

XIV

TERRY: AFTER THE DUEL

I don't want no pardon for what I was or am.
I won't be reconstructed and I don't give a damn.
"The Rebel's Song," 1865

For Terry and his family the duel ended three years of comparative peace and serenity. We are told that Terry was "ostracized in business" after the duel. He was no longer a judge, and any future career as lawyer and politician seemed hopeless. His wife and sons sought refuge in a long visit to relatives in Texas. This was the time of the great Comstock discovery in Nevada, and Terry hoped he could find a new livelihood in mining the silver to be found in Washoe — almost next door. In the spring of 1860, as the nation drifted into secession and war, Terry, sick with loneliness and self-blame, joined a few friends who set out for the Nevada mining country. He staked some claims, practiced some law, and took an active hand in the feverish secessionist plotting. By early 1861, it was clear that the Territory of Nevada would be an arena for conflict between pro-Unionists and Southerners. Southern zealots believed that if the Confederacy could lay hands on the mineral wealth of Nevada, it could be used, along with cotton, to finance the impending struggle. Terry was suspected of planning a stroke to seize the territory for the South. It was rumored that Jefferson Davis had sent him a secret commission as governor of the Territory. But there was a strong federal garrison at Fort Churchill that discouraged any *coup de main*. The notion of a Pacific Republic allied with the South had haunted the imagination of California's secessionists for years. They thought the war would give them the opportunity they dreamed of, and Terry may have been a member of the Knights of the Golden Circle, the secret band of Southerners in California who conspired to establish the Pacific Republic. But for once, the Union leadership was equal to the emergency, and the Southern leaders were either jailed or fled to join Lee and Jackson in the East. Gwin, the natural leader of the West Coast Secesh, gave up the struggle as hopeless and left California to serve the Confederacy as its commissioner in France to labor for recognition.

In 1861 Terry rejoined his family in Stockton. For two years he rejoiced over the news of Manassas, Seven Days, Chancellorville and the glorious victories of the South. He was sure that before long there would be two

Albert Sidney Johnston, in his uniform as a Confederate general, 1862

republics on the North American continent, and there would be a place of honor for him in the new Confederacy. It was time to go and join the fight. It is strange that a man with Terry's convictions and propensity for violence should have waited so long. From the day that word of the attack on Fort Sumter reached the West, there was an eastward exodus of the Chivs. The federal military were alerted to intercept Southerners trying to break through into the Confederacy. They caught Gwin, but he escaped; they trapped a party of more than a hundred under Terry's friend, Daniel Showalter. A special watch was set up for Terry, but Terry did not come. News came of the death of his brother, Frank, at the head of his Rangers in Kentucky; then brother Clinton died in a Union ambush. By early 1863, the urge to join the Confederate Army became irresistible. The overland route was dangerous for Terry; it was too closely watched by Union patrols. Mexico was the only safe escape route.

Of course, the air was filled with talk of rebel plots and Terry's name was bruited about as a leader. Ironically, the only real conspiracy was foiled when Albert Sidney Johnston, still wavering between North and South, was placed in command of the Department of the Pacific in January 1861. Edmond Randolph of Virginia, a leader of the San Francisco bar, a fiery secessionist, and an intimate of Terry, tried to persuade Johnston to surrender the federal garrisons. The general spurned his blandishments; to the fastidious Johnston there were limits to treason. His refusal to surrender the Benicia arsenal to Randolph and the Southern sympathizers was expressed in a ringing pronouncement: "I will defend the property of the United States with every resource at my command and with the last drop of blood in my body," said Johnston. Then he turned the federal command over to General Edwin V. Sumner, Massachusetts-born and unwavering in devotion to the Union, and slipped through the federal cordon to die for the South at Shiloh. When the Randolphs and Terrys heard of Johnston's refusal to arm the rebels, they knew there was no hope for armed insurrection in California. In January 1863, Terry and ten Southern sympathizers left San Francisco by steamer for Mexico. Terry's escape was not unnoticed. The press said that his traveling expenses were paid by Confederate sympathizers, "sneaking rebels"; that he had a Confederate brigadier's uniform in his saddlebags; that he had been presented with a $2000 war-horse.

Terry's party worked their way from Mazatlan, in Mexico, to Texas and north. They rode saddle horses across the vast distance, arriving in the vicinity of Jackson, Mississippi, in June 1863, just as General Joseph E. Johnston was trying to raise the siege of Vicksburg. Vicksburg fell to Grant and Johnston fell back out of the fighting. There seemed no glory to be won in the western theater, so Terry continued on to Richmond to offer his services to the Confederacy.

In Richmond Terry met with James A. Seddon, the Confederate secretary of war, from whom he demanded a commission as a major general and the command of a department. Why he felt he was entitled to such rank and responsibility is not recorded, but Seddon bluntly told him that this was out of the question, that "such positions were reserved for those who had borne the heat of the conflict and earned such honors by distinguished services." The secretary, already plagued with lawyer-politicians who saw themselves as military commanders, granted Terry authority to raise a regiment in Texas. Terry visited President Davis, and started for the West, carrying with him a commission as colonel and authorization to raise a cavalry regiment in Texas.

In later years, Terry related that en route to Texas he fell in with the Confederate Army under General Braxton Bragg, on the eve of Chickamauga. As he told it, he learned that the Eighth Texas Cavalry, recruited by his brother Frank, who died leading it in battle at Green River, was on the front before Chattanooga, under the command of a Texas friend, a Colonel Harrison. Terry promptly offered his services to Harrison. Terry also alleged that in the bloody engagement that followed, "he received a flesh wound in the right arm, near the shoulder." If he fought at Chickamauga and was wounded, it was the only military action he saw in the war.

Terry's military career may have earned him no glory, but it included at least one experience typical of the tragedies that haunted him through life. In Texas, he formed his regiment of conscripts, and became its colonel. From the beginning of the war, the Confederate leaders had dreamed of conquering the Southwest by a force striking west from Texas. This was one of the favorite military schemes of Secretary Seddon. Back in Richmond, Seddon had hinted that Terry might even command the western invasion. But the project fell apart, and Terry stayed in Texas commanding an undermanned and feebly-armed garrison regiment around Houston.

Terry's polarity for attracting tragedy followed him into the Rebel army. The only casualty in his command occurred when his friend, Major General John A. Wharton, conferred on him the temporary rank of brigadier general over the head of Colonel George W. Bayler, a fellow colonel who outranked Terry in seniority and experience. Bayler was understandably miffed to be passed over; he expressed his indignation to Terry in an emotional explosion in which the disappointed officer told Terry what he thought of him and of General Wharton. Terry informed Wharton of Bayler's remarks: "The General visited the headquarters of Bayler to settle the dispute in a friendly way, and while the two were alone, General Wharton was shot dead." Bayler was arrested and tried, and having presented "a clear case of self-defense" before a civil tribunal, he was acquitted.

In late April 1865 came the news of Lee's surrender. Terry's command was in the ragged, starving western army under the command of Kirby Smith, not included in the terms of Appomattox. It was the last place of refuge for the diehards of the Confederacy. But it, too, vanished on June 2, 1865, when Kirby Smith came down from the Red River to Galveston to affix his signature to a surrender document. From Houston, Smith urged his officers and men to go home and resume the occupations of peace. But a return to peaceful pursuits in California was not for Terry. While the presidential Proclamation of Amnesty to the rebels gave pardon to all who had participated in the rebellion, Terry was told it excluded "officers above the rank of Army Colonel." Since Terry had been a temporary brigadier general, he may have had cause to expect a period of imprisonment. So, when he heard the terms of the amnesty, he set out for Mexico, emulating his chief, Kirby Smith, who read the Proclamation, and crossed the river into Mexico "to place the Rio Grande between myself and harm." Terry should have been more patient, but his fear of incarceration went back to Fort Gunnybags. The

Federal fortifications on Alcatraz Island, early in the Civil War. There was an obsession that a well-armed Confederate cruiser would attack the harbor.

Proclamation hinted that amnesty would be "liberally extended" to higher ranks, and, though the rebels did not trust Andrew Johnson and Stanton, by October, Confederate generals, governors and cabinet members were clearly amnestied.

Whatever his reasons, whether he feared imprisonment or found it repugnant "to live in a conquered country," Terry led a band of six hundred horsemen across the Rio Grande into Mexico. Again, he was in the grip of his fatal penchant for lost causes; he planned to commit himself to a new life and career in Mexico, where the French army of occupation had installed Maximilian as emperor. The country was in the throes of a sanguinary civil war between Frenchmen and Juarez's republican *guerillerros*. Terry's wife and family were left behind in Texas, where they had joined him in 1864, after enduring a terrible passage from California through Mexico, during which one of the children died. Now Cornelia and her three surviving sons stayed back in Texas, while Terry tried to find a new life for them in Mexico.

Terry's force entered an area of Mexico not yet under French control. He was following a loose plan for several Confederate refugee columns to rendezvous around Mexico City. Terry met at least once with General Joe Shelby, who had led his own column of rebels into Mexico. The large party Terry brought across the Rio Grande soon broke into scattered fragments when it encountered a determined republican general, Juan Cortina. General Phil Sheridan was encouraging Cortina from across the Rio Grande to resist rebel refugees as well as the French invaders, but Cortina allowed Terry's personal group of about twenty-five Confederate horsemen to proceed to the Monterrey area without interference. Here Terry encountered his old friendly enemy from California, William M. Gwin.

Gwin had occupied himself during 1864 and part of 1865 trying to win support from Napoleon III to establish a colony of Confederate refugees in one of the northern provinces of Mexico. Louis Napoleon liked the plan and recommended it to Maximilian, who was receptive. But with Sheridan's formidable veterans hovering on the Texas border, the project was deemed too provocative to the northern giant, and it was dropped. Terry came to Maximilian's attention through Gwin's influence. The emperor liked the Texan firebrand and proposed that Terry should accept a "high command in the French army." Whether the French commander in chief, the crusty Marshal Bazaine, knew or approved this offer we do not learn. But the imperial offer was declined, and Terry turned to less warlike pursuits.

It was a season of tired patriots. When Terry encountered Gwin in Monterrey in the summer of 1865, the ex-senator had given up hope and was on his way north to surrender to the Yankees. He told Terry he hoped for amnesty and exile in France. He expressed his despair over the chances of a permanent Confederate sanctuary in Mexico, castigated Maximilian's Empire as "imbecile" and "unstable," and left Terry to his own devices. "Your excellent judgment, my dear Colonel, will be your best guide as to your future movements."

One Confederate refugee did establish some short-lived rebel colonies in Mexico. Matthew Fontaine Maury had the ear of Maximilian, and the celebrated oceanographer, who had fought bravely in the Confederate Navy, enlisted his son and rebel General J. B. Magruder in the project. A considerable agricultural development was started near Cordoba in the state of Vera Cruz. It was called Carlotta Colony, after Maximilian's ill-fated empress. Terry conferred with Maury and made careful notes about his project, including a compact with former slaves that if they served the Colony they would be emancipated in seven years. Terry decided to form his own colony in Jalisco.

Maury left a single enduring monument: he introduced the cultivation of cinchona in the neo-Virginian colony. To this day, the area remains an important and valuable source of that vital pharmaceutical. But Maury's colony languished and died; his few remaining years were spent first in England where he lived on the charity of fellow scientists, until 1868, when he accepted the American government's amnesty and was professor of meteorology at Virginia Military Institute until his death in 1873.

Terry's "colony" was little more successful than Maury's. He tried sheep-raising with stock that Cornelia bought in California and transported to Mazatlan, but there was trouble with Mexican landowners who resented the intrusion of the Southerners, and the sheep were liquidated. Next, Terry turned his hopes to cotton-raising in Jalisco. When the French withdrew their support of Maximilian, his shadow empire collapsed, and Juarez, the republican, came back to power. Terry contrived to come to terms with the new regime. But Santiago, Jalisco, offered no opportunity for educating the children and in 1867 Cornelia, who had joined her husband in Jalisco, took her three sons back to California. Finally, Terry surrendered to Mexican hostility and followed them. On July 2, 1868, the steamship *Sierra Nevada* steamed into San Francisco. David S. Terry, home at last from the wars, was among the passengers. His return was greeted with a notable lack of hospitality by the local press.

There were allusions to his escape from the vigilantes, the Broderick duel, and his part in the later rebellion. "Rebel!" "Murderer!" "Traitor!" were among the epithets applied to him. When he tried to reestablish his law practice in Stockton, clients shunned him and no money came in. Once again he took to the road; he went back to the White Pine section of Washoe County, where he had tried his luck as a prospector at the outbreak of the war. He had heard stories of new rich strikes in the Treasure Hill diggings.

In early March 1869, Terry arrived in Hamilton, the center of the recent mining development. Here there was so much turmoil and litigation over mining claims and titles that it was easier and more profitable to be a lawyer than to toil in the mines. Terry won a few cases and invested the fees in lots. But money was scarce in Hamilton; it was even scarcer back in Stockton where Cornelia and her boys were living in actual want. In May 1870, Terry had earned a little money from some fees, and he resolved to return to California.

*"Blood Will Tell!" A broadsheet circulated when Terry ran as a presidential
elector. Note the portrayal of the duel.*

XV

TERRY: LAWYER AND POLITICIAN IN POSTWAR CALIFORNIA

Stanford and Huntington so long at outs,
Kissed and made up. If you have any doubts,
Dismiss them, for I saw them do it, man;
And then — why, then I clutched my purse and ran.

Ambrose Bierce, *Wasp*, 1882

The society of the California to which Terry returned in the spring of 1870 was different from the one he had left behind in 1863. The war was over, the old factions were gone, the issue of slavery which had exacted such a terrible toll in blood was laid to rest. Even the agonies of reconstruction that convulsed the rest of the country were far-off echoes in the Far West. Hostility toward Terry from the stabbing of Hopkins was slowly fading from memory. The duel with Broderick was dim in the minds of men. His service in the rebellion was easily forgiven; by this time Confederate brigadiers were back in Congress, and to Californians, the bloody shirt that Stanton and Thaddeus Stevens were waving back in Washington was a distant blur.

New issues, new struggles were emerging that would soon engross minds and passions. The growing dominance of the railroads, the influx of Orientals, municipal corruption — all came to the front during the decade after 1870, and Terry's role in these affairs was not much different from that of most lawyer-politicians of that time. By 1871, he was again at war, this time with Leland Stanford and the Central Pacific Railroad, the California "Octopus," fighting the legal battles of farmers, ranchers and settlers, whose cruel oppression by the railroad magnates was growing into a national scandal. He did well in the defense of criminal cases. He gained considerable praise (and a good fee) when he successfully defended the publisher of the San Francisco *Chronicle* in a criminal libel action.

The steady climb toward local respectability and financial security was marred by a personal tragedy in 1873. Terry's son David began to be rebellious and indifferent to his studies. In our time he would have been sent to a psychiatrist. Terry and his wife sent him to a ranch near Bakersfield, in the hope that "fresh air and vigorous exercise" would restore him to health. In December, Judge and Mrs. Terry went to the ranch to bring their son home for Christmas, only to learn that he was dead by a shot from his own revolver. The local newspapers called his death an accident, but there is little doubt he was a suicide. It was the third son the couple had lost. Cornelia

*When Terry returned from Mexico in the late 1860's, he made his office
in this block in Stockton.*

began to sink into an illness from which she would never recover.

By 1875, Terry had resumed an active place in Democratic politics. He
ran for no elective office, but he addressed many political gatherings and
earned the respect of the party's leaders for his eloquence and professional
attainments. By 1878, he was ready to assume a more important part in
resolving some of the troublesome legal, social and political problems that
the state was facing. His own troubles were receding into the past, and he
was being accepted — at least in Stockton and throughout the San Joaquin
Valley — as a respectable citizen. Recognition of the aging firebrand's new
standing came in 1878, when the Republicans and Democrats of San Joaquin
County joined in a bipartisan nomination to send Terry as a delegate to the
Constitutional Convention. At the time, a local paper characterized the
nominee

> *as a man of the highest sense of honor; a man of ability equal to any
> in the State; of the highest integrity; one whom no interest can pur-
> chase; and a lawyer of large experience in the affairs of the State.*

California held its Constitutional Convention in 1878 in the shadow
of a revolutionary threat akin to the Know-Nothing movement of 1856. The
economic agonies of the nation in the 1870's came late to California, but by
1878 the farmers and workingmen of the state were in distress. Unemployed
men with hungry families looked for a scapegoat and they found him in the
"Chinaman." By 1880, Orientals were almost ten percent of the state's population — there were between 75,000 and 100,000. The "workingman," who
saw the Chinese as a threat, found a voice and a leader in the Irish-born demagogue, Denis Kearney. Kearney formed a Workingman's party in San Francisco with the slogan "The Chinese Must Go!" Kearney inflamed the lowest
elements in the city against Orientals, chiefly because they were "cheap
labor" and as he put it: "The beef-eater has no chance against the rice-eater."

"The Chinese Must Go!"

Kearney's wild rantings appealed to laborers and miners throughout the state. But Kearney and his cohorts fixed on another target that endeared them to the have-nots: the railroads. Leland Stanford and his cohorts were justly despised by ranchers and farmers for the cruel monopolistic practices and the tactics — often violent and illegal — by which they accomplished their aims. To modern readers, Frank Norris's *The Octopus* may sound like romantic fiction, but it gives a true picture of the depredations of the railroad trust. The Kearney movement not only led to riots and insurrection and produced a brief but bloody civil convulsion in San Francisco, it brought its own new wave of vigilantism against the railroads. In the end, Terry supported the Kearneyites against the railroads, and thus drew on himself the fierce enmity of the California establishment.

The disorders of the Kearney movement had frightened the "regular" politicians of both major parties into choosing a bipartisan slate of nominees, including Terry, for the Constitutional Convention. The shadow of his past rose briefly to embarrass him when he appeared to take his seat. The Kearneyites had won the election for delegates from San Francisco, and when Terry appeared to be seated in the convention, one of the San Francisco delegates, C. J. Beerstecher, challenged him under the old Constitution which debarred from public office any participant in a duel. Terry was seated only after an acrimonious squabble. But one unsuccessful candidate, feeling affronted by Terry, sent him a challenge "in the old style." According to the Sacramento papers, Terry "refused to have anything to do with the matter, professing to have had sufficient experience of that character before."

It was generally thought that Terry was one of the ablest and most useful participants in the convention. His view of the big corporations, the monopolists, was closer to that of the Workingman's party than to that of the moderates who had elected him to the convention. He sponsored a

Denis Kearney

measure to prohibit state agencies from investing in private corporations; he joined in the movement to establish a railroad commission to protect the public from the corporate depredations of the Railroad "Big Four": Mark Hopkins, Collis P. Huntington, Leland Stanford and Charles Crocker. He shared the popular hatred and distrust of these moguls expressed by Ambrose Bierce and other liberals. As the convention progressed, Terry joined with the Kearneyites in a proposal to forbid California corporations "from employing in any way, any Chinese or Mongolians." He led furious attacks on the railroad monopolists. His hostility to the Chinese and the corporations alienated him from the more moderate delegates, but made him the darling of the Workingman's representatives.

> In opinions and temper Terry was a good deal like the Workingmen delegates, and having about ten times as much brains as the smartest among them, he soon became their actual though not their acknowledged leader. The man they had so recently execrated and called by all the vile names they could invent, really directed the movements of the Workingmen party during that long and eventful session.

That Terry's political attitude in the convention earned for him the admiration and support of the Kearneyites should have surprised nobody. Their ideas were not distant from those of the Know-Nothing American party which had elected Terry to the California Supreme Court in 1856. But the disclosure of his radical, populist, anti-establishment opinions drew on him the hatred of the "corporations." Back in Washington, Field expressed disgust when told of Terry's expressions. It was another step in their growing enmity, and before long their antipathy would have a significant effect on the Sharon-Hill litigation and on the aftermath of Terry's death at Lathrop.

Terry's work in the Constitutional Convention gained him statewide attention. Even those who remembered him as the foe of the vigilantes, the slayer of Broderick, as a rebel general, were forced to concede that he had exhibited high qualities of professional skill. He even essayed a new political career; he ran for attorney general in 1879 as a candidate of the New Constitution party, but he ran fourth, behind the candidates of the Republican, Democratic and Workingman's parties. And in 1880, when he was a candidate for presidential elector on the Democratic slate, he was roundly defeated. According to one account, Terry lost "by the refusal of a number of the old friends of Broderick to give him their votes." For the next few years, Terry was a quiet participant in Democratic politics. The comparative tranquility of his life was shattered in December 1884, when Cornelia died. By then, Terry's descent to total ruin had already begun. In March 1884, he was retained by a new client, Sarah Althea Hill, and he came face to face with an old enemy, Stephen J. Field.

Executive Mansion
Washington June 22d 1863.

Whereas the Act of Congress approved the 3d day of March A.D. 1863, entitled, "An Act to provide Circuit Courts for the District of California and Oregon, and for other purposes" authorized the appointment of one additional Associate Justice of the Supreme Court of the United States, and provided that the Districts of California and Oregon should constitute the tenth circuit, and that the other circuits should remain as then constituted by law; and Whereas, Stephen J. Field was appointed the said additional Associate Justice of the Supreme Court since the last adjournment of said Court and consequently he was not allotted to the said circuit according to the fifth section of the Act of Congress, entitled an Act to amend the judicial system of the United States, approved the 29th day of April 1802; Now I, Abraham Lincoln, President of the United States, under the authority of said section do allot the said Associate Justice, Stephen J. Field, to the said tenth circuit.

Abraham Lincoln

Attest.
Titian J. Coffey
Attorney General ad interim.

The warrant signed by Abraham Lincoln, appointing Field to the federal Circuit Court for California

XVI

FIELD BECOMES A JUDGE

The rising unto place is laborious; and by pains men come to greater pains; and it is sometimes base; and by indignities men come to dignities.

Francis Bacon, *Of Great Place*

Because he played so vital a part in the last tragic scenes in the saga of Terry, the career of Stephen J. Field is germane to our story. Field, who started out as Terry's friend on the California Supreme Court, became his archenemy, his nemesis. When Terry resigned as chief judge of the California Supreme Court in 1859 to fight his duel with Broderick, Field succeeded him as head of the court. Field was elected to the court in 1857 by a substantial majority, with Broderick's support, in the Know-Nothing contest of that year. He was the only Democratic winner. He made the usual noises about sacrificing a professional income of $42,000 to take a judgeship that paid only $6,000, but in the manner of lawyers through the ages, the honor outweighed the sacrifice, and he ascended the bench. His first two colleagues on the bench were Terry and Peter H. Burnett, a former governor.

Field's six years on the California Supreme Court were marred by accusations of corruption never substantiated, but revived from time to time by his enemies and critics. He was a member of the three-judge court that passed on *Biddle Boggs* v. *Merced Mining Company,* the case which established the all-important principle that mining rights belonged to the owners of the land and were not subject to a general license to miners to enter on the land and remove the minerals. Today, the decision seems reasonable and salutary, but in its time it provoked enormous controversy. Charges of bribery were made against all three judges.

Field's judicial services were outstanding in clearing up the vagueness and imperfections which surrounded titles to land among miners, settlers and farmers. Viewed historically and objectively, he was a leader in eliminating an area of dangerous confusion. But again, he was charged with corruption and bribery, with speculating in property affected by his decisions, and of letting interested litigants influence his decisions. Field and his fellow jurist Joseph Baldwin earned a significant place in the legal history of California when, in 1860, they upheld a San Francisco ordinance (the notable "Van Ness Ordinance") which confirmed titles to land to those who had possession on or before January 1, 1855, and ousted subsequent purchasers and squatters. At this distance it is clearly a proper and salutary piece of judging. But at the time, he was bitterly criticized. This was Field's comment on the recriminations over his decision in *Hart* v. *Burnett:*

> *Attacks full of venom were made upon Judge Baldwin and myself. No epithets were too vile to be applied to us; no imputations were too gross to be cast at us. The press poured out curses upon our heads. Anonymous circulars filled with falsehoods, which malignity alone could invent, were broadcast throughout the City, and letters threatening assassination in the streets or by-ways were sent us through the mail.*

In 1860, there appeared in San Francisco an anonymous pamphlet entitled *The Gold Key Court or the Corruptions of a Majority of It,* dripping with charges of venality and corruption against both Field and Baldwin. The screed accused Baldwin of buying up squatter interests to be confirmed in his decision. It alleged that Field was bought with "the sum of $10,000 in coin" paid to him by a Marysville friend and by stock interests in other property. Despite these attacks, Field earned the respect of California's lawyers and judges. The anonymous slanders plainly emanated from disappointed litigants. Most sensible people dismissed them.

During his few years on the California bench, there was one important change in Field's personal life. When Field visited San Francisco, he boarded with a charming widow, Mrs. Isabel Swearingen. One of her daughters, Sue Virginia, twenty years younger than the judge, captured his heart and they were married at Sacramento in 1859. It was an idyllic marriage. She remained his "beautiful Sue" to the end.

Of course, Field was unflinchingly loyal to the Union in 1860, but there is no reliable record that he took any important part in the counterplot to preserve California from the secessionist conspirators, led by Randolph, Gwin and Terry. During the first three years of the war, he stayed quietly at his judicial tasks in Sacramento. In December 1863, the United States Supreme Court was riddled by war, death and secession. Chief Justice Roger B. Taney was a jurist hated in the North for the *Dred Scott* decision, suspected of sympathy with the rebels, and despised by Lincoln and the administration for his opinion in Ex parte *Merryman.* When Lincoln took office in 1861, the three vacancies created by the rebellion had been filled by the administration by the appointments of Noah H. Swayne of Ohio, Samuel F. Miller of Iowa, and David Davis of Illinois. All three were selected less for judicial attainments than for their demonstrated loyalty to the Union. In the minds of Lincoln and his influential advisers, at that moment loyalty was more weighty than judicial skill or experience.

In the midst of the war, the Court under Taney had split five to four in the *Prize* cases. In effect, four judges of the nation's highest Court held that the war and the naval blockade of the South were "illegal." The administration was understandably alarmed. In March 1863, Congress responded to this threat by enacting changes in the organization of the federal court system, including a new circuit on the Pacific Coast, with the incumbent circuit judge assigned as a tenth justice of the United States Supreme Court.

Field's friend, Leland Stanford, was the wartime governor of California, a position that invested him with great responsibility and prestige. He led a movement to name Field to the new vacancy; he wrote a personal letter to Lincoln urging the nomination in the warmest terms. Lincoln was reminded by many of the high opinion of Field held by his friend, Colonel Baker, martyred at Ball's Bluff. Secretary of War Stanton, at the height of his political power, backed Field. The most persuasive voice was that of brother David Dudley, one of Lincoln's most influential advisers, who had been an active agent for Lincoln's nomination and election and was one of the administration's most powerful voices in New York. David Dudley sent John A. C. Gray, of New York, himself a close friend of Lincoln, to ask the president to appoint Field. Lincoln asked nothing about the candidate's fitness. "If David wants his brother to have it, he shall have it," said Lincoln. On March 10, 1863, Stephen J. Field was confirmed as a justice of the United States Supreme Court. Since the new circuit court was in session in San Francisco, he moved to that city from Sacramento. In September, he and his wife went to Washington, where he assumed his seat on the high Court. They remained in Washington for at least eight months in each of the next thirty-five years.

Before he left for the East, Field had an opportunity to demonstrate his devotion to the Union cause. Even as Lincoln and his cabinet were agonizing over the secessionist sympathies of Chief Justice Taney, exemplified in Ex parte *Merryman* and the *Prize* cases, Field gave encouragement to the administration by holding in the new circuit court that giving aid and comfort to the rebellion constituted the offense of levying war against the United States. This was in a case where a group of Confederate sympathizers fitted out a privateer to attack Union shipping. They were apprehended by naval forces and brought to trial in San Francisco before Field, acting under his brand-new commission as a federal circuit judge, and a jury. Field's vigorous pro-government charge was decisive. The defendants were found guilty of treason, to the delight of San Francisco's preponderantly Unionist press and public. Congratulations were heaped on Field, and when he reached Washington to take his seat on the high Court, he was received as something of a hero by Lincoln, Stanton and Gideon Welles, secretary of the Navy.

For the next twenty years, between sessions of the Supreme Court in Washington, Field would preside over the circuit court in California. In the decade after the war, many regarded the Supreme Court with little respect because it presented the spectacle of cringing before politicians, the press and the cries from the mob. In Mr. Dooley's celebrated phrase, the Supreme Court followed the election returns. Field was an exception. As far as the general public knew, he conducted himself with dignity and vigor on the bench. He refused to be intimidated by the radical Republicans and the public saw him as one of the few men in authority and power who toiled for moderation and reconciliation in the sectional struggles after Appomattox. But if he was a moderate in matters affecting reconstruction, he soon made it clear that on any question involving property, or the interests of business and industry, he could be counted on as a conservative stalwart. The dubious propriety of Field's relationships with the rich and the powerful, whose interests repeatedly were adjudicated in his court, was not known or understood until much later.

A leading scholar of the United States Supreme Court makes a forceful argument that Field was "one of the most powerfully creative justices ever to sit on the Court." But even his admirers must concede that Field's judicial mind, shrewd and resourceful as it was, belonged to big business, to the industrial robber barons who in the second half of the nineteenth century were transforming America from a predominantly agrarian society into the world's greatest industrial complex. In matters affecting California, Field was always on the side of the railroad trust, the vicious Octopus created by his close friends, Stanford, Crocker, Huntington and Mark Hopkins. His judicial accomplishments in the social and economic milieu in which he passed his life were narrowly confined to the interests of his friends. When the post–Civil War Congress and the legislatures of the victorious North spawned the Thirteenth and Fourteenth Amendments, in their minds they were freeing the slaves, investing them with basic civil rights, and protecting those rights from encroachment. In 1873 the Supreme Court was called on to characterize the purpose of the Fourteenth Amendment. In the *Slaughter House* cases Mr. Justice Miller, writing for the Court, had no doubt: "the one pervading purpose of the due process clause was to protect the newly-made freeman and citizen from the oppression of those who had formerly exercised unlimited dominion over him." Field did not agree.

His mind was stimulated by a vision of America emerging as the world's biggest and best business machine, a vigorous turbulent country devoted to money-making. This vista was opened to his eyes by the Stanfords and Huntingtons and other men of their type. They may have been robber barons to some; to Field they were empire builders, and their dynamism activated his own tremendous energy and intellect. Over the three decades that followed his elevation to the Supreme Court, Field was more than the voice of big business; he formed such personal relationships with the great business leaders that the liberal press would repeatedly question his judicial integrity. Under Field's guidance, the "due process clause," designed to protect the newly-emancipated slaves from oppression, became the prime bulwark of big business against regulation and control by state and federal government.

It is clear now that for more than three decades in the last third of the nineteenth century, Field was one of the principal architects of a judicial process by which the ingenuity of the American bench and bar was used to protect the interests of American industry from any intrusion of popular control. Swisher writes that the California judge

> *must be classified as one of the great men of the country — great as one of the master builders of the legal structure needed for the housing of a particular economic order through a dramatic era of our history.*

Field, and those of his colleagues on the bench who finally came around to agree with him, created this economic order, indispensable to the superbusinessmen of that time, the Morgans, the Rockefellers, the Fricks, the Carnegies, if they were to build their empires in oil and steel and banking. It was equally vital to the great railroad tycoons, men who were personally close to Field, too close for public comfort. Stanford and Huntington were outspoken in their gratitude to Field for his part in developing a doctrine that kept the government's hands off business and industry. The reactionary and repressive economic forces of the time realized their greatest triumphs as the Court,

THE CURSE OF CALIFORNIA.

"The Octopus," as seen by the Wasp. *The houses in the upper left corner belonged to Hopkins and Stanford, and can be seen in the photograph on page 166.*

Field blithely ignores his detractors in this Wasp *cartoon, "Dignity and Impotence."*

with Field as the fugleman, struck down the income tax, hamstrung attempts at governmental regulations and suppressed the aspirations of the working class.

Field's detractors claimed he was susceptible to big business because he wanted the support of the rich for his presidential aspirations. They contended that it was his personal ambition that led him to cultivate the wealthy and powerful. This may have been true, in part. But it was Field's character and training, his own patrician background that drew him inevitably into the society of the rich and powerful, and to their interests and ideas. He had been born into an establishment and he changed only as the establishment changed. The price Field paid for his twisting of the due process clause into an instrument of reactionary oppression was the contempt of liberal commentators in his own time and in this century. When Theodore Roosevelt began thwacking his big stick in the early twentieth century, its blows fell on the heads of men Field had seen not as miscreants, but as heroes. His opinion in *Butchers Union* v. *Crescent City* was called the fountainhead

> *of a line of decisions which, in the name of "liberty of contract"*
> *struck down statutes to redress the inequity between the power of*
> *working men, women and children and that of their employers.*

In a celebrated article that castigated Field and his brethren for their reactionary stand against legislative restrictions on the "right to follow lawful callings," i.e., to contain and rectify economic and social imbalance, Roscoe Pound sneered that "Mr. Justice Field was eminently the man to lead this belated individualist crusade." When the country, in the decades that followed the Civil War, became a cockpit in which the burgeoning capitalist economy contended with working men and "populists," the due process clauses of the Fifth and Fourteenth Amendments became capital's sharpest talons. Field was the not so subtle alchemist who devised this paradoxical legal alloy.

Field's close identification with "the interests," the California establishment, made Terry an object of execration to him. To Terry, Field was despised as a tool of "the interests." When the two men became adversaries, as they did in the Sharon-Hill litigation, a violent explosion was unavoidable.

This cartoon portrays Field dealing humanely with the Chinese, an attitude which he reversed when it proved unpopular.

XVII

FIELD FACES THE CHINESE
AND THE OCTOPUS

The railroads are not run for the benefit of the dear public.
That cry is all nonsense. They are built for men who invest their
money and expect to get a fair percentage on the same.

William H. Vanderbilt, 1882, as quoted in a letter
from A. W. Cole to the editor of the *New York Times*,
August 25, 1918

Before we deal with the tragic conflict that arose between Field and Terry, let us examine some of the other influences that made them fatal adversaries. In fame and the respect of his fellows, Field by the 1870's had left his old colleague Terry far behind. Field even aspired to be president of the United States. His presidential ambitions became known to his friends as early as 1868, when the California delegation described him as "a wall of fire against the encroachment of radical domination" and "the guardian of the Constitution of his country against all the power of the Radical party." He was so self-righteous, so sure of the virtue in his every act that he felt no hesitation in offering his name for the presidency, although he was a sitting judge. When many urged Chief Justice Morrison Waite to seek a presidential nomination in 1875, he declined with a statement of principle: "The office of Chief Justice came to me covered with honor and when I accepted it my chief duty was not to make it a stepping-stone to something else, but to preserve its purity." He pointed out that if a judge became a candidate for elective office there would be public suspicion that his judicial decisions were made with an eye to public favor and political self-interest. This was a principle honored by Charles Evans Hughes in 1916, when he resigned from the Supreme Court to seek the Republican nomination. Even William O. Douglas, whose aspiration to the presidency was chronic, recognized that "political ambitions are incompatible with performance of our judicial functions." Field had no such modest compunctions. In the end, he received only fifteen votes at the 1868 convention, and Governor Seymour of New York won the doubtful right to contest the election with Grant. But Field kept trying. He was again a candidate for the Democratic nomination in 1880. One of his loudest supporters at the convention was John Norton Pomeroy, an eminent lawyer in California, who covered Field with fulsome praise for his "broad liberal and national interpretation of the Constitution," and for his "high view concerning the supremacy of the United States government," as exhibited by his dissent in the *Slaughter House* cases.

Field's campaign run off the rails. Field is portrayed as the clown beneath the locomotive, circa 1884.

Field's dissent in that case foretold his forging of the instrument that became so helpful to his friends in industry and finance. In the gospel according to Field, the operation of the Fourteenth Amendment was not confined to the emancipated Negro; it afforded the equal protection of the laws to all classes of persons — including the Stanfords, Crockers, Huntingtons and Vanderbilts. Field, the judicial architect, was an egalitarian in reverse; he saw the Fourteenth Amendment as Anatole France perceived the law, in his celebrated jibe, as allowing the rich as well as the poor to sleep under bridges and to beg in the streets for bread. Pomeroy and some of Field's other admirers spent the year 1879 in preparing for their champion's candidacy in the forthcoming election. They produced a campaign biography: *Some Account of the Work of Stephen J. Field as a Legislator, State Judge and Judge of the Supreme Court of the United States.* This transparently self-serving campaign document was a compilation of Field's accomplishments printed privately at the expense of his affluent brothers. Again Field fell short at the convention and had to console himself with the comparative obscurity of the high Court.

Included in the volume was Pomeroy's quoted encomium on Field. There was no reference to Pomeroy's employment by the railroad trust in the cases he argued before Field. In a biographical sketch of his father, J. N. Pomeroy, Jr. later wrote that there was a "warm and devoted friendship" between the two men, an intellectual sympathy at almost every point. By today's fastidious code of professional ethics such an intimacy would suggest that Field should not sit in Pomeroy's cases. But Pomeroy argued before Field in *San Mateo* v. *Southern Pacific,* and won. Next year he argued before the same bench in *Santa Clara* v. *Southern Pacific,* and won that, too!

In 1884, Field was still trying for the White House but the Democratic State Convention gave the *quietus* to his hopes. On June 10, it declared its preference for Tilden, Thurman or Hendricks, in that order, and then took the unprecedented step of adopting a resolution that the convention "unanimously repudiates the presidential aspirations of Stephen J. Field" and "requires that California's delegates pledge to use their 'earnest endeavors' against him." Field may have been the only presidential candidate in history to have suffered the indignity of being his state's least favorite son.

He probably attained this remarkable distinction by his early protection of the Chinese and by the almost universal belief that he had sold himself to Stanford, Huntington and the other corporate predators who were detested at every level of California society except the San Francisco financial oligarchy. While Terry was getting friendly attention in California by opposing Chinese immigration and attacking the corporations, Field was drawn into both subjects in a far more serious way that would affect his judicial career, and probably served to eliminate him from consideration as a candidate for the presidency. Californians could not ignore the "coolie" problem. When the Chinese swarmed to California in the early years after the discovery at Sutter's Mill, they were welcomed as a source of cheap much-needed labor — until they began to compete with white labor. Prejudice, discrimination, hatred and violence were inevitable. They suffered general personal mistreatment, and legislation aimed at restricting their rights and liberties poured out of state, county and municipal legislative bodies.

In the beginning, Field had been a leader in the judicial struggle to protect the Chinese from vicious oppression. He expressed shock and humiliation at anti-Chinese measures which, in his own words, were "shameful . . . unworthy of a brave and manly people," and "brought disgrace upon the state." Field's humane pronouncements in the area of discrimination against the Chinese came as early as his days on the state's supreme court. In an address to a grand jury in San Francisco in 1870, he denounced the maltreatment of Orientals as "base and cowardly . . . unchristian and inhuman." In 1874, a state statute aimed at excluding Chinese women from California was declared unconstitutional by the circuit court, led by Field. Of course, by 1880, Field's personal and judicial protection of the downtrodden Chinese made him the special target of Denis Kearney and his Workingman's party.

When the Kearneyites, abetted by Terry, fought to enshrine discrimination against Chinese in the California Constitution in 1878, Field used all his influence to prevent this injustice. In 1879, he spoke for the circuit court in striking down the notorious "Queue Ordinance," the infamous San Francisco enactment that prescribed that male prisoners in the San Francisco jail have their hair cut to a maximum length of one inch. Among Chinese of that time, the loss of the queue was a disgrace in the eyes of friends and countrymen.

By these pronouncements Field became a hero to the Chinese of San Francisco, and an object of abomination to many Californians. He and Judge Lorenzo Sawyer, who concurred with him in the "Queue Ordinance" decision, were derided in the local press as "sickly sentimentalists."

Looked at through the blue spectacles of a New England Sunday School teacher, it [i.e., the decision] may go down, but to those who stand in this verge of the continent, confronting the incoming hosts of barbarians who threaten our civilization and our government, it is altogether ridiculous.

In his early days on the California Supreme Court, and in the state legislature, Field had indeed shown some "liberal" signs, some awareness that there was a need to regulate business and property to conform with social needs. As a legislator, he had been an active sponsor of a liberal debtor's law; as a state judge, he had written a vigorous opinion defending the right of the workingman to enjoy at least one day of rest in the workweek.

But by 1880, Field recognized that his stand against Chinese discrimination was alienating most white Californians and endangering his chances for their needed support in the presidential campaigns of 1880 and 1884. He began to shift with the political winds. It is one of the shabbiest chapters in his history that, spurred by a wish to recapture the affection of his fellow Californians, he first wavered and then retreated on the subject of Chinese immigration. The change in front came too late to regain for him the affection and trust of most fellow Californians. It is not easy to forgive Field's transparently selfish motives for abandoning principle and embracing a cynical self-interest. Swisher explains his insensibility to social needs thus:

Field was a statesman — his enemies would have said a politician — as well as a judge. . . . In his use of legal principles he chose one type on one occasion and another on another occasion. . . . Back of it all was the man who used principles and rules of evidence for the achievement of ends which he thought most worthwhile.

His biographer might have added two more words: "to him."

Many believe that the novelist Frank Norris bestowed the epithet "The Octopus" on the predatory California railroad trust, but it was already known by that name long before his celebrated novel appeared in 1900. Bancroft, the California historian, had earlier referred to the Central Pacific as "our pet octopus, the four-armed cuttlefish." To the people of the state, the vast network of lines reaching into every aspect of life and enforcing the will and interests of the railroad men with brutality and corruption, was an all-powerful, ever-present corporate beast, whose tentacles reached into the legislature, the courts and local politics. To California's farmers and stockmen in the nineteenth century, Leland Stanford became the incarnation of the oppressor. His name lives on in honor as the founder of a great American university, established as a memorial to his dead son; into this great institution he poured the millions that most Californians felt he took out of their pockets, as Rockefeller, Frick and Carnegie turned their "ill-gotten" gains into vast and useful educational enterprises. To the farmers and merchants of his time, Stanford was a vicious bloodsucker. But to Field, he was a friend, a patron and a benefactor. Stanford had first become friendly with Field in 1862 when Stanford was governor of California and Field was chief justice of the California Supreme Court. As we have seen, in that early time he used all his influence with Lincoln to get Field appointed to the United States Supreme Court. Out of Field's gratitude and Stanford's admiration grew a warm friendship — rewarding to both men. During Field's yearly visits to California, he spent much time with Stanford, socializing and philosophizing. A true intellectual harmony developed between the two men.

Joining of the rails, Promontory Point, Utah, May 10, 1869

But Field's well-known relationship with Stanford was even more destructive to his popularity in California than his early protection of the Chinese. The Central Pacific Railroad, in which Stanford and his associates were the principal stockholders, began to dominate the economic life of the state after the Civil War. It received generous donations of land, rights and financial subsidies from the national government; it had the exclusive right to build the line eastward to meet the Union Pacific being constructed at a forced pace westward from Missouri. When the two roads were joined at Promontory Point, Utah, in 1869, the transcontinental rail line, over which Broderick and Gwin had contended in the 1850's, became a reality. Control of the western portion of the line gave Stanford and his associates — Huntington, Crocker and Hopkins — a tight monopoly of transportation facilities in California.

The ruthless exploitation of this monopoly drew on its proprietors the hatred of many Californians. The railroad exacted exorbitant subsidies from local communities for building branch lines; in an era when freight and passenger rates were not regulated, they squeezed money out of small businessmen with the ingenious avarice of medieval barons. Officials who opposed them were beaten down by shady political deals, by corruption, even by physical attacks by hired bullies. A pervasive stench of dark villainy and chicanery hung in the air over their actions. This aura moved the California Constitutional Convention of 1878–79 to adopt measures to protect the

Leland Stanford, as governor of California   *Huntington in the 1880's*

Crocker in the 1880's   *Mark Hopkins in the 1880's*

public from the predators. The railroad men felt sincerely that their brains and labors had built California, and they owned it. Their attitude toward "reform" was well expressed in the rhymed jibe of Eugene Field:

Out on reformers such as these
By freedom's sacred powers
We'll run the country as we please
We saved it, and it's ours.

Of course reform and regulation would come in the end, but by the time its effects were felt, Stanford and his pirate crew were so deeply entrenched, they had acquired such vast wealth, that neither belated reform nor rigid regulation could shake their tremendous power.

The intimacy between Mr. Justice Field and Leland Stanford was no secret. The liberal press printed frequent reminders that the railroad man had used his personal influence with Lincoln to place Field on the Supreme Court. The relationship between the two men that bloomed over the next twenty years was so obvious that it received regular attention in the press. Field's name was usually in the list of guests at Stanford's Medicean palace in San Francisco; Field was a trustee of the university Stanford founded; Field advised Stanford "informally" on legal and business matters. When Stanford died and the government sued his estate for $15,237,000 — on the theory that Stanford, as a stockholder of the Central Pacific, was personally liable on bonds for railroad construction — Field "gave assistance to Mrs. Stanford in protecting her interests." This was a dubious role for a justice of the Supreme Court, especially since the government's appeal from the circuit court's dismissal of the case came before Field's court. Neither good taste nor sense led Field to refrain from participating in the affirming decision on March 2, 1896. The government did not get its money, and in November 1896, Jane Stanford, the tycoon's widow and executrix, wrote Field assuring him of her "prayers for years of usefulness here in this life." There were countless other evidences of the personal and social ties between Field and the Stanford family and the other banking and railroad satraps of California. To the liberal press, even more galling was Field's commitment as a judge to the pecuniary interests of the rich and powerful.

In 1878, public revulsion against the rapacity of the California railroad builders led to a statute that imposed on the railroads the onerous obligation to establish sinking funds to pay off their bonds when due. Led by Huntington, the railroad men fought the measure with ferocity. They denounced the legislation as an expression of "communistic tendencies." One of them, David D. Colton, anticipating a court struggle over the bill confided to Huntington, "I have had several long talks with Judge Field and the hope of the country is in the Supreme Court if the nation is to be saved from disgrace."

Albert Gallatin, one of the railroad men, sued in the federal court in San Francisco to have the new act declared unconstitutional. Field stayed out of the case. His alter ego, Judge Sawyer, ruled *pro forma* and the case moved to the Supreme Court. It is known now that Field's abstention in the circuit court was not an expression of judicial taste or of any consciousness of prejudice. It followed a deliberate plan which, had it been known at the time, could have precipitated a national scandal. In 1885, Colton's widow sued the railroad tycoons over her husband's share of some joint property. Letters

Mark Hopkins's mansion on Nob Hill in San Francisco. Leland Stanford's mansion can be seen just behind, and slightly down the hill. These sites are now occupied by the Mark Hopkins Hotel and the Stanford Court Hotel.

turned up in the court proceedings from which it is plain that it was prearranged for Field to stay out of the *Gallatin* case in San Francisco and to leave the decision to his impressionable colleague, Sawyer. Colton wrote Huntington that Field would

> reserve himself for his best effort (I have no doubt) on the final termination of the case at Washington before a full bench. I think it is wise, as then Judge Sawyer will hear the case here, and if Judge Field should take our view of the case on final argument before the Supreme Court, it would have more weight with that court than if he had rendered a decision before in our favor in California.

Huntington agreed:

> I think you are right about Field not sitting in the Gallatin *case.*

Of course, Mr. Justice Field did take "our" view of the case. The majority held the act constitutional, but Field carried two of his colleagues in a bitter dissent in which the judge seems to have had his eye fixed on the railroad crowd back home in California and on his own chances to win their support for his presidential hopes. Swisher wryly suggests that

> The observer should not take Field's legal arguments [*in* Gallatin] *too seriously. The heart of his attitude was in his fear of creating "insecurity in the title to corporate property in the country" or we must suspect, in making insecure the titles of Stanford, Huntington, Crocker, Hopkins and the others to the winnings of the Central Pacific.*

Rarely do we find such cynical comments on the purity of motive of a justice of the United States Supreme Court by a scholar respected for objectivity.

The railroads were deeply aggrieved when the new California Constitution permitted taxes to be levied on them. They attacked these taxes unsuccessfully in the state courts. Their lawyers, men who often shared Stanford's banquet table with Field, turned to their most dependable judicial friend: Stephen J. Field. In *San Mateo v. Southern Pacific R.R.,* their friend in court first contrived a high-handed and daring technique for the circuit court in San Francisco to assume jurisdiction. For eight full court days, the railroad lawyers argued their cause, chief among them John N. Pomeroy, Field's disciple. As usual, Field and Sawyer agreed with the railroads; the tax assessments were invalidated, the money remained in the grip of the Octopus, and the public scored up another bitter point against Field. Public reaction was expressed in the San Francisco *Chronicle* of September 28, 1882, which bemoaned the fact that "the Circuit in which California is unfortunately included is presided over by Justice Field . . . [who] whenever he has a case before him in which the community and the corporations are arrayed against each other, his lights always lead him to discover points against the people."

San Mateo went to the Supreme Court. Under the system that then prevailed, justices of the Supreme Court who had ruled on cases in the circuit court would frequently sit in the Supreme Court on appeals from their own decisions in the lower court. It was neither novel nor startling that Field sat on the *San Mateo* case in the Supreme Court; but it was decisive. It *was* novel and startling that when Leland Stanford gave a dinner party at a Washington restaurant for the railroad lawyers who had argued *San Mateo,* on the day after the argument, Mr. Justice Field was among the guests. In the end the Supreme Court, with Field working from within, protected the railroads. Scholars report that a study of Field's record on cases involving the California railroads discloses no single instance in which his vote was antagonistic to the interests of the Octopus.

In 1887, Stanford was called as a witness before a congressional commission investigating loans from the government to the railroads. At one point, the witness denied any recollection of certain questionable payments to legislators for favors to the railroads. The commission applied to the federal court in San Francisco to compel responses. For the court the faithful Field upheld Stanford's position. Field treasured his status as a charter member of the California establishment. In the few decades since 1848, there had arisen on the West Coast a patriciate founded mostly on sudden riches, but membership was not confined to the wealthy. Admission was granted to their professional servitors, the lawyers and bankers and publishers who protected their interests from a hostile and ungrateful public. It was useful to number among those the presiding jurist of the highest federal court on the Pacific Coast. Field was gratefully embraced by the railroad moguls and the Bonanza Kings. The day would soon come when membership in the oligarchy would be vital to Field's personal interests. He would invoke his rights as a member of the club, and in the Sharon litigation the club would serve him well.

Senator William Sharon, circa 1880

XVIII

THE BONANZA SENATOR

*Surely every man walketh
in a vain show;
Surely they are disquieted
in vain:
He heapeth up riches, and
knoweth not who shall
gather them.*

Psalms XXXIX, 6

William Sharon was born in Ohio in 1820 of Quaker parents. He studied law in Steubenville, Ohio, as a pupil under Edwin M. Stanton, Lincoln's secretary of war. He came overland to California in the Gold Rush in 1849. From the beginning, he had the Midas touch, the special ability to make money out of everybody else's mistakes. To the newspapers he became known as the "Bonanza Senator," the "California Croesus." Sharon's first wealth came when he was appointed agent for the Bank of California at Virginia City, the chief depository for gold found in the area. The envious said that a lot of the dust stuck to Bill Sharon's fingers. By 1870 he owned the Reno-Virginia City Railroad which was reputed to bring him more than $3,000,000 per year. His railroad entitled Sharon to membership in "The Club," the tight little group of California transportation magnates who controlled most of the state's business. Through Huntington, Crocker, et al., he became friendly with Stephen J. Field. He became a partner in the mining business with Darius O. Mills and William C. Ralston, two of California's legendary moguls. In 1852, Sharon married a charming and modest Canadian lady, who spent the rest of her life trying to keep up with her dynamic spouse, and doing her best to ignore his flagrant infidelities. In 1874, she gave up trying and quietly died.

While Sharon was busy making his millions and climbing to the pinnacle of San Francisco's financial and social world, he contrived to find time for a series of transient amours. His penchant for harlots would poison his old age, and even after his death would make his name a local byword for the prurient. Still, for many years, until Sarah Althea Hill entered his life, no public scandal seemed to touch him. By 1875, Sharon was at the zenith of his power and wealth. He controlled the Union Mill & Mining Co.; he owned at least seven producing silver mines; he had snatched the famous Lucky Ophir mine from the fabulous "Lucky" Baldwin. San Francisco watched in awe as he acquired one of the state's great fortunes and a succession of glittering and ephemeral female companions. In 1875, at fifty-four, Sharon was known as the "Bonanza King," "King of the Comstock." He had annexed the

William C. Ralston, shortly before his death

*Belmont—the baronial estate built by Ralston and taken over
by Sharon after Ralston's death*

Territorial Enterprise, Nevada's most influential newspaper. With this power-ful organ and by sharing a small part of his wealth with the legislature of Nevada, he became United States senator from Nevada in 1875.

Sharon's partner, Darius Mills, took his fortune to New York where he became the progenitor of one of the city's richest and most powerful fami-lies. His mansion across from St. Patrick's Cathedral ranked with those of the Astors and Vanderbilts; his monuments still endure in the New York's Metro-politan Club (which he commissioned) and the noble Villard mansion, now a landmark on Madison Avenue. Sharon's other partner, William C. Ralston, built his monuments in San Francisco. The Grand Hotel on Market, New Montgomery and Second streets was the city's showplace. In 1870, Ralston presented his townsmen with the California Theater. He was a sought-after patron of the arts. His *chefs d' oeuvres* were architectural: his suburban pal-ace, Belmont, and the Palace Hotel. Belmont, about twenty miles out of town in Cañada de Diablo, was one of the most magnificent private resi-dences in America. "Its grandeur," said an admiring press, "would have satis-fied a Medici." But the Palace Hotel on Montgomery Street was to be the realization of Ralston's most extravagant dream. Ralston did not live to see it completed. His empire collapsed in 1875 undermined, it was said, by secret enemies who had pretended to be his closest friends. Ralston's admirers claimed that the "Bonanza Crowd," including former partners Sharon and Mills, had plotted his ruin. Ralston himself charged that the market manipula-tions of the two men abetted by eastern bankers had wrecked his bank.

HOME OF W. C. R

3. Major William A. Hammond 12. Mrs. Herron and M
4. General Alexander D. Mc Cook 1. President Hay
6. Secretary Ramsey 7. Mrs. Irvin McDowell
9. Charles W. Howard 10. Senator Francis G.

Ralston entertaining Rutherford B. Hayes at Belmont in 1874

ON AT BELMONT

...nt 2. General T. Sherman and Daughter
...d Wife 5. Senator Leland Stanford
...ator Sharon 13. Mr. Jamison 8. Mayor Alvord
...nds. 14 CON. JACKSON 15 THOMAS BROWN

Black Point—the scene of Ralston's death

On August 26, 1875, Ralston rode out to his favorite swimming place at Black Point, donned a bathing suit, and swam out into the Bay. He never came back. Enemies said it was suicide; his friends blamed a sudden cramp, a swimming accident. Whatever caused his death, Bill Sharon profited from Ralston's disgrace and death more than anybody else. He took over the wobbly Bank of California and restored it to vitality; he took over the unfinished Palace Hotel which he completed to regal splendor; he even succeeded Ralston as the seigneur of Belmont! With Ralston's death, Sharon was the acknowledged *numero uno* in San Francisco's glittering society, the instant aristocracy of Nob Hill, feverishly engaged in America's Gilded Age in aping the extravagant excesses of eastern society. The 1870's were a *Belle Epoque* in San Francisco. Newly-found wealth was being lavished on newly-discovered luxuries, and Bill Sharon made some of the headiest contributions to the air of opulence.

A glimpse of Sharon's imperial life-style comes from the publicity that attended the wedding of his daughter, Clara. A single headline in the San Francisco *Chronicle* of November 20, 1874, tells the story:

TWO ENTIRE PAGES DEVOTED TO THE SHARON WEDDING: A BRILLIANT MATRIMONIAL DAZZLE. SPLENDID CELEBRATION OF THE NEWLANDS-SHARON NUPTIALS. A DESCRIPTION OF THE SHARON MANSION. HOW A CITY MILLIONAIRE SURROUNDS HIMSELF WITH LUXURY. THE MOST ELEGANTLY APPOINTED RESIDENCE ON THE COAST. BIOGRAPHY OF THE NEVADA MINING KING. CLIMBING THE THORNY WAY TO FAME AND FORTUNE. LOVE IN A PALACE. ELEGANT TOILETS OF THE QUEENS OF SOCIETY.

In the most dazzling hymeneal celebration in the city's history, Princess Clara was united to Prince Francis Griffith Newlands. Mark him well; we meet

The Palace Hotel. The Grand Hotel was across the street, connected by a second-story bridge spanning Montgomery Street.

Frank Newlands again in these pages. In 1874 he was twenty-eight years old, educated at Yale and regarded by San Francisco's *bon ton* as a young lawyer of great promise; he had the confidence of the Stanfords, Crockers and Huntingtons, and would prove himself a useful tool of the Central Pacific crowd.

Ralston's final monument, his envoi to the city, was the Palace Hotel, erected across from the Grand on Montgomery Street and connected to it by a little bridge, proudly emulating its Venetian prototype. The Palace became the center of the city's social life; until it was destroyed in 1906 in the fire that followed the great earthquake, it was one of the largest and most luxurious hotels in the world. Its amenities were legendary. When the Bank of California closed its doors in the summer of 1875, Sharon took personal control of the almost-finished Palace, and he spared no expense in its decoration and amenities. The inaugural function at the Palace was a dinner in honor of General Philip H. Sheridan on October 14, 1875, with Sharon as master of the revels. His welcoming speech was "a model of self-effacement"; he said nothing of his part in the enterprise, shed tears over Ralston's death and mourned the absence of "the proud and manly spirit of him who devised this magnificent structure." Several important San Franciscans maintained luxurious suites at the Palace — among them, Mr. Justice Stephen J. Field, who made the hotel his home during the four months of each year he spent in the city. Since all records were destroyed in 1906, it is impossible to determine what rent he paid, if any.

Ulysses S. Grant, America's greatest hero, paid a triumphal visit to San Francisco in 1879. As a matter of course, Sharon accommodated Grant's party at the Palace. One of the most spectacular events of the visit was a reception at Sharon's pleasure dome, Belmont. Guests were conveyed in private railroad cars in special trains provided at the station at Third and Townsend streets; they detrained at Belmont's private station, where Sharon and his daughter, Flora, received the president and his party.

Flora brought joy and pride to the heart of the Bonanza Senator when she married a genuine British nobleman, Sir Thomas George Fermor-Hesketh, in a resplendent affair at Belmont. The press compared her conquest of Sir Thomas with California's most celebrated romance: Admiral Count Rezanov's love for the beautiful Concepción Argüello, daughter of the *commandante* of the presidio at the beginning of the century. The dashing British baronet sailed his yacht into the Bay and captured Miss Flora. He was luckier than Nicolai Petrovich de Rezanov, the czar's ill-fated Pacific admiral. In 1806, Rezanov wooed and won, but he sailed away and never came back. Concepción spent the rest of her life watching the empty sea. Sir Thomas landed his American Princess.

The first intimation to the public of a connection between Sharon and Sarah Althea Hill came when that lady provoked an ugly little scene at Flora's marriage ceremonies. Sarah Althea, as Sharon's mistress of the month, tried to force her way into the reception. She was physically barred from the wedding ceremony by young Fred Sharon, home from Harvard for his sister's wedding. Sarah Althea insisted that she had a right to attend as a member of the family — as indeed she was in a way!

Flora went to England, where she became one of the great hostesses of the Edwardian era. Son Fred inherited little of his father's talent for making

FRANK LESLIE'S ILLUSTRATED NEWSPAPER

No. 1,041—Vol. XLI]   NEW YORK, SEPTEMBER 11, 1875.   [Price 10 Cents.

THE SAN FRANCISCO BANK FAILURE.

THE failure of the Bank of California has fallen upon the public like a thunder-clap; and the excitement has naturally enough been increased by the almost simultaneous announcement of the self-destruction of its President. Financially, in the first instance at least, it must be regarded in the light of a calamity; for, in addition to the direct and immediate losses, it is feared that it may lead to disastrous results, not only on the Pacific Coast, but all over the Union. Morally it re-reads and enforces a lesson which our people seem slow to learn. Most undoubtedly this fresh failure is the result of unwise and extravagant speculation. So far as we know the facts, it has been brought about, not by any outside or incalculable influence or misfortune, but by deliberate and systematic misdoing. Omnipotence is not granted to mortals, even if they should happen to be bank managers; neither is omniscience. It would seem as if the managers of the Bank of California believed themselves possessed of the one attribute, and as if they were resolved to possess themselves of the other. Not contented with a wealth which princes might have envied, they sought to make half a continent their own, to own its Senators and Congressmen, to control its Governors and Judges, and to make its vast mineral and agricultural resources contribute to their avaricious love of gold and their boundless ambition. Made mad, they have finally reached

SAN FRANCISCO.
SUSPENSION OF THE BANK OF CALIFORNIA, AUGUST 30TH—SCENE ON CALIFORNIA STREET IMMEDIATELY AFTER THE ANNOUNCEMENT OF THE FAILURE. FROM A PHOTOGRAPH BY BRADLEY & RULOFSON.—SEE PAGE 7.

The scene before Ralston's bank when it closed its doors in 1875

money. In San Francisco society he became a favorite as "a good amateur singer and very popular." Clara's husband, Frank Newlands, had brains and energy enough for the whole family.

During the years that followed his wife's death in 1874, Sharon regaled every important visitor to San Francisco with lavish parties at Belmont and the Palace. His entertainments were reported with gusto in the local press. He maintained a *pied-à-terre* at the Palace where, attended by a discreet little Chinese seneschal, Ki, he gave quiet poker parties and other virile entertainments. When his daughter Clara, Frank Newlands's young bride, died in 1883 the whole city mourned with the bereaved rich man, and there were many pious observations about the empty futility of great wealth. "The Lord giveth, The Lord Taketh Away," intoned the local clergy and press, *ad nauseam.*

Then, without warning, in September 1883, the grieving Sharon was dealt a second blow that would embitter what was left of his life. Out of the blue, William N. Nielson, an Australian-born unemployed self-styled journalist and an habitué of the city's Barbary Coast, filed a criminal complaint against Sharon, charging the crime of adultery. He alleged that while Sharon was the lawfully-wedded husband of one woman, he had violated his marital vows with another. A warrant issued, and the senator was actually arrested! It was to be the first shot in *Sharon* v. *Sharon,* a litigative war that would occupy the city's courts, newspapers and gossips for the next seven years.

Nielson held a press conference at which he explained vaguely that he had taken this action in a spirit of "good citizenship." But he did clear up the mystery of the wronged woman's identity: she was a "lone, fatherless and motherless woman" who had aroused his pity and concern. Her name: Sarah Althea Hill Sharon! Nielson neglected to mention that on the day before he appeared in the police court and filed his affidavit charging Sharon with adultery, he had made an audacious attempt to blackmail the senator. He had invaded Sharon's private apartment at the Palace and demanded money for Sarah Althea. Sharon had him thrown into the street.

Citizens of San Francisco familiar with many facets of Sharon's life were shocked and confused. What aroused a wild local surmise was that Sharon was known to be a widower. Who was the abused wife? How could a widower be guilty of adultery? The explanation, according to the plumed knight Nielson, was simple: Nielson claimed to have in his possession a written contract of marriage dated August 26, 1880, between Sharon and Sarah Althea, which recorded a secret marriage. The complaint alleged that while married to Sarah Althea, Sharon had committed adultery with Miss Gertrude Dietz. There was no mystery in the city about Gertie Dietz; she was known to be one of the senator's successive doxies who had gracelessly become pregnant. There was a child, and the senator had paid the damages with as much pride as anger. So what? Nielson charged that Sharon had married Miss Hill!

The episode gave off a smell of blackmail, of the kind of shakedown that is an occupational hazard to men of Sharon's wealth. The purported marriage contract was not exposed to the public gaze. But the press and public asked for the first time: "Who is Sarah Althea Hill?" The answer would occupy the city's gossipmongers, journalists and judges for the next decade.

The Grand Courtyard of the Palace Hotel

San Francisco Bay from Oakland, 1870

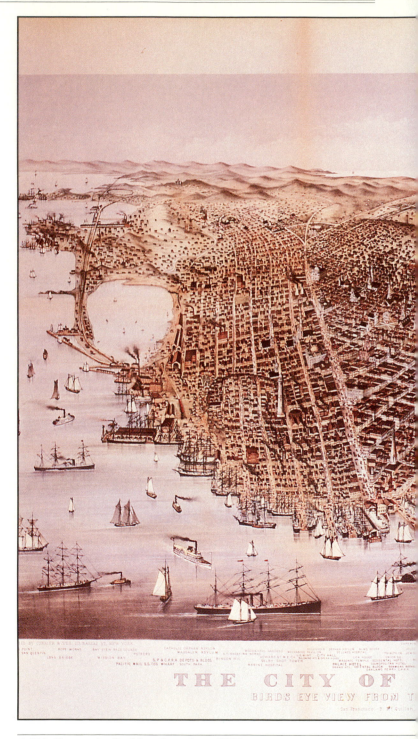

A "bird's-eye view" of San Francisco, 1878

Sarah Althea Hill

XIX

NEW GIRL IN TOWN

Here's not a modest maiden elf
But dreads the final Trumpet,
Lest half of her shall rise herself,
And half some sturdy strumpet.
Thomas Hardy, "The Levelled Churchyard"

In 1883 Sarah Althea Hill was a well-upholstered strawberry blonde in her middle thirties, who caught the eyes of men as she flounced through the hotel lobbies of San Francisco. She had come to the city from Missouri in 1870. From the first, the young lady put on grand airs; she gave out that she was an orphan of good family, reared by affluent grandparents on a plantation near Cape Girardeau, Missouri. Little was known of her background until the home-folks back in Cape Girardeau heard of her ill-treatment at the hands of that old satyr, Senator Sharon. Then, some of them rallied to her support. The San Francisco *Bulletin* of October 4, 1883, printed a letter from a Missouri judge, an old friend of the lady's family: "An orphan . . . daughter of a lawyer . . . descended from Revolutionary stock . . . niece of a governor . . . cousin of a Senator!" Sharon's millions, he wrote:

> *would hardly compensate a handsome and accomplished young woman for his age and reputation, and certainly no one can have a higher family connection than she has. I had always expected she would make a wiser and better alliance.*

The Missouri judge's letter did raise a question about her age; if she was indeed twenty-seven at the time of her "marriage" to Sharon in 1880, as the press reported, she was only sixteen when she left Missouri. Her first engagement had been announced four years earlier which would make her quite precocious, even for that time and climate.

But then, Sarah Althea had a demonstrated talent for making favorable impressions on elderly gentlemen. The good people back in Cape Girardeau could hardly know about her sojourn at the "boardinghouse" maintained by Mammy Pleasant, the city's best-known Negro procuress, or about her meretricious liaison with local lawyer Reuben Lloyd, or that she had been the paid concubine of old Senator Sharon, making nocturnal transits across the little bridge between the two hotels. Even the few details of her former life in Missouri that Wagstaff reluctantly records make her out a somewhat less than decorous Southern belle. She had "a spirited temper"; she was "a schemer above all things"; though "she was a spendthrift, she worshipped money, and gave her attention to those who possessed it." She was "a flirt"; she was "engaged to marry three young men at the same time." She was "fast." Jilted in Missouri by one Will Shaw, "in September 1870, disgusted and broken-hearted, with only the shadow of her fortune, she started for California."

It is recorded that Allie and her brother arrived in San Francisco in 1870 to take up residence with a well-to-do uncle, William Sloan, and his mother, Allie's maternal grandmother. But Sloan's attentions to the fair Allie were less avuncular than they should have been, and precipitated a family *brouhaha*. He had brought her into his mother's home, but according to Wagstaff, "Sarah and the old lady did not live in harmony, and Sloan gave the girl a fine suite of rooms in a hotel." There, Wagstaff suggests, she encountered Senator Sharon. Not quite. A number of years would pass before she met Sharon, and she would encounter quite a few local gentlemen before she climbed into the old man's bed.

Most of all, she would encounter Mary Ellen Pleasant, "Mammy" Pleasant to her and to much of San Francisco, and her life would never be the same thereafter. She met Mammy Pleasant after her relationship with Uncle William cooled and she had to vacate the "fine suite of rooms" he had provided her. She needed shelter, and she found it in the boardinghouse-bordello maintained by Mammy Pleasant, the flamboyant queen of San Francisco's Negro community. It was there that she formed a tempestuous liaison with one of the customers, Reuben Lloyd, a leading lawyer of the city. Lloyd was rich, successful, handsome, blond-haired and hag-ridden, the only child of a pious Irish widow, who kept him tied to her apron strings. He would steal away from mamma for assignations with Sarah Althea in hotels or in Mammy's discreet bagnio on Octavia Street. Sarah Althea's passion flamed into love; she began to talk of engagement and marriage, which led to a dreadful scene in the lawyer's office.

The stormy intrigue ended on May 10, 1880, when Sarah Althea, her repeated demands for marriage rejected, swallowed the contents of a vial of poison she had drawn from her reticule. The barrister rushed out for the aid of a physician, who applied a stomach pump to the forlorn maid, prostrate on the law office floor. She recovered temporarily from her broken heart as well as her gastric injuries. The incident did not attract much public attention at the time. Later, it would be dredged up as bearing on the lady's reputation for virtue and emotional stability.

There is no doubt that, however grandiose were her airs, Sarah Althea was a denizen of Mammy Pleasant's Octavia Street house in January 1877; she remained "in residence" until May of that year. Teresa Percy also lived in the house and "a close friendship, which seemed to please Mrs. Pleasant, sprang up between the two beautiful women." It would be strange indeed if, as one of the resident ornaments, she did not participate in the entertainment of the gentlemen visitors. Mammy Pleasant planned for Sarah Althea to marry Reuben Lloyd and enjoy the same sort of profitable career she had designed for Teresa Percy: marriage to a local millionaire. For Teresa the plan worked out: she became the wedded wife of Thomas Bell, a respected local financier. For the ill-fated Allie, the black lady's plan miscarried. There is little doubt that when the Lloyd project failed, it was there in the black woman's brothel on Octavia Street that a conspiracy was contrived to lay hands on the Sharon

Sarah Althea Hill, at the time of her "marriage" to Sharon

fortune by perjury, trickery and forgery. Mary Ellen Pleasant was not only the architect of this scheme of spoliation, she was its financial backer and chief tactician. As the part played by Mammy Pleasant in the Sharon-Hill contest began to emerge, the local press began to ask a question that could have been answered by many of the city's leading businessmen and politicians: "Who is Mammy Pleasant?"

"Mammy" Pleasant—the only known photograph, taken at age 87

XX

MAMMY PLEASANT

The miners came in forty-nine,
The whores in fifty-one;
And when they got together
They produced the native son.
Contemporary California Song, circa 1860

The little we know of "Mammy" Pleasant's origins comes in part from her own febrile diary, a document so obviously replete with fantasies and fictions that it is difficult to winnow the truth. Her elemental character stands out clearly: she was a female as fatal as could be designed. The combination of the crafty, unscrupulous Negress with the dotty beauty who came under her tutelage had to produce melodrama. It spawned *Sharon* v. *Sharon*. When Mammy laid eyes on Sarah Althea, she recognized a weapon she had dreamed of for years.

There is not much reliable evidence about Mammy's origins. She enjoyed telling her listeners a romantic yarn that she was the daughter of a white planter and a light-skinned creole from Santo Domingo. She described her mother as a "voodoo queen" — "surely, the spirit of the Great Serpent could speak through her." Her fanciful pedigree includes a convent education and a heroine's role in the operation of the Underground Railroad that rescued fugitive Southern slaves. This heroic activity, she said, had brought her into intimate relations with the great abolitionists of New England — William Lloyd Garrison and Wendell Phillips. In her "memoir" she even concocts a marriage to a New England magnate. She portrays herself as using her husband's wealth to provide the chief financial backing of John Brown's rebellion. This was all pure invention.

The truth is that she was born a slave, that she was a cook on a plantation near New Orleans and ran away to California in November 1852. It is certain that she arrived in San Francisco in April 1853, a passenger on the S.S. *Oregon*. On the voyage from Panama, she bedded in with a well-heeled young Scotsman, Thomas Bell, coming to California to seek his fortune. Bell became a prominent financier in the Bonanza days. To Mary Ellen, he became lover, patron and employer; to him, she became concubine, procuress, supplier of voluptuary delights and finally, "housekeeper" in a bizarre *ménage à trois* on Nob Hill. When she first arrived in San Francisco, Mary Ellen was a tall, well-formed beauty who apparently "passed" as white. In the woman-starved San Francisco of the 1850's her complexion was not important; she had little difficulty in finding gentlemen to whom she sold her services, culinary and sexual. She was passed from kitchen to kitchen and from bed to bed. In the transit, she acquired a considerable reputation in more than one *métier*. Her services as a cook were so prized that she sold them at auction for five hundred dollars a month "with the stipulation that she should do no washing, not even dish-washing." Her versatile talents made her the uncrowned queen of the city's blacks, and in the 1860's and 1870's she became the town's most successful flesh merchant and a successful real estate operator.

When Mammy Pleasant died in 1904, aged eighty-nine, the obituaries in the San Francisco press remembered her as "a schemer," as "a philanthropist," but chiefly as one "who numbered among her staunch friends many men and women who stood and stand high in the world's esteem." Another obituary noted that "it was always asserted that she never betrayed a secret of even her worst enemy, either for gain or in revenge."

Her memoir includes the story that in September 1856, when she was "housekeeper" for Mr. Selim Woodworth, a leading citizen, she organized an elaborate party, complete with qualified females, attended by both Broderick and Terry. If true, it would disclose proclivities in both men concealed from their other biographers and hardly consistent with their established characters. Her dubious memoir also includes the fable that in 1859 she traveled east to Cape Girardeau, Missouri, where she worked for a time as a cook. She contended that

> *the only leavening happiness which she had at all during the months she remained at Cape Girardeau came from the visit to her kitchen of a neighbor's child. This girl, named Sarah Althea Hill, was an orphan, and she, with her younger brother, Morgan Hill, lived with their grandfather, Mr. Sloan, on the adjoining plantation.*

According to Mary Ellen, the two became "fast friends" and it was Sarah Althea who conferred on her the name "Mammy" Pleasant by which she later became famous in San Francisco, at least to the male population. The encounter in Cape Girardeau with Allie is almost certainly a piece of claptrap devised years later to explain her seemingly incongruous relationship with Sarah Athea.

By 1869, Mary Ellen owned a prosperous house of assignation, where she entertained many local potentates, including (if she is to be believed) the Bonanza Kings, William Ralston, Darius Mills and William Sharon. She also continued her relationship with Thomas Bell, the young Scotsman first encountered on the ship. She would relate to her girls and their guests that it was her fiscal acumen imparted to Bell that was transforming him into one of the town's financial moguls. There is authenticity in the tale that she plotted to have Bell take one of her girls, Teresa Percy, to live with him. In the end, Bell married Teresa, and when she lost her real estate fortune, Mary Ellen became their "housekeeper." The conspiracy to have Sarah Althea become the wife of Senator Sharon may have had its seeds in the Teresa Percy-Thomas Bell-Mary Ellen triangle. It was Mammy's practice to encourage her girls by relating that she could find them rich husbands. What better target than the widowed multi-millionaire senator? What better bait than the alluring Allie?

Thomas Bell's mansion on Octavia Street. "Mammy" lived here with Bell and his wife, Teresa Percy.

By September 1869, business was so flourishing for Mary Ellen that she built a second pleasure palace in the city's outskirts, at Geneva and San Jose roads. Here she gave alfresco stag parties that became the talk of the town. Financiers, politicians and mining kings drove out to Geneva Cottage in parties limited to ten, at five hundred dollars the head. The fee entitled each gentleman to a carefully-selected dinner companion.

> *Seated at the dinner table, lighted only by [a] magnificent French candelabrum, upheld by the figures of the unabashed nudes, were the dinner companions provided by Mrs. Pleasant. Ten beautiful girls in low-necked dresses of satin and gauze, trimmed with velvet ribbons and garlands of tiny pale roses, sat with their puffed crinoline skirts gracefully outspread on the rosewood chairs.*

The girls were mostly Caucasian, although there is mention of some pulchritudinous "creoles." Parties at Geneva Cottage were held down to two a week. The clientele was limited to twenty tycoons, each of whom was privileged to attend one hebdomadal orgy at the established rate.

One of the saturnalias got out of Mammy's control, and caused a mild local scandal when the details leaked out. It was a voodoo party for which the high priestess gathered "ten beautiful quadroon girls" who danced the Haitian "calinda" with the chosen ten patrons to the beating of the jungle drums. At a signal given by Mary Ellen, the nymphs ran off into the darkness leaving a trail of abandoned finery, pursued by the satyrs who shed their

*The 900 block of Washington Street, San Francisco, in the 1880's, the block
on which "Mammy" maintained her "boarding house"*

broadcloth and linen integuments during the chase.

Mary Ellen's operations made her rich and made most of her girls ephemerally happy. Some of them did indeed find well-to-do husbands and rewarded Mammy for her successful brokerage; some of them moved to other cities where they emulated the *cordon bleu* cuisine and other refinements they had learned from the voodoo queen. The success of San Francisco's better class of prostitutes in finding husbands among the early citizens was celebrated in local song and story. Some of the city's plushest matrons had served apprenticeships on the Barbary Coast.

Here and there, one of Mammy's girls would become "difficult" and disappear from sight. Inevitable gynecological and obstetric complications were handled in an affiliated establishment at 711 Sutter Street owned by Mammy Pleasant and presided over by Dr. S. M. Mouser. Since Mary Ellen's girls did not furnish a full-time professional practice for this devoted healer, Mary Ellen and the doctor developed a side business in disposing of unwanted babies for non-professional ladies. This activity spawned its own by-product: blackmail. Amateur patrons received carefully-worded messages requesting "a liberal donation" for the "charities" maintained by Mammy Pleasant. Nobody asked for an accounting of the sums disbursed.

When Mary Ellen opened a new "boardinghouse" at 920 Washington Street on September 6, 1871, the occasion was celebrated with elaborate bacchic revels. The "hosts" were Newton Booth, the newly-elected governor of the state, and Drury Malone, his secretary of state. Dozens of notables attended, including William Ralston, the brightest comet flashing across the western skies and his "partner" in the Bank of California, William Sharon, the Bonanza King. As he cavorted with Mammy's young ladies, Sharon could not have known that in the dark lady's mind a plan was fermenting that would embitter his last days.

At about this stage of her life, when she felt rich and powerful, there creep into Mammy Pleasant's memoir some errant words and phrases that suggest something *outré* in her relationships with her young ladies, particularly with Teresa Percy and Sarah Althea Hill. There are repeated allusions to their "blonde hair and china-blue eyes." One girl has "the grace and delicacy of a Dresden figurine." Another has "a heart-shaped dimpled face." The references suggest a sapphic quality to her relationships that may explain her tigerish devotion to Sarah Althea in terms other than pure avarice.

When the Ralston-controlled Bank of California collapsed on August 26, 1875, Mary Ellen was one of the victims of the debacle. She is reported to have lost a great part of her hard-won savings. Many San Franciscans felt that Sharon's machinations contributed to Ralston's ruin and the ensuing losses. Sharon did profit enormously; he acquired control of the bank and almost everything else the financier had amassed. In Mary Ellen's mind Sharon was a villain, and this too may have contributed to the design forming in her mind. She threw out veiled threats of revenge. In Sarah Althea, she found at close hand an instrument of reprisal and profit.

Sarah Althea's appearance at Octavia Street in January 1877 is recorded in Mammy's diary. It notes that she was "a sensationally beautiful girl with red-gold hair" and that she remained for many weeks before she left to take up residence in a nearby hotel. It is significant that Allie had been in San Francisco almost seven years before she became a denizen at Octavia Street. Three more years would pass before she would move into the Grand Hotel as Sharon's lady-in-waiting. There are intimations that Sarah Althea's departure from Octavia Street in May 1877 was hastened by competition with another nymph, India Howard, a newcomer brought from the East by Mammy Pleasant to be the chief ornament of her establishment. She was almost ten years younger than Sarah Althea, "tall, slender and blonde." India Howard herself later described her first weeks in Octavia Street with Mary Ellen as "very profitable." Mammy's most faithful protégée, Teresa Percy, recorded in her diary that Mary Ellen "blackmailed a lot of men with a mulatto girl named India Howard." Teresa was in a position to know. She, too, was blonde and blue-eyed; she had been one of Mary Ellen's ladies since 1869, moving back and forth from the urban branch of the business to the suburban annex. As I have related, she wound up her career married to Mary Ellen's patron and protector, the bibulous Scot, Thomas Bell.

"General" William H. L. Barnes, at about the time of the Sharon-Hill litigation

XXI

ROSE OF SHARON

There was a young lady of Kent,
Who said that she knew what it meant
When men asked her to dine,
Gave her cocktails and wine,
She knew what it meant — but she went!

Langford Reed, *The Limerick Book*

Nielson's charge against Sharon transformed Sarah Althea overnight into a municipal — and eventually — a national celebrity: the press called her "the Rose of Sharon." Some attributed the sobriquet to Ambrose Bierce, the caustic editor of the city's *Wasp*. Headline writers would use and abuse the epithet for years to come.

Before the adultery charge came to trial, Sarah Althea gave press interviews in which she said that she had met Sharon "by chance" in Redwood City in the spring of 1880. They had discussed mining stocks, and he invited her to call at his San Francisco office. After the two had discovered their common interest in securities, Sharon visited the young lady at her modest room in the somewhat shabby Baldwin Hotel. "He made himself agreeable for an old gentleman, recited some poetry and sang 'Auld Lang Syne,'" Sarah Althea wistfully recalled. Then Sharon regaled the young woman with a dissertation on his tastes in females, and wondered if she could learn to like an old man like him. She could try. It would come out later that in the learning effort she moved to a rent-free room in Sharon's Grand Hotel, across the street from his *pied-à-terre* in the Palace. The two hotels were connected by a convenient covered bridge. Nor did Sarah disclose, in these pre-trial interviews, that the learning process had lasted at least a year, or that tuition was at the rate of about a thousand dollars per month, payable to the pupil.

On October 3, 1883, before the adultery charges could come to trial, Sharon's attorney, "General" William H. L. Barnes, responded to the charges by filing a suit in the United States Circuit Court in San Francisco seeking a declaratory judgment that Sharon had never been married to the woman and adjudging that any marital contract was a forgery. He asked the court to enjoin Sarah Althea from holding out that she was the wife of the senator and from asserting the validity of the alleged marriage contract. Federal jurisdiction was based on diversity of citizenship, since Sharon claimed to be a citizen of Nevada. Little would be heard of this case, *Sharon* v. *Hill,* for a considerable time; not until December 26, 1885, would the federal court render a decision. But before that, the whole scandalous affair would be aired in a different forum, in still another action brought by Sarah Althea in the state superior court.

From the beginning, the San Francisco press was fascinated with the personalities of opposing counsel. Sarah Althea's lawyer, George Washington Tyler, was a Vermont Yankee who came to San Francisco in 1849 in his teens. He found no gold and returned to the East for a legal education. He came back to San Francisco in 1860, where he gained some notice as a staunch defender of the Union. He had a pronounced limp, which he facetiously described as a "war wound." He told the press that his political enthusiasm so deeply offended the Southern zealots that one of them shot him in the leg. Tyler limped (proudly) through the rest of his life because of the wound. The press called him "Judge" Tyler because he had served briefly as a magistrate in the lower courts of the city. His practice was mostly in the defense of squalid criminal cases and the brahmins of the local bar did not esteem him. The newspapermen found him an endless source of delight and good copy. "He can be mild and pleasant as his mother's milk," one reporter observed, but "when the storm breaks," his victims on the witness stand endure "all the horrors of hell-fire and damnation." "A bulldog!" "A sledgehammer!" "A Yeoman armed with a broad axe!" Before the case was over, he would also be revealed as a shyster! In the early stages of the litigation he was supported by his son and two shield bearers: "Colonel" George Flournoy and Walter H. Levy, who would use the case to wangle a minor judgeship for himself, a role in which he would one day commit his former client to a lunatic asylum.

Sharon's lawyer, William H. L. Barnes, came from the most exalted stratum of New York society. In his press interviews he preened himself on his academic accomplishments, his graduation from Yale, his legal apprenticeship with the Grand Panjandrum of the American bar, Joseph H. Choate, one of Field's close associates. From the moment he arrived in San Francisco with credentials endorsed by the great Choate, Barnes was accepted in the highest social and professional circles. He was not among the most experienced trial lawyers of the city, and there were some expressions of surprise when Sharon selected him for this all-important contest. In the end, the choice was not a happy one. But it was made by the grandest nabob of the American legal establishment and endorsed by Field himself. There was an explanation: when Sarah Althea first threatened to sue, Sharon went East to consult with Field, who suggested that the old senator discuss the matter with Choate, who recommended his former student, Barnes. It is not recorded that Field felt that his part in the process of selecting Sharon's counsel affected his right to judge the case. To the press, Barnes was "perfect in scores of arts and graces that combine to make a gentleman's life enviable." The trial would expose this social paragon as a clumsy blunderer in the courtroom, a blowhard and an unprincipled adventurer, deficient in elementary principles of legal ethics and professional loyalty.

"General" Barnes (his claim to military rank was never established, but he was "General" to everybody) had only one aide, O. P. Evans. There was a brief flurry of excitement on the second day of the trial when Tyler unexpectedly announced that the formidable — and notorious — advocate, David S. Terry, had joined the plaintiff's forces as associate counsel.

George Washington Tyler during the Sharon v. Sharon *trial*

None of the principals appeared at the adultery hearing, to the disappointment of curious spectators and the press. Tyler was appointed special prosecutor by the police court judge, and he craftily moved to dismiss the charge on technical grounds. He had concocted a new plan, and the feeble "adultery" charge did not fit in with it. The charges were promptly dismissed, but Tyler's design did not become clear to all until November 1, 1883, when he filed a plenary action on Sarah Althea's behalf — *Sharon* v. *Sharon* — in San Francisco's superior court for divorce on grounds of adultery.

Tyler understood that the criminal adultery charge could not prevail without clear and convincing proof from Gertie Dietz; but she had taken off to the East with her infant son and a purse full of consolation provided by Sharon. Tyler saw an easier road: a suit for divorce in which he would prove the marriage contract through the testimony of Sarah Althea, and Sharon's adulterous conduct with "at least nine women." Barnes promptly demanded an inspection of the alleged marriage contract, and Superior Court Judge Finn directed Sarah Althea to produce it in court on November 9. On the appointed day, while routine legal business was in progress before Judge Finn in superior court, a procession of local celebrities came into the courtroom: Sharon, Sarah Althea, Barnes and Tyler, each with a retinue of well-wishers and spear-carriers. The press, suitably forewarned of great events, was present in force. The prosaic case on trial was suspended as counsel in *Sharon* v. *Sharon* took their places at the bar, with an air that according to *The Daily Chronicle*'s observer said plainly, "everybody must give way for us — this is a millionaire's case!" Sarah Althea threw back the veil which obscured her features, and a reporter noted that "the mental anguish which she must have endured during the past three years, if her solemnly declared statements are true, had left its blighting marks upon her features."

Tyler opened the hostilities on a bizarre note. He announced that he had tried to have the paper brought to his office, but "my client will not consent." Sarah Althea stepped front and center, and "visibly affected," drew an envelope from her *poitrine* and waved it toward the bench. In a hysterical voice and excited manner she declaimed: "The paper is in this envelope!" Barnes demanded to examine it. The judge directed her to hand it to him. Sarah Althea clutched the envelope to her bosom with both hands, as if shielding the Holy Grail from profane hands. With a gesture worthy of a Duse or a Bernhardt, she held the paper out toward the bench and appealed to the judge:

Sarah Althea: *Judge, this paper is my honor. I cannot leave it out of my hands.*

The Court: *Just show it to Mr. Barnes.*

Sarah Althea: *If Your Honor will take all the responsibility upon yourself, and compel me to, I will deliver the document.*

The Court: *I cannot take any responsibility. Is the paper inside this envelope?*

Sarah Althea: *I desire that neither Mr. Sharon nor Mr. Barnes should handle it. I consider it my honor, and have regarded it as my honor for three long years. . . . Mr. Sharon knows all about it.*

Barnes: *I object to this lady standing here and making these statements. Mr. Sharon knows nothing about it. It is a fraud and forgery from end to end.*

Sarah Althea: *He knows every word in this paper, so help me God. He dictated it to me, and knows all about it.*

Mr. Sharon: *I tell the court it is the damnedest lie that was ever uttered on earth.*

Sarah Althea: *I do not like to offend Your Honor, but he has got his millions against me. I have been driven from my home. He has taken my money, and I have got no money to defend this with.*

There was more play-acting and more bickering between Barnes and Tyler. There was a private strategy session among Sarah Althea, her counsel and her dusky Clausewitz, Mammy Pleasant. Finally, Judge Finn ran out of patience:

The Court: *I will tell you . . . if you refuse to deliver that paper to the clerk for the inspection of the opposite side, the paper cuts no figure in this case. It is so much waste paper.*

Sarah Althea: *As Your Honor orders it, I, in your presence, deliver it to the court and hold you, Judge, responsible for my document.*

The Court: *You can save yourself the trouble of making any speech like that. You understand that there is no responsibility in the matter. Now, Mr. Clerk, you will have a photographic copy of that taken today.*

With this, there was handed to the court the document that would engross the state and federal courts of California for the next decade, that would evoke rivers of printing ink and satisfy gossip-hungry citizens for years. In the end, the paper would lead to bloodshed and death, to tragedy and destruction, to insanity and doom. On November 9, 1883, it drew only the stares of the curious and the leers of the prurient. It was a single sheet of paper with writing on two sides, all in a single feminine hand (admittedly Sarah Althea's) except a purported signature at the bottom of the second page. This is the text:

> *In the City and County of San Francisco, State of California, on the 25th day of August, A.D. 1880, I Sarah Althea Hill, of the City and County of San Francisco, State of California, age 27 years, do here in the presence of Almighty God, take Senator William Sharon, of the State of Nevada, to be my lawful and wedded husband, and do here acknowledge and declare myself to be the wife of Senator William Sharon of the State of Nevada.*
>
> *Sarah Althea Hill*
> *August 25th, 1880, San Francisco, Cal.*
>
> *I agree not to make known the contents of this paper or its existence for two years unless Mr. Sharon himself sees fit to make it known.*
>
> *S. A. Hill*
>
> *In the City and County of San Francisco — State of California, on the 25th day of August, A.D. 1880, I Senator William Sharon, of the State of Nevada, age 60 years, do here, in the presence of Almighty God, take Sarah Althea Hill, of the City of San Francisco, Cal., to be my lawful and wedded wife, and do here acknowledge myself to be the husband of Sarah Althea Hill.*
>
> *Wm. Sharon, Nevada*
> *Aug. 25, 1880.*

When the paper was exhibited, Sharon turned to the ranks of journalists and spectators and "in a voice dripping with outrage" proclaimed it a forgery. This triggered the judge's wrath, and the senator was ordered to leave the courtroom. Court was recessed while arrangements were made to photograph the document.

Journalists friendly to Sharon's cause opined the following morning that it was plain that the scheming woman had succeeded in getting an autograph from Sharon (why else "Wm. Sharon — Nevada"?) and had composed the contract to fit the signature. Sarah Althea's champions were relieved to learn that at least there really was a paper, and that the signature it bore seemed genuine.

Sarah Althea's "honor" was locked up in the court's safe overnight. The paper seemed to breed melodrama. Next morning, at the time appointed for its return to Sarah Althea, Judge Finn mounted the bench and sheepishly announced that "there is something wrong with the combination" of the safe, but a locksmith was on the way. Sarah Althea looked on in anguish, announcing to press and public that it was all a trick to steal her "honor." But the safe was opened and her "honor" was restored to its normal resting-place, adjacent to her heart.

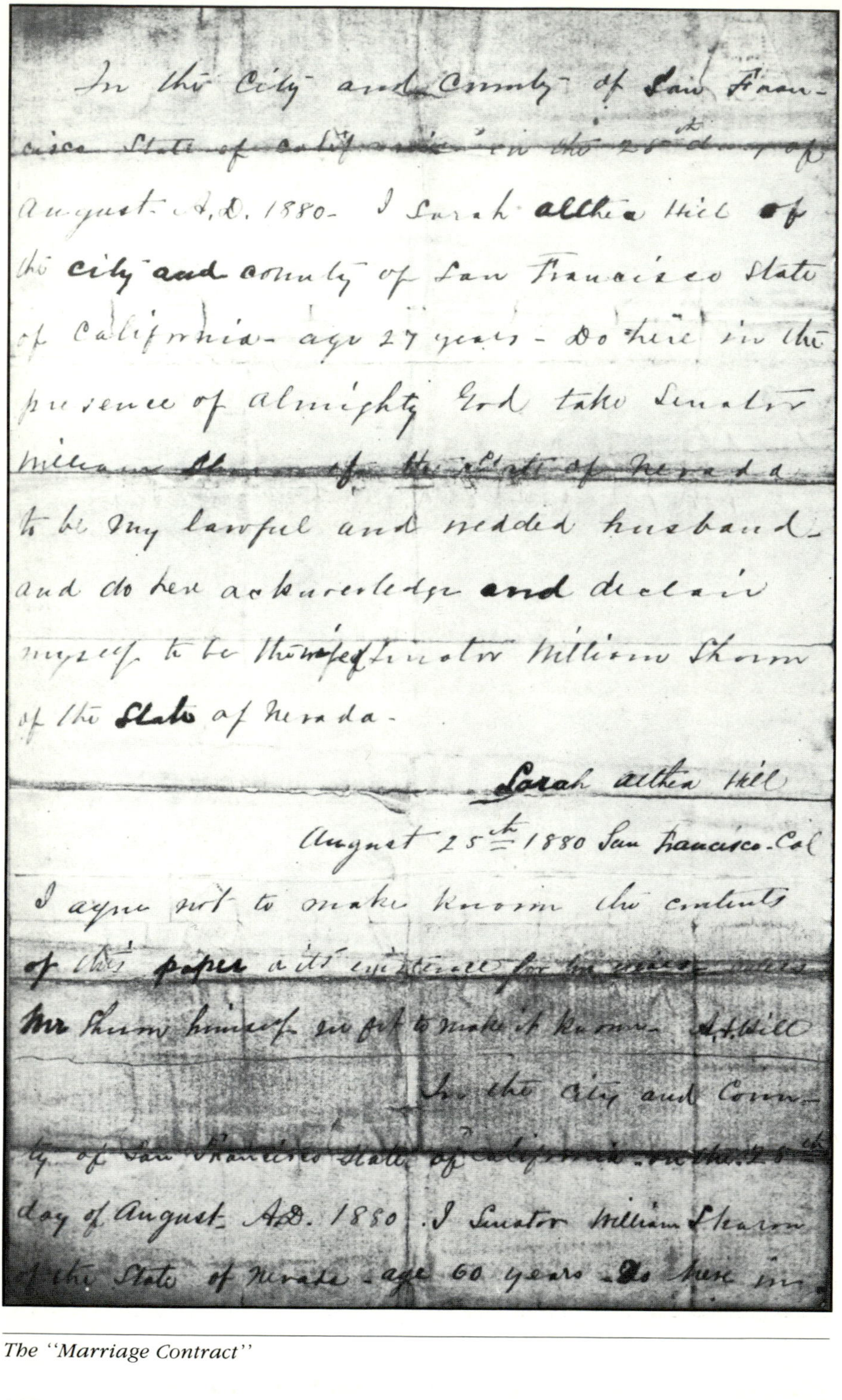

In the City and County of San Francisco State of California on this 25th day of August A.D. 1880— I Sarah Althea Hill of the city and county of San Francisco State of California— age 27 years— Do here in the presence of Almighty God take Senator William Sharon of the State of Nevada to be my lawful and wedded husband— and do here acknowledge and declair myself to be the wife Senator William Sharon of the State of Nevada—

Sarah Althea Hill

August 25th 1880 San Francisco. Cal

I agree not to make known the contents of this paper a it's existance for two years unless Mr Sharon himself see fit to make it known— S.A. Hill

In the City and County of San Francisco State of California on this 25th day of August A.D. 1880— I Senator William Sharon of the State of Nevada age 60 years— Do here in

The "Marriage Contract"

the presence of almighty God take Sarah althea
hill of the city of San Francisco. Cal __ to be my
lawful and wedded wife- I do here acknowledge myself to be the husband of Sarah althea hill __

Wm Sharon Nevada
"   "

Aug 25 1880
"   "

While Sharon, his lawyers and handwriting experts studied the "contract," the press began to understand Tyler's moves. Obviously, he was an ingenious rascal: not for him the simple stratagem of a suit for breach of promise to marry, the conventional technique of the blackmailer; his device was the comparative respectability of an action on a marriage "contract" concocted by Allie and her helpers. It not only invested his case with unusual quality, it invested his client with "virtue." He knew that the cohabitation of Sarah Althea and Sharon in the Palace Hotel apartment would come out in the proof. It had to be a "wife" who made the nocturnal crossings of the bridge, not a concubine. Tyler's complaint included the remarkable allegation that when Sarah Althea and Sharon first "intermarried," Sharon's worth was a mere $5,000,000, but that in the period of their conjugal relationship, the devoted couple had "by their joint prudent management of mines, railways, banks, fortunate speculations, manipulations of the stock market and other business enterprises" increased the familial fortune to at least $15,000,000. The press could not resist speculating to what financial heights Sharon would have ascended had he met the auburn-haired fiscal genius a few years earlier.

At this point, Barnes made the first of a series of tactical mistakes that would have far-reaching consequences. The divorce suit brought by Tyler, *Sharon* v. *Sharon,* had been removed by the senator to the federal court. But Sharon's own federal case, *Sharon* v. *Hill,* designed to stop the divorce case, had itself become bogged down in technical jurisdictional matters, so Barnes consented to have the divorce case returned ("remanded") to the state court where it got a prompt trial. Thus, while Tyler's delaying tactics in the federal action were slowly being overcome, the divorce case moved swiftly to trial in the state superior court, to be tried without a jury by the Honorable J. F. Sullivan. In the end, while both cases would turn on the validity of the marriage contract, the results in the two cases would be diametrically different.

But what of Nielson, the altruistic "journalist" who had first come forward as the champion of Sarah Althea's marital rights? In his first interview, Nielson told reporters that he had made the adultery charge against Sharon because he was "an incorruptible journalist dedicated to exposing the truth and obtaining justice for the wronged." A few inquiries by a curious press disclosed that he was an alcoholic who had fled Australia after a conviction for forgery. As for his "altruism," when the "contingency fee" contract between Tyler and Sarah Althea came to light in the fall of 1884, it would be learned that Nielson had a direct pecuniary interest in the outcome of the case. He was designated as the plaintiff's "agent" to be compensated out of the recovery. In the end, he would prove one of the frailest of Sarah Althea's allies; she had him arrested on a charge of embezzlement, and he would shuffle off the stage into the murky shadows of the city's underworld, never to reappear. The staunchest of Sarah Althea's supporters would prove to be Mammy Pleasant, who supported her to the tragic end. One other supporter, David S. Terry, would stand stoutly at her side to the end and his devotion would cost him his life.

Before the climax of a trial was reached, there was some diverting preliminary legal skirmishing. Sharon and Barnes filled the air with so many accusations of forgery, perjury and conspiracy, that a grand jury was empaneled and directed to investigate, sparking another peripheral proceeding.

The "Bridge of Sighs," linking the Palace and Grand Hotels

In early November 1883, the grand jury issued subpoenas to both Sarah Althea and the senator. Tyler was unenthusiastic about any investigation; he moved in superior court to divest the grand jury of its powers. It was all a frame-up of his client, he asserted. Sharon had corrupted several members of the grand jury, and they would do his bidding. He wrote to each of the grand jurymen, repeating his accusations of corruption. This drew upon him a conviction for contempt and a fine of five hundred dollars. The California Supreme Court sustained both the conviction and the fine.

Now the parties girded themselves for the first major battle: the trial in superior court before Judge Sullivan. Sharon's forces won the first significant — if ephemeral — victory. At the end of November, the grand jury handed down indictments charging both Sarah Althea and Nielson with forgery, perjury and criminal conspiracy.

The San Francisco City Hall, site of the Sharon *v.* Sharon *trial.*
The building was destroyed in the earthquake.

XXII

SHARON v. SHARON:
AN ACTION FOR DIVORCE

Full of grief and full of love.
Impatient for my Lord's return
I sigh, I pine, I rave, I mourn.
Was ever passion cross'd like mine?
Joseph Addison, *Rosamond*

Everybody expected the trial of the divorce case in the state superior court to be the most exciting event of the San Francisco season in 1884, and nobody was disappointed. But before the trial got started, there were a few comic curtain-raisers.

Barnes hired detectives to scour the city for men who had known Sarah Althea over the years, and could testify to the frailty of her character. They should have been easy to find, but the gumshoes encountered the understandable reluctance of the local Lotharios to talk. Barnes had to go afield. He turned up one Freddie Burchard, an eastern dandy who averred that during a visit to San Francisco in 1881 — more than six months after the alleged marriage contract — he had enjoyed a whirlwind courtship with Sarah Althea, and they had become "affianced." "How could the duly-wedded wife of Senator Sharon accept a proposal of marriage?" The answer to that question, Barnes reasoned, should wreck the plaintiff's case.

Freddie seemed like a great find for the defense, until the redoubtable Tyler raked him on cross-examination. Freddie's memory suddenly became clouded; he could not remember his own birthday! Under Tyler's pummeling, Freddie sounded the depths of oblivion. When he could not recall even the date and circumstances of his "betrothal," Tyler taunted him: "The day of all days that you ought to remember, the day you became engaged to this lady!" Hapless Freddie had testified on direct examination that he had terminated the engagement because he had learned of Sarah Althea's gamy reputation. Tyler shot him down like a pigeon with a paper bullet: a maudlin letter from Freddie to his former *inamorata,* weeks after the "engagement" was broken, a fatuous *billet-doux* dripping with puppy-love remorse, in which Freddie confessed his own shortcomings as a lover, acknowledged that the breach was caused by his own faults, and pledged eternal fealty to his goddess of love, Sarah Althea. Tyler did not relent until Freddie admitted not only the commission of perjury, but that his noticeable limp was the result of a venereal disorder. Sarah Althea promptly brought charges against him and had him arrested for perjury. The charge was soon dismissed and the stricken swain left the arena for good.

With Freddie Burchard disposed of and the comedy over producing the plaintiff's "honor" played out, Tyler directed his talents to the pending indictment against Sarah Althea for perjury. There was much gossip in the town that Sharon had procured this charge by corrupting the grand jurors. Tyler set out to prove the "fix." A supreme court decision blocked him from examining individual grand jurors, but Judge John F. Sullivan, the trial judge in the divorce case, put an end to this fribble by ruling that the senator had indeed used "undue influence on the grand jury." He dismissed the perjury indictment.

The trial opened on March 10, 1884. Few trial-watchers gave much attention to a ruling by federal Circuit Judge Lorenzo Sawyer on March 9, over-ruling Tyler's motion to dismiss the federal case. That proceeding would lie smoldering silently, one day to explode in the faces of Sarah Althea and her supporters. For the moment, most San Franciscans fastened their attention on the sensational divorce trial before Judge Sullivan in the state court, *Sharon* v. *Sharon*.

The San Francisco papers published the most minute details of the trial and the telegraph carried every story all over the country. To them it was a rich theatrical spectacle. Of course, the journalists paid less attention to the legal issues than to the glamorous personalities of the contestants. The fair plaintiff's appearance and raiment on the opening day drew this journalistic dithyramb:

> *Sarah Althea looked as demure, innocent and sweet as the arts of the toilet could make her. Her costume was black silk over which she wore a brocaded velvet dolman faced with black fur around a throat which, if the truth must be told, is no longer as round and full as it no doubt was not many years ago. The face is shapely and oval. The features are regular; the mouth is well cut; the lips are rather full and are the most expressive feature. They look resolute but betray also that their owner has a temper. The nose also looks spirited. It is cast on the Roman model. The eyes lack the expression of trustfulness. . . . The whole face betrays intense nervousness, quickness of perception and mirrors faithfully all that is going on within her mind. Her hair is auburn and, if it is not false, is of luxuriant growth.*

The Bonanza Senator, "a veritable game-cock," was described as "in fighting trim bodily as well as legally." His forehead was

> *round, full and even. Under it are two piercing brown eyes, which look out inquisitively over a nose which tells nothing, not even Greek or Roman descent.*

The press went beyond Sarah Althea's millinery and Sharon's physiognomy. It sketched the personal histories of the judge and the legal gladiators; it described their attire, down to the color of their handkerchiefs.

As judges go, Jeremiah Francis Sullivan, the trial judge, was young and inexperienced. In 1883, when *Sharon* v. *Sharon* was tried before him, he was only thirty-three. He was born in Litchfield, Connecticut, in the foothills of the Berkshires, not far from Field's birthplace. His background was humble, but admirable. Unlike the other participants, he was less than a year old

Judge Jeremiah Sullivan

when his Irish immigrant parents carried him to California by way of Nicaragua. He had taught Latin, Greek, mathematics, geography, history and English in the San Francisco schools "during his spare hours" while studying law. In 1879, after five years of petty prosaic practice, he was elected to the superior court. His legal experience hardly equipped him for the demands of *Sharon* v. *Sharon*. The press observed of Judge Sullivan that in the conduct of the trial,

> *his greatest trouble is with Mr. Tyler, and though conscientious to a fault, he has oftentimes allowed that sturdy gentleman undue licence and has refrained from punishing him or rebuking him for contempt of court through fear of causing a suspicion that he was fluctuating to the side of wealth and power.*

In fact, Sullivan's paltering and lack of firmness during the trial would do much to prolong the case and to confuse the issues. He conducted himself like a ferryboat captain who suddenly finds himself commanding an oceanliner during a typhoon.

The lawyers exchanged salvos in opening statements to the court. For hours, the fustian flowed from both Tyler and Barnes, and as the two men interrupted each other with well-honed barbs, the journalists remarked on the "bad blood" that flowed between them. At last it was time for witnesses, for proof. The spectators leaned forward in anticipation of Sarah Althea. Not yet! Tyler was too skilled a courtroom impressario to open with his diva. His first witness was a tiny black seamstress, Martha Wilson. She testified that in October 1880, Sarah had "drawn a piece of paper from her bosom." It was the marriage contract, known to the press from that moment as Plaintiff's Exhibit Number One. Alas! Martha Wilson was illiterate: she could not read the paper. But by good fortune, at that moment another black lady, Mrs. Vesta Snow, "happened by." Mrs. Snow was but a charwoman, but she had the gift of letters and she read the paper to Mistress Wilson. Now the redoubtable Barnes thundered: "Produce it!"

Of course, the defense had already seen the document and had made photographs. Somehow, any reference to the alleged marriage contract seemed to drive Barnes into voluble rage. "Produce it!" he thundered as if to suggest he had cause to believe it did not exist. Judge Sullivan mildly suggested that this would indeed be a good time to show the paper to counsel. The complaint alleged that Sharon and Sarah Althea had lived together as man and wife pursuant to the contract for more than a year; that in November 1881, Sharon had demanded its surrender; that he had threatened her with "brutal force" if she refused, and that he had violated his marriage vows by having adulterous intercourse with Gertrude Dietz, and at least eight other women. After all, the trial would turn on the authenticity of this "marriage contract." Clearly, if it was genuine, there could be a valid marriage under California law. No one could dispute the relationship with Miss Dietz: it was attested by the lusty infant in Philadelphia now supported by a stipend from the old senator. There were even those who could tell of Sharon's expressed pride in his autumnal fertility. During the early days of the trial, journalists speculated about the legal effect of the alleged marriage contract and about the extent of Sharon's wealth. His fortune was estimated at more than $20,000,000, his income about $1,500,000 per annum. In her complaint,

Sarah Althea professed to be content with only an equal share of the conjugal property, "about $10,000,000."

Despite her illiteracy, Mrs. Wilson was permitted to testify that Plaintiff's Exhibit Number One was the very paper she had seen in October 1880. Mrs. Wilson had performed another function for Miss Hill. She had served as the custodian of the lady's "honor." After the plaintiff was ejected from the Grand Hotel, she had brought the paper to the black seamstress, who secreted it "behind a picture on a wall . . . packed between the picture and the wooden frame." One day when Miss Hill was absent, she "had so much curiosity to know what the paper was that she took it out." Again, her literate friend, Mrs. Snow, "happening to call at the house," assured her it was the same paper she had read to her when Miss Hill was present. Vesta Snow, the charwoman-amanuensis who so conveniently "happened by," corroborated Mrs. Wilson. Tyler and Mammy Pleasant had done their work well. But "General" Barnes had committed a boner — the first of many. The press failed to observe that the testimony of the two black ladies would have been inadmissable had not the blundering Barnes asserted the position that the paper was "a recent fabrication." The testimony of both women was admitted as "proof" that the paper existed in 1880. Thus ended the first day of what one newspaper promised would be "the nastiest case on record in California's courts." Tyler still withheld his leading lady. His next witness was billed as the "mysterious Irish beauty," Nellie Brackett.

"*Judge Sullivan's Nightmare,*" *from the* Wasp

XXIII

NELLIE BRACKETT

A little still she strove, and much repented,
And whispering "I will ne'er consent" — consented.

Lord Byron, *Don Juan*

According to the reporters, Nellie was "a lovely colleen, not yet twenty, with a fresh, pretty face." She furnished excellent copy to the reporters and much excitement for the spectators. One reporter observed that while she was testifying, Nellie's gaze was fixed on Sarah Althea, and "she bore an expression of complete and almost childish delight in looking at her patroness." Nellie had become acquainted with Sarah Althea when the wicked old senator had tumbled that dear lady out of the Grand Hotel into a boardinghouse maintained by Nellie's mother. The two had become friends. Nellie's parents objected to Sarah's influence over their daughter and asked Sarah Althea to find other quarters. Considering the mode of life to which the older woman introduced Nellie, the concern of Nellie's parents is pardonable. Sarah Althea moved out and Nellie went with her. By now, Sarah Althea was her "loving friend," her preceptress and protectress.

Tyler's artful questions elicited that Nellie was a young lady of such delicate sensibilities that, before she consented to become the companion of the older woman, she found it necessary to catechize Sarah Althea about her relationship with Senator Sharon. She asked her preceptress if she had indeed been the old man's mistress, "as was rumored about?" With her lovely eyes turned up to the courtroom ceiling, Nellie piously explained that if such rumors were true, she would have to sever the relationship; she could not "associate" with a kept woman. But Sarah had met the Brackett test of respectability by exhibiting to Nellie documentary proof of her probity: the marriage contract and the correspondence which would become famous as the "Dear Wife Letters." Indeed, Nellie was herself present with Sarah Althea and the senator when the cruel old man had addressed her dear friend as "Wifie." Now, with her eyes averted in shame, with every possible expression of modesty, Nellie let Tyler draw from her the lubricious story at which the press had hinted and for which the spectators were panting.

She had accompanied Sarah Althea to the Palace Hotel to spy on the old man. She told how the two women entered the senator's bedroom while he was absent and Sarah Althea directed Nellie to hide behind a bureau. When Sharon appeared, he asked Sarah Althea: "Don't you want to brush my hair?" She brushed his hair. Next, he told her his feet were cold. "Don't you want to rub my feet?" he asked. She rubbed his feet. After this exciting sexual foreplay, he asked Sarah Althea: "Don't you want to go to bed with me?" At first, Dear Wife demurred, "she did not come to stay all night, and her relatives would wonder where she was." Finally, she yielded (as usual). When the senator left for the bathroom Sarah Althea coached Nellie to remain hidden behind the bureau and observe. Nellie witnessed the lovemaking of Sarah Althea and Sharon, during which the senator "several times called Sarah his wife." "Who is my own little wife and nobody knows about it?" were the precise words of ardor she remembered. When the spent lovers were asleep, a fact confirmed by the senator's snoring, she "tiptoed out."

While this Boccaccian tale was told, the press observed that tears moistened the eyes of spectators and there was a flurry of handkerchiefs among the ladies present. Their Victorian sensibilities were offended that an innocent girl — hardly more than a child — should have been subjected to such a scene! At this point, Tyler, a superb showman, withdrew Nellie for a few moments to produce one Frank Rodney, a youth who seemed always in attendance on Sarah Althea and Nellie. He testified to the delivery of a letter to Sharon at the Palace in June 1882, shortly after Nellie's introduction to voyeurism. The letter is one of Sarah Althea's most artful confections:

June 1882

My Dear Senator. — I send Frank with this note so as to make sure that you get it to-night. I am afraid it will be impossible for us to go to Belmont with you on Saturday; besides, you say you want this business kept quiet for a little while, and you know my dear "Sen," what you wish is my law. This terrible pressure is killing me. Why do you hesitate to come out and acknowledge my rights and my place by your side? Have I not suffered enough already by it all? Have I not been ignored and snubbed already by the world, by my friends and relations, and yet I have kept my secret. Oh, what a thousand deaths I have suffered in these months of separation! But I suppose I should not recall the past as to our promise now — 'twill only be a short time until you will relieve me of this burden and allow me to take my place by your side and take me forth into the world relieved of this — this terrible odious stigma.

You said the other night that I was your own little wife and only we two knew it. How glad I was to hear you again tell me that! . . . Why do you hesitate to call me to you day and night and tell the world that all these years I have been your wife?

There was a furious wrangle between Tyler and Barnes over the admission of this letter. Sharon stoutly denied that he had ever received it. But Judge Sullivan received it in evidence as "corroboration." There was more "corroboration" to come. Nellie testified that in July 1882, Sarah showed symptoms of pregnancy. "How nice it would be," Sarah Althea told her, "to be the mother of Sharon's baby." Besides, it would strengthen her "wifely claims." She sent Nellie as her ambassadress to report this happy event to the senator. "Whom does she suspect?" asked Mrs. Sharon's alleged spouse. "She does not suspect anybody; she knows it is you," responded the ambassadress. "Well," said the senator, "send Mrs. Sharon down." Then, said Nellie, she negotiated with Sharon for several months for a house "suitable" for the accouchement of a senator's spouse. Alas, Sarah Althea was not pregnant, there was no need for a suitable house, and the matter was dropped. The important fact was that during her negotiations, Nellie stoutly maintained the senator repeatedly referred to Sarah Althea as "Mrs. Sharon."

When Tyler turned Nellie over to Barnes for cross-examination, Sarah Althea's purpose in introducing Nellie into her relationship with the senator began to emerge more clearly. In the manner of Cyprians through the centuries, as Sharon's interest in Sarah Althea cooled she was tempting him with younger and firmer flesh. Sarah Althea was not the first faded courtesan to turn to procuring. The earliest intimation of her vicious purpose is in a letter she wrote in August 1882 when the "terrible odious stigma" letter failed to produce results. She was at one of her lowest points of despair, suffering the cumulative trauma of her eviction from the Grand Hotel and the failure of all attempts at reconciliation. Worst of all she was penniless. The August letter was pure nectar to the press; it was immediately dubbed the "Egg in Champagne Letter," and the telegraph carried it all over the land. Here it is:

> *My Dear Senator:*
> *Don't I wish you would make up your mind and go down to them* [*local spas*] *with Nellie and I, wherever they be, on Friday or Saturday. We all could have such nice times out hunting or walking or driving these lovely days in the country. The jaunt or little recreation would do you worlds of good, and us girls would take the best care of you, and mind you in everything. . . . I am crazy to see Nell try and swallow an egg in champagne. I have not told her of the feat I accomplished in that line, but I am just waiting in hopes of seeing her some day go through the performance. . . . What a lovely evening this is, and how I wish you would surprise us two little lovebirds by coming out and taking us for a moonlight drive. But gracious me, it's too nice to think of; but I really wish you would. 'Twould do you good to get out of that stupid old hotel for a little while, and we'd do our best to make you forget all your business cares and go home feeling happy.*

One day this letter would be shrewdly described as an artful trick "to put young Nellie in the foreground as a fresh lure to the wary old bird." But the wary old bird was unmoved by the "Egg in Champagne Letter" and the delights of a moonlight drive with "us two little lovebirds." There was no answer. So the temptress again took Nellie Brackett to visit the old man at the Palace. Sharon ordered both women out of the hotel. They were escorted to the street by the house detective. This indignity drew a letter signed by Nellie Brackett. By this time, press and public were familiar with Sarah Althea's prose style, and they understood it was written at her dictation:

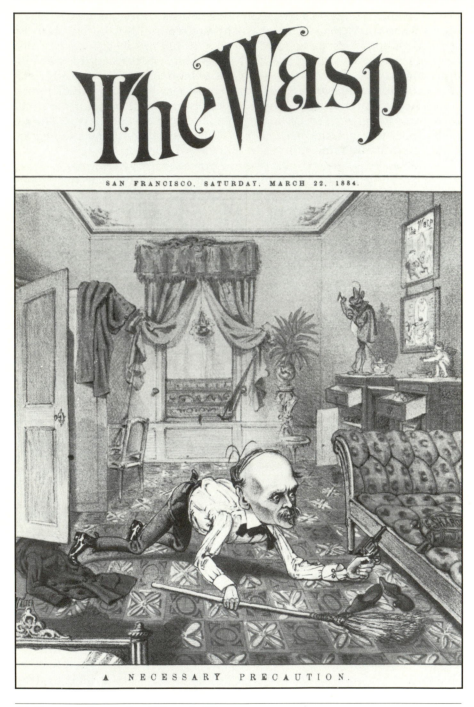

The Wasp

SAN FRANCISCO, SATURDAY, MARCH 22, 1884.

A NECESSARY PRECAUTION.

"A Necessary Precaution," from the Wasp

Old Sharon:

When I first met you I felt quite honored to think I had on my list of acquaintances a United States senator, but to-day I feel it a double disgrace to know you. If you are a specimen of the men that are honored by the title of rulers of our country, then I must say that I pity America; for a bigger coward or upstart of a gentleman never existed, in my opinion, since last Thursday night. I was present with the lady who called on you; and to think of what a coward you must be! Your own conscience would not allow you to see her and politely excuse yourself, but you must send one of your Irish hirelings to do your dirty work. I hope God will punish you with the deepest kind of sorrow, and make your old heart ache and your old head bend. I am one not to wish evil to people generally, but with all my heart I wish it to you. You did her a mean, dirty trick, and tried in every way to disgrace her, — a motherless, fatherless girl, — because you knew she leaned on you, and was alone in the world; and a few weeks after God took from you your much loved daughter. Be careful that, after this disgraceful outrage of Thursday night upon her, God does not again bring you grief, or some great misfortune. . . . I should think you would be so ashamed of yourself that you couldn't do enough to atone for the wrong you have done her. I love her, and I just hate you. It is well I am not her, or I would advertise you from one end of the world to the other. But she feels herself so much of a lady that she too timely submits to your insults. Why, you are not good enough for me to wipe my shoes on, much less her. . . .

Miss Brackett.

Even this broadside left the old man unmoved; he had had enough. He was not to be seduced by alfresco jaunts, Nellie's pristine charms or the fear of divine retribution.

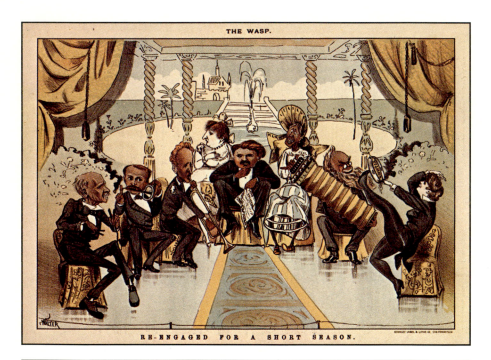

"Re-engaged for a Short Season," from the Wasp

XXIV

MAMMY PLEASANT
THE VOODOO QUEEN

O what a tangled web we weave
When first we practise to deceive.

Sir Walter Scott, *Marmion*

Mary Ellen Pleasant was the next witness for Sarah Althea, and she was impressive, although on objective analysis, every word she uttered was undoubtedly false. She showed a devotion to the plaintiff's cause that would be better understood later in the trial, when it was learned that she had a financial stake in the outcome of the case: she had invested at least $5,000 of her own money in the case as "sinews of war." She was in court throughout the trial, draped in a green shawl, her head "adorned with a huge poke bonnet." She sat in a chair immediately behind Sarah Althea, and consulted frequently with the plaintiff and her counsel. She signalled to the press her delight over points scored by Tyler, her disgust with the defense, and her chagrin when Sharon's troops made a hit.

Her testimony starts off with a palpable falsehood: "I first met the plaintiff in the Grand Hotel about two years ago." That would be in 1882. "I saw her there one day crying." Her own diary records that Sarah Althea was an inmate of the Octavia Street house in 1877, and Mammy's memoir records that the two women met in 1859, in Cape Girardeau.

Of course, to a woman of Mammy Pleasant's pursuits, a damsel in tears was a clear and present opportunity. Of course, she volunteered her aid. She went on:

> I have lived in San Francisco since 1849. I met the plaintiff in the Grand Hotel about two years ago. She wanted me to furnish a house for her. I asked to see the marriage contract to see if she had any guarantee for her money. The plaintiff showed the contract, and then I went to Mr. Sharon. I told him that I heard that he had some kind of relation with Miss Hill and owed her money, and asked him if it would be all right if I furnished the house. Mr. Sharon said all right, go ahead and furnish it and he would pay the bills.

Mammy Pleasant further related that only a month later, Sharon not only refused to pay for her "services" to Miss Hill, he denied even knowing such a person. Next thing she knew, she received a visit from Captain W. I. Lees of the San Francisco police, sent by Sharon to question her about her

"Mammy" Pleasant at the trial, from the Alta

relationship with Sarah Althea. Mammy spoke of a conversation with Sharon in which she told him that Miss Hill wanted nothing from him but "her reputation" and the money she had entrusted to him. But the senator said "he could not comply with her wishes." He said that Sarah Althea had "fooled her like she had so many other persons." He also said that Sarah Althea "was a very bad woman and he would have nothing to do with her."

Significantly, the old sorceress was subjected to only the most perfunctory cross-examination by Barnes. All San Francisco rightly surmised that Mammy Pleasant was financing Sarah Althea's litigation. The journalists did more than surmise: "The proceedings are a gamble as far as Mammy Pleasance [sic] is concerned, for she is risking some money with a chance of losing it against one of winning a good deal more." But Barnes would not even touch on this. Surely, her testimony strained everybody's credulity. Why should the wife of one of California's great tycoons need help in furnishing a house from a Negress who at best was Thomas Bell's housekeeper, and at worst was a notorious procuress?

One can only assume that Mammy was one of those witnesses "loaded for b'ar" that are best treated with delicacy. Obviously Barnes was afraid of the formidable black lady. He made no effort to expose her for what she was or even to probe for her part in what he must have recognized as a conspiracy. Perhaps he was impressed by Mammy's considerable "style." Every day she rode to and from the courthouse "in a top buggy, drawn by a neat pair of bays." She comported herself as an important person in the case — as indeed she was. But Barnes held back on her, as he had on Nellie Brackett. His cautious handling of these witnesses caused much comment — and much suspicion. The author's suspicion is that Barnes was fearfully avoiding the revelation — which came later in the trial — that he had been approached to take Sarah Althea's case, and had expressed some views unfavorable to Sharon.

Now came some more dubious "corroboration" of the plaintiff's case. Two former employees of the Palace testified that Sarah Althea was frequently in the senator's suite for breakfast, that the senator told them to obey her orders "as if they were his own." The last witness, before Sarah Althea herself took the stand, was one Harry Lovidore Wells, a name out of Gilbert and Sullivan, and a character that could have been drawn by Dickens or Trollope. As later proof would show, he was a witness bought, but not paid for.

Mr. Wells began his yarn by telling that he had a friend, Mr. H. M. True, who was an acquaintance of Senator Sharon. One day in the spring of 1881, while strolling in the street with Mr. True, they encountered Sharon in the company of a lady whom he believed to be Sarah Althea. He could identify her as the senator's lady companion by "the peculiarity of the eye, a rather sharp look." "And what happened at this street encounter?" asked Tyler. When Mr. True greeted the senator, Mr. Wells withdrew four or five paces, but he remembered that the senator introduced the lady companion as "Mrs. Sharon" and "my wife." As we shall see, the Wells's testimony is a piece of manufactured perjury. But again Barnes did little to expose this piece of claptrap by cross-examination. He was not living up to the encomia showered on him by Mr. Choate.

San Francisco at the time of the trial

XXV

AT LAST, THE HEROINE:
SARAH ALTHEA TAKES THE STAND

Yet beauty, though injurious, hath strange power.

John Milton, *Samson Agonistes*

All the trial-watchers were relieved on March 12, 1884, when the prima donna made her entry. "She was rather richly dressed, but some floating locks of hair about her forehead and ears gave her an untidy look," reported the *Alta*. The "fair plaintiff" told her story in the clear and refined accents she so assiduously cultivated, marked, it is true, by occasional solecisms. Tyler led her through the circumstances of her meeting with the goatish senator. There emerged a self-serving account of her relationship with Sharon.

She first met her "betrayer" at the end of the summer of 1880, when she was just recovered from "an illness" (the *sequelae* of the incident of the stomach pump in Lloyd's law office). She neglected to tell the court that financially she was at one of her periodic low points, and that her meeting with Sharon providentially rescued her from disaster. In fact, she had eleven dollars in the bank, an unpaid hotel bill of $339, and all prospects had vanished. She was (at least) thirty-two years old, her reputation tarnished, her looks fading, she had quarreled with her family and even with her staunchest friend, Mammy Pleasant. She needed an angel, and she found one in the lecherous old senator.

As she began to describe her first meeting with Sharon "the fair Althea . . . began to weep and sob as though it were the most wretched time of her young life," reported the press. The "introduction," she said, was in the spring of 1880 at the depot in Redwood while she was seated in a buggy, and so she had no chance to tell him how much he attracted her. But shortly after, she met him "by chance" at the Bank of California. They exchanged some pleasantries and a few days later the elderly faun piped his first few provocative notes:

> *My Dear Miss Hill:*
> *Can you meet me this evening, say about five o'clock, in the parlors of the Grand Hotel? Something I want to tell you of interest to*

*yourself. Will not do to meet you at the Baldwin; so, if you cannot
see me at the Grand, name place and hour.*

*Very truly,
Wm. Sharon.*

"Mr. Sharon talked love almost every time I went to see him." With
appropriate expressions of maidenly contrition, heavily larded with blushes
and tears, Sarah Althea described his advances, his revolting offer of money
for the use of her body. He offered her $1,000 a month and Flora's white
horse if she would let him love her. Of course, this proposal was offensive
to an alumna of Mammy Pleasant's Finishing School for Young Ladies. She
said:

> *I told him he had made a mistake in the Lady. . . . that I was an
> honest girl and had my own affairs to look after. Then he . . . said
> that he had only said that to tease me; that he had inquired about
> me and learned that I was a respectable girl of good family, and he
> wanted to marry me. I said that was a different matter, and we sat
> down again and talked. . . . He said that if we should be married it
> would have to be done secretly. I said I would not consent to that, and
> he said it was necessary, as he had sent a girl to Philadelphia with
> her mother who would create a scandal about him if he got married.
> The girl had no reputation to lose, and would come out and ruin his
> chances of election in Nevada if he got married. I told him I did not
> believe that story, and he took out a letter from the girl and showed
> it to me. He tore off part of it and gave it to me.*

She told how she had tried to keep her friendship with the senator "on
a business basis," talking about "the stocks and the weather and all those
kinds of things." "Why," she said, with an air of outrage, "I gave him $7,500
to invest for me." Sarah Althea's insistence that the money she received from
Sharon was in repayment of this spurious transaction is one of the most amusing of her lies. Asked where she had obtained $7,500, she said blithely, "Oh
Mr. Charlie Gummer, at the Bank." Charlie Gummer, it turned out, was an
embezzling bank teller who had recently committed suicide.

Before the platonic summer of 1880 slipped into autumn, the senator
took her to dinner and on horseback rides, during which he proposed marriage. On August 25, 1880, at Sharon's office, she agreed to become his wife.
But he said there was need for the highest degree of secrecy because of the
menace of the jealous young woman in Philadelphia. So their nuptial rites
could be celebrated only on a piece of paper — Plaintiff's Exhibit Number
One. She wrote it, she said, at Sharon's dictation, and he signed it.

Now, he visited her hotel almost nightly to collect a husband's dues.
But his visits were causing "talk," and he arranged for Sarah Althea to move
into a suite at the Grand, so she could avail herself of the little connecting
bridge. In early October, Sharon was in Virginia City fighting for reelection
to the Senate. He lost. Sarah Althea wrote that she was having some problems
with Mr. S. F. Thorn, the hotel manager, who was withholding the honors
due a senator's consort. This, she related, evoked from Sharon the first of
the critical "Dear Wife" letters:

One of the "Dear Wife" letters. It was later determined that the words "My Dear Wife" were forged.

My dear Wife:
In reply to your kind letter, I have written Mr. Thorn and enclose
same, which you may read and then send it on to him in an envelope,
and he will not know that you have seen it. Sorry that anything should
occur to annoy you and think my letter will command the kind of
courtesy you deserve. Am having a very lively and hard fight. But
think I shall be victorious in the end.

With kindest consideration believe me as ever,
Wm. Sharon.

On the second day of her testimony, Sarah Althea suffered from a competitive disadvantage. Adelina Patti, the famous European singer, opened at the local Grand Opera House, diverting some attention from her own performance. She met the competition head on. The *Alta* reported that when the courtroom doors opened "standing room was at a premium and reserved places were being filled at prices far in advance of Patti speculators' prices." Sarah Althea was "handsomely attired in black, with a beaded horseshoe bonnet surmounting her strangely-tinted locks." She resumed her description of the brief halcyon days with Sharon.

According to "Dear Wife," the lives of the married couple fell into a pattern as regular as it was blissful. Nightly, she would cross the little bridge from the Grand to the Palace to enjoy the senator's society. His horses and carriage were at her disposal. His servant, Ki, performed her errands. Sharon took her to Belmont, but daughter Flora objected to her presence, so she had to forego those rustic splendors until Flora left for England with her titled Englishman. Then, Sarah said, she "went everywhere" with the senator, meeting all his important friends, including a Vanderbilt from New York! She testified that Sharon gave her five hundred dollars each month for her personal expenses. Plainly, the old man was enjoying the romp with his "dear Allie." At Christmas 1880, he sent her a penciled note:

My Dear Allie:
Come over and join me in a nice bottle of champagne, and let us be
gay before Christmas.

W. S.
If you don't come over and take part in the bottle, I may hurt myself.

Sharon was paying for his fun. The "Dear Wife" letters, introduced through the plaintiff's testimony, all deal with the five hundred dollars per month that Sarah Althea received for her "personal expenses."

My Dear Wife:
Inclosed send you by Ki the balance, two hundred and fifty, which
I hope will make you happy. Will call this evening for the joke.

Yours, S.
April 1, [1881.] [Exhibit 29.]

My Dear Wife:
You have had one hundred and twenty. Then twenty and before I left
one hundred. In all, two hundred and forty, (240.) The balance is just
two hundred and sixty, for getting extravagant.

May 5, 1881. [Exhibit 11.]

My Dear Wife:
Inclosed find three hundred and ten dollars to pay bills with, etc.

W. S.
August 29, 1881. [Exhibit 16.]

Palace Hotel, San Francisco, October 3, 1881.

My Dear Wife:
Inclosed find five hundred and fifty dollars, which will pay expenses
until I get better. Will then talk about your eastern trip. Am much bet-
ter to-day. Hope to be up in three or four days.

Truly, S.
[Exhibit 37.]

In the fall of 1881, the idyll was interrupted. The senator began paying court to a vibrant New York beauty and neglecting Sarah Althea. There were some unpleasant scenes, and about the beginning of November there was a climactic quarrel. Sharon accused Sarah Althea of having violated the secrecy of their "marriage" in a meeting with a lawyer. Sarah Althea told Sharon that she had consulted counsel "only" about the $7,500 she had entrusted to him. The truth, which did not emerge until later, and then from testimony other than hers, was that Sharon accused Sarah Althea of filching money from his pockets during his slumbers, and with stealing some important papers relating to the Belcher Mine from his room. She denied the theft, although she later admitted "finding the papers in her trunk." Whereupon, she said the senator had given her $3,000, a promissory note for $1,500, and undertook to repay the balance (of her $7,500, of course) at the rate of $250 per month. In return, he demanded that she sign a "release" paper affirming that she had no claims against him and return to him the marriage contract, Plaintiff's Exhibit Number One.

With an air of hauteur, she told how she refused to return the marriage contract to Sharon; to do so would be to surrender her "honor." At this, he had been seized by a wild rage and attacked her physically: "He choked me until I fainted." Then he locked her in a bedroom closet until she lost consciousness and had to be revived. Somehow, the precious paper was not taken from her. Next, Sarah Althea related the harrowing saga of her eviction, not only from the senator's bed and affections, but from her own snuggery at the Grand.

On November 19, the manager of the Grand Hotel, at Sharon's orders, wrote Sarah Althea, directing her to vacate her room "on December 1st prox.'' She ignored his letter, but the harrowing indignity of her prospective eviction led her to write Sharon on November 19:

> *Mr. Sharon:*
>
> *I received a letter from Mr. Thorn in regard to my room. Of course I understand it is written by your orders, for no human being saw you; and would you, who wished me to come to this house, whom I have been up with nights and waited on and cared for, and would have done anything to help you, be the one to wrong and injure me? — a man whom the people have placed enough confidence in his honor to put him in the United States senate, to stoop to injure a girl, and one whom he has professed to love!*

There was no answer. On December 5, manager Thorn had the door of the room removed from its hinges and the carpets taken up. Stoically, she remained in the doorless, uncarpeted room, barricaded by furniture piled up in the doorway. On December 5, a second *cri de coeur* came to Sharon:

> *My Dear Mr. Sharon:*
>
> *I cannot see how you can have any one treat me so — I, who have always been so good and kind to you. The carpet is all taken up in my hall. The door is taken off and away, and it does seem to me terrible that it is you who would have it done.*

At this point in her letter, the desperate woman's prose rises to a level of pathos that could come from the most tragic of Italian grand opera heroines. She writes:

> *Oh, senator, dear senator, don't treat me so! Whilst every one else is so happy for Christmas, don't try to make mine so miserable. Remember this time last year. You have always been so good; you don't act so. Now let me see you and talk to you. Let me come in after Ki has gone, if you wish, and be to me the same senator again. Don't be cross to me; please don't. Or may I see you, if only for a few minutes? Be reasonable with me, and don't be unjust. You know you are all I have in the world, and a year ago you asked me to come to the Grand. Don't do things now that will make me talk.*

Still no answer came from the obstinate old man, so she changed her approach and filled the air with the smoke of her burning bridges. On December 6 she wrote:

> *My Dear Mr. Sharon:*
>
> *I have written you two letters, and received no reply, excepting to hear that they have been read and commented upon by others than yourself. I also heard you said you were told that I said I could and would give you trouble. Be too much of a man to listen to such talk, or allow it to give you one moment's thought. I have never said such a thing, nor have I had such a thought. If no woman ever makes you*

any trouble until I do you will go down to your grave without the slightest care. No, Mr. Sharon, you have been kind to me. I have said I hoped my God would forsake me when I ceased to show my gratitude. I repeat it. I would not harm one hair of your dear old head, or have you turn one restless night upon your pillow through any act of mine. If you are laboring under a mistake, and not bringing the accusation for the purpose of quarreling with me, the time will come when you will find out how you have wronged me; and I believe you too much of a man at heart not to send for me and acknowledge it to me. . . . Mr. Sharon, I have never wronged you by word or act; and were I to stay in this house for a thousand years I would never go near your door again until you felt willing to say to me you knew you had spoken unjustly to me. You once said to me there was no woman who could look you in the face and say: "William Sharon, you have wronged me." If that be the case, don't let me be the first to utter the cry. I had hoped to always have your friendship and best will throughout life, and always have your good advice to guide me, and this unexpected outburst and uncalled for action was undeserved. . . . Think how you would like one of your daughters treated so. If you have any orders to give, or wish to, make them known in any other way than through your servants or through Thorn. Don't fight me. I have no desire or wish to in any way be unkind to you. I have said nothing to any one about the letter I have received, nor do I even wish to speak to Thorn on the subject. You have placed me in a strange position, senator, and all the pride in me rebels against speaking upon the subject.

As ever,   A.

Sharon remained unmoved. Before she left the hotel, in a last-ditch effort to revive the liaison, the distraught woman stole into Sharon's suite and locked herself in a closet. The ubiquitous Ki discovered her and with the aid of hotel employees, literally threw her into the street. Finally, Sarah Althea left the Grand, one step ahead of Thorn and the house detective. She moved first to the Mary Street house of the kindly Negro woman, Martha Wilson, and then to several "boarding places."

Sarah Althea testified how, from her places of exile, she tried unceasingly to renew her relationship with Sharon. She almost succeeded. There is evidence that in the winter of 1882, she spent a night with Sharon at the Palace. But any reconciliation was ephemeral. The old man rejected her advances and, in the early spring of 1882, she wrote:

Senator:
I hear you are quite ill. I should like if you would let me come and read to you, or sit with you of evenings and wait on you. Perhaps I may prove entertaining enough to help drive away both your cares and your pains and you know no one would do so with a more loving heart than I. You surely have not forgotten what a nice little nurse I proved myself in your last illness, and you cannot but remember

227

how willing I was to be with you. . . . And I assure you, you will find
me as willing and agreeable now. . . . Please don't deny me the pleas-
ure of being with you while you are sick. . . . I should like to see you
today, anyway, it being the first of the month, and I would like to get
some money. I don't like to have to ask for it while you are ill, but
you know house bills have to be paid. . . .

With love, I am always,
A.

In the end, she gave up her effort to regain the nest and rented quarters on
Ellis Street, near the home of Nellie Brackett's parents.

A month or two passed of separation between the lachrymose plaintiff and her dear but obdurate old senator. In late May 1882, she gave it another try. She dined with the old man several times and again spent at least
one night with him. Sarah Althea said that on one of these visits to the Palace
suite she was accompanied by little Nellie Brackett, whom she secreted behind some furniture in the senator's bedroom. Her purpose, she stated, was
that Nellie might overhear words between herself and the senator that would
be evidence that the pair were man and wife. With suitable blushes she admitted that finding no way out, she did spend the night with him, conscious
that the virginal Nellie was behind the bureau, making notes. After this flutter
of passion, Sarah Althea heard nothing more from Sharon. So she resolved
to restore her honor in the courtroom.

At this point, Tyler turned his client over for cross-examination in a
courtroom filled with press and spectators, all athrob with curiosity and excitement. There was some surprise when Barnes delegated the task of cross-
examining the plaintiff to his associate, Evans. When Sarah Althea learned
that Evans, not Barnes, would conduct her cross-examination, she was furious. She asked Judge Sullivan to make Barnes question her, as he had all
other witnesses. The judge said counsel could "please themselves" and
Evans took over. His style seemed turgid after the flamboyant Tyler. The duel
of wits between Evans and Sarah Althea was not rollicking sport, although
the press thought it "a contest of well-matched adversaries." At first, Evans
bored spectators and infuriated the witness with tedious attempts to trap her
on specific dates, places and amounts of money. But when he touched the
subject of Sharon's insistence that the "marriage" be kept secret, reporters
and trial-watchers were rescued from their temporary ennui.

Evans: *What reason did the Senator give for requiring that the mar-*
riage remain secret for two years?
Sarah Althea: *He had a young woman in Philadelphia with child. If*
we were openly married they would come out and make trouble in
Nevada for him. They had nothing to lose and all to gain. He was
afraid they would make trouble and prevent him from being re-
elected.

Next, in a prelude to the "magic show" at which Barnes had hinted
and the defense had carefully planned, Evans turned to the supernatural. He
questioned the plaintiff about putting charms and love potions in the old
man's food, clothing and bedding. She denied invoking magic or the spirits

Judge Oliver P. Evans, one of Sharon's lawyers, as sketched during the trial

of the underworld to capture Sharon's love. Evans confronted her with an allegation that in company with Nellie Brackett she had stolen some articles of Sharon's underclothing and buried them under a coffin in a local cemetery. Some of the knowledgeable journalists winked at each other; they recalled that Mammy Pleasant claimed descent from a voodoo queen. If Sarah Althea had a cabinet Cagliostro, a sortileger in her retinue, it must be Mammy Pleasant. Scornfully, Sarah Althea denied enlisting the spirit world in her cause.

Next subject: "Why was she estranged from her own family, especially her brother?" The haughty maiden answered,

because my brother did not consider Mr. Sharon my equal by any means, but thinks he is of very low birth. We are somebody by birth, and Mr. Sharon is like a thistle in a field by birth!

On this note, Evans quit for the day. Apparently, it never occurred to him to ask if her brother, that proud Southern gentleman, had social views on her intimacy with Mammy Pleasant.

When court resumed in the morning, Evans began chipping away at some of the plaintiff's questionable activities: excursions to places of ill-repute with casual acquaintances, her ill-fated dalliance with the mamma-ridden barrister, her attempt at suicide. "Lies! Slander! Calumny!" Sarah Althea screamed. "Are you through with this dirt?" demanded the outraged maiden and appealed to Judge Sullivan's chivalrous instincts. The jurist coldly told her to answer the questions.

Evans then shifted to a new line, "Did she ever threaten to kill Sharon?" Now, for the first time, the redoubtable Judge Terry came to his client's defense. There was a bitter confrontation between the Texan and "General" Barnes. The press had been puzzled by Terry's sudden emergence as one of Sarah Althea's legal champions. Some of them opined that Tyler was "feeling

JUDGE DAVID S. TERRY.

David S. Terry, as he looked at the time of the Sharon v. Sharon *trial*

the heat," and had invoked Terry's considerable reputation as a "divorce" lawyer. Wagstaff, always prickly about his hero's motives, wrote later that Terry was

> *assigned the position of special counsel and protector to the plaintiff, as there were intimations based upon well-grounded suspicions that she was in danger of being kidnapped or "spirited" away.*

In fact, Terry's services were sought as a lawyer, not as a bodyguard. Tyler wanted his prestige and experience in matrimonial litigation, not his Bowie knife. Certainly, Terry's presence endowed her case with an ingredient of professional respectability that was greatly needed. Terry was a lawyer of standing, despite his history. His unhappy past was only dimly remembered and his erratic behavior in the Sharon-Hill litigation lay in the future. It has never been explained why Terry undertook the Sharon litigation. He must have been susceptible to the plaintiff's personality.

Terry suffered heavy personal tragedies during the winter and spring of 1884–85. Cornelia Terry died on December 16, 1884, after an illness of many months. His son, Sam, the only companion left him in the Stockton home, had already developed an infection from an operation in 1883 and on April 1, 1885, he died. Nor had Terry ever fully recovered from the "accidental" death of his son, David, in December 1873, shot with his own pistol. Terry's familial world was crumbling, and successive disasters had left their mark on his mind and character. But in the spring of 1884, his professional lights certainly outshone those of the Tylers and George Flournoy.

Whatever were Tyler's motives in projecting Terry into his case, from the moment in the trial when Evans accused Sarah Althea of plotting to kill Sharon, the Texan became an impressive gladiator for the plaintiff. His courtly manners and polished speech had already captured Sarah Althea's heart. Here, at last, was a gentleman who was her equal "by birth." As we shall see, a delicate *amourette* was developing between lawyer and client that did not go unnoticed; Isolde had found her Tristan, and their relationship flowered into a moonstruck passion that would overwhelm the old warrior, recently widowed, and the much younger courtesan, who was running out of elderly protectors. What seems to have begun as an exercise in antebellum courtesies, soothing little smiles and compliments, palliative glasses of water, the helpful hand to and from the witness box, reared up into a love-storm that would bring the roof of their world crashing down on both of them. She saw Terry as a Southern Agamemnon, but to the press and the spectators, he gradually assumed the role of an infatuated Pantaloon.

At first, the journalists and the corps of trial-watchers were told that Terry would furnish "the major portion of the law in the case" and "argumentative powers." He was regarded as "ponderous in frame, mind and language," but observers saw him transformed during the trial into a plumed gallant "of the old school."

> *The greater portion of his time is taken up by his client. . . . Their seats are invariably side by side and to the lady's hard-worked tongue does Mr. Terry ever lend a kindly ear. All her confidences are made to him, and all her many stage-whispered sarcasms, directed to the defendant, his witnesses and counsel reach him before they do their targets. Oftener than not, he escorts her to and from lunch, and it is a not*

infrequent sight to behold them arm-in-arm in the street or at the theatre, each as merry and full of glee, and oblivious to criticizing spectators as a pair of freshly-betrothed lovers of more recent date of conception.

Prophetic words!

But strangely, like Barnes, when Evans cross-examined the plaintiff, there was no attempt to probe her relationship with the old brothel-keeper who was providing "the sinews of litigation." Just before Evans completed his cross-examination of the plaintiff, Terry had a chance to display his chivalry. There was "a scene that those in the courtroom will not soon forget."

Evans: *Did you ever threaten to take Senator Sharon's life?*

Sarah Althea: *I told Mr. Barnes that if Senator Sharon succeeded in convicting me criminally when he knew I was innocent, I would, if it lay in my power, kill him and myself both.*

Barnes immediately shouted a denial, and called her testimony "False! False!" This provoked the plaintiff's special Galahad. Terry rose to his full height and thundered an accusation at Barnes:

His conduct is most unprofessional, and is insolent in the highest degree to the witness whom he accuses of perjury. I believe the story of the witness notwithstanding the denial of counsel.

Barnes retorted with a sneering gesture and a denunciation of Terry. He concluded with:

Judge Terry attempted to insult me by his remarks. I appreciate the insult, but shall disregard it. I will not take it up. I will send him no challenge, for I fight no duels.

According to the newspapermen in the court,

loud applause greeted this pointed allusion to Judge Terry's past. Judge Terry turned a ghostly white and his hands trembled as he slowly responded to Barnes.

The spectators expected Terry to explode with violence. His face bore an expression of rage, but he controlled himself and said, in measured tones:

I have no apology of any kind to make, nor have I in this matter changed my mind.

At this, there passed from the witness to her protector such a look as Andromeda must have bestowed on Perseus.

There were still a few bonbons for the hungry trial-watchers in the plaintiff's reexamination by Tyler. He elicited from his heroine that her Uncle Sloan was so solicitous of her reputation and the good name of his family that he once trailed her to a restaurant where she was dining with Sharon. When she returned to the Palace with the old man, Uncle Sloan made an avuncular scene:

[He] began to upbraid me, telling me that the restaurant where I had been was a disreputable place and that he would send me to the Magdalen Asylum [a prison for prostitutes] or that he would kill me before he would let me disgrace the family. He said that he would tell my brother of what I had done. I begged him not to do so and began to cry. . . . It was then, as he felt so badly about it, I told him I was Mr. Sharon's wife, and that we had been secretly married.

This seems to have satisfied the family honor, although Uncle Sloan never appeared in court to confirm the incident. On this note, "Mr. Tyler created a sensation by announcing that the plaintiff's case was closed." When Sarah Althea tripped down from the witness stand, the consensus was that she had weathered the storms.

"Judge Sullivan's 'Happy Family,'" as seen by the Wasp

XXVI

THE DEFENSE: ACT ONE

. . . no more heart than a piece of marble!
Mrs. Eliza Stagg

Barnes opened Sharon's defense with a lady from Oakland who described herself as "a social hotel acquaintance" of the plaintiff. She had seen Sarah Althea a number of times during the time when she had been the senator's companion and claimed that there had never been any mention of marriage. Although Sarah Althea had once confided to the lady that she and the senator were "engaged," at another moment she had said her interest in the old man was "purely monetary" and that she was still deeply in love with the bashful barrister, Reuben Lloyd (who was now the law partner of Sharon's son-in-law, Frank Newlands). The witness recounted that while Sarah Althea was the "companion" of the senator, she had joined her in several visits to the law offices of Reuben Lloyd. How happy the plaintiff had seemed, the witness recalled, because "Lloyd had been induced to dine with her at last, and it seemed so nice that she and Reub had made up." She quoted the ecstatic Allie as saying, "Oh Reub! Oh sweetest; oh it is so nice to be caressed as of old." The witness continued, "I asked her if she loved Lloyd better than Sharon. She said, 'What do I care for old Sharon! Only his money!'"

Next came Mrs. Eliza Stagg, an eastern lady, who, with her husband, had been a guest at a weekend party at Belmont in April 1881 that included Sarah Althea and the celebrated eastern tycoon, Cornelius Vanderbilt. There was another weekend at Belmont when Freddie Burchard was of the company, and Sarah Althea confided to Mrs. Stagg that Freddie had proposed marriage. The Staggs had asked Sarah how the senator would feel about such a marriage, but, according to Mrs. Stagg, "his feelings made no difference for she did not love the old man. She had no more heart than a piece of marble!" There was so much laughter and merriment from the spectators during Tyler's cross-examination of Mrs. Stagg that Judge Sullivan cleared the courtroom. "The Court," he said, "should not be regarded as a low place of entertainment like a Kearny Street cellar."

J. R. Reigart, another visitor at Belmont, recalled a number of conversations with Sarah Althea, in which she had besought him to testify in her behalf, "to save her honor at the expense of my own; she would give me anything in the world to testify on this stand that Senator Sharon had introduced her to me as his wife." There were intimations that Mr. Reigart's compensation for perjury would be more than mere lucre! "I told her that I was on record as an honest man and could not do it. She repeated this proposition several times and our friendly relations ceased from that time." His wife corroborated his testimony. The press regaled the nation's breakfast tables with accounts of the bravura pageant being staged in the courtroom, including some earthy speculation on what the plaintiff meant when she offered "anything in the world" to Mr. Reigart.

The San Francisco *Chronicle* titillated public curiosity by pointing out that one of Sarah Althea's most devoted supporters had vanished from the courtroom. "Where is Nellie Brackett?" it asked. Tyler gave out that the Irish beauty had been abducted by the defense, and sought a court order from Judge Sullivan to search a departing steamer on which he believed she was to be taken off. Before Sullivan ruled, reporters found Nellie in the most likely and most prosaic place: her mother's kitchen. Nellie's evanescence was explained on the mornng of April 1, 1884, when Barnes called to the stand Mrs. Mary Brackett, Nellie's mother. "A buzz of expectation ran through the little audience of lawyers and reporters" (the public was still excluded) as the matron testified how Sarah Althea had come into the life of the Bracketts after her eviction from the Grand, when she moved into the building next to the Brackett boardinghouse. Had she discussed the senator? "Of course," said Mrs. Brackett, who then told how Sarah Althea had displayed some costly French undergarments which had been imported for her by her "protector," Mr. Sharon. But there was no talk of marriage, according to Mrs. Brackett. Indeed, Sarah Althea had said she would never marry the senator, or any other man, for "she loved her freedom too much." Sarah told Mrs. Brackett that she had been engaged to the senator, but had broken the engagement at the insistence of her brother "because the Sharon pedigree was inferior to the Hills'." Then, Mrs. Brackett related how Sarah Althea had snatched her beloved Nellie from the family bosom.

The *Chronicle* reported that Nellie was now "under guard" in her mother's home and had told reporters that she had done all she could for Miss Hill and would now do something for her own parents. The "something," it was intimated, would be a $25,000 payment by the senator to Mr. and Mrs. Brackett in return for which Nellie would reveal that her prior testimony was false, suborned by the plaintiff and her counsel.

Barnes next called Mrs. Harriet Kenyon, who described herself as a "ladies' companion" hired by the plaintiff to be "a companion and chaperone" on a trip to the East and Europe, where Sarah Althea would devote herself to the study of music and art. Had the plaintiff discussed the senator? Of course. The plaintiff told her she was jealous of the other women with whom Sharon consorted. Mrs. Kenyon recalled that Sarah Althea told how she had secreted herself in the old man's bedroom to observe his love-making with "other women." Any talk of marriage? "No," said Mrs. Kenyon, "but there were repeated professions of her love for 'her only man' — Reuben Lloyd." Allie had confided: "I love him better than any person I ever knew. I would give up everything if he would only come back to me again!"

Now Barnes scored a big point, at least with the press. He called John Hornblower, Esq., a respected San Francisco lawyer, who testified that a Mrs. Samson, a friend of Sarah Althea, first spoke to him about a breach of promise case against Mr. Sharon.

Then, a few days later, Mrs. Samson introduced the prospective plaintiff to Hornblower:

> *At that time Mrs. Samson introduced me to Miss Hill. She said: "This is the lady I have spoken to you about, that desires to bring an action against Mr. Sharon for breach of promise of marriage." . . . Mrs. Samson introduced me to the lady who was veiled. She said, "This is the Miss Hill," and I think I bowed to the lady, and this lady said, "Well, I have fifty letters from Mr. Sharon." I told her all I wanted was three good, square letters that had good, square promises. The reply that she made was that she hadn't yet looked over her letters sufficiently but that she would come back in a few days. This is the last I saw of her. I never saw her since until I saw her in this court room. I cannot say that the statement that I made to her about the three letters was advice given her as a lawyer, because I was not her lawyer.*

It struck the reporters as "peculiar" that in March 1883 Sarah Althea should have been looking for a lawyer to sue Sharon for breach of promise to marry her, when she claimed she had a paper that said he had "married" her three years before.

The next witness for the defendant was Mrs. Mary Shawhan. To the press, she was "one of the city's great beauties." She had known Sarah Althea for a number of years, including the roseate period of the Sharon-Hill liaison. Sarah Althea had accused her of trying to lure the senator away. There had been a slanging match between them that sounded like a couple of Barbary Coast harlots quarreling over a drunken sailor. Mrs. Shawhan said Sarah Althea told her that her "engagement" to the senator was at an end and that she "proposed to sue the old man for breach of promise." On cross-examination, Tyler sniffed out that Mrs. Shawhan's background was as full-flavored as his own client's. He started with her own marital status. There seemed to be no Mr. Shawhan, but there was a son. Tyler shouted that he intended to prove that Mrs. Shawhan was a woman of ill-repute, a *demi-mondaine* "who is in the habit of visiting disreputable places in the company of a large number of men . . . houses of assignation," including "the Poodle Dog and the California House and other places of resort for the evil-minded." This assault on his mother's virtue stimulated some angry threats from the witness's son, who was seated in the courtroom. Tyler, Jr. leaped to his father's support — brandishing a pistol! "An Exhibition of Guns in the Sharon case!" "Four Ready Revolvers!" trumpeted the *Daily Alta*. The pistoleros were disarmed and from then on the courtroom was guarded by police officers.

Next, Mrs. Samson, the lady who had introduced Sarah Althea to lawyer Hornblower, testified that Sarah Althea had offered her a large sum if she would testify that Sharon had described her to Mrs. Samson as his wife. But then cross-examination revealed that for many weeks she had been engaged, together with Mrs. Shawhan, in seeking out witnesses for the senator in the murkier strata of local society. It must have been plain that both women shared with Sarah Althea a certain kind of life, a certain calling. In fact, they were drawn from San Francisco's version of the *grandes horizontales* who in that era were making such a mark on Parisian society.

Now came Mr. H. M. True, the subject of Harry Lovidore Wells's testimony. He denounced Wells's story as complete perjury. He did not know Sharon, had never met him, never heard him introduce the plaintiff as his wife. But he did know Tyler. True confessed he had written the lawyer offering for a fee to testify for the plaintiff. He had produced Wells as "the other man" who had been with him when the fabricated meeting was supposed to have taken place. Plainly, True and Wells were a pair of scoundrels trying to make a few dollars from both sides of the case.

Ah Ki, the senator's faithful Chinese servitor for thirty years, provided some of the richest moments of the trial with testimony that might have come from the pen of Bret Harte. After Sarah Althea moved to the Grand, the senator had sent him to her rooms to exhibit Miss Dietz's baby to her:

> Ki: *She say not look like Misser Sharon. I say yes it do. Miss Hill not like it and tell me to steal it away and kill it.*
> Evans: *What for?*
> Ki: *Oh, she say not like baby get any of estate, and tell me she give me three, four hundred dollars if I kill it or stole him away.*

Ki confirmed that Sarah Althea spent about three nights a week with his employer during the winter of 1880–81. "Yes, sir, she sleep there two, three times week." He knew of their quarrel in the spring of 1881, when Sharon accused Sarah Althea of stealing papers and money from his clothing during the night. Once, after the quarrel, she had slipped into Sharon's bedroom and the old man tried to choke her, called her a whore, and threw her out. Ki told how Sarah had forced herself into the senator's room, had sprinkled her love potions on the bed, on furniture, on his clothing; how Sarah Althea had tried to enlist his aid in her effort to make the senator marry her:

> "*Oh, Mr. Sharon marry me for sure, and I give you one thousand dollars every month if you help me.*"

The next turn on the bill was Barnes's long-awaited "Magic Show." A cemetery attendant testified:

> *I went with [Sarah Althea and Nellie Brackett] to the lot of the Oriental Lodge, to a grave prepared for the remains of a man named Anson G. Olsen. . . . Miss Hill came down into the grave. She took a package out from under her cloak and placed it through the hole and under the board and whispered something to herself. Then she went up out of the grave and Nellie Brackett came down. . . . Nellie said: "I want you to take this," giving me a silver dollar. I said I wouldn't take anything, but Nellie said that the fortune teller told them that they had to pay for everything they did about the charm or it would not work. So I took the silver dollar and took it home and gave it to my wife.*

What Sarah Althea and Nellie took from the grave was a sack to be made into a love charm, following a reliable voodoo formula provided by Mammy Pleasant. They planted the grisly object in Sharon's room, but it proved a dud. The old man's ardor was not revived.

Barnes next called Laura Scott, an ancient black disciple of Mammy

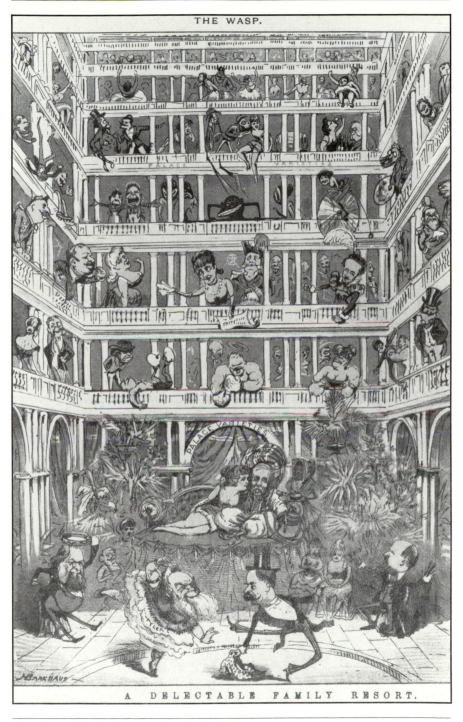

THE WASP.

A DELECTABLE FAMILY RESORT.

"A Delectable Family Resort," from the Wasp

Pleasant, by profession a sorceress and purveyor of charms, magical incantations and love potions. She told of several visits from Sarah Althea:

> She had been to other fortune tellers, she said, and got some stuff which she gave the senator, and it seemed to make him sick at his stomach. She was afraid it was too strong. I told her she should bring me some of it and she did so in a black bottle. It smelled awful strong. . . . When she came next time I gave her a love draught. . . . Nine drops of molasses, nine pinches of sugar, and the balance of the vial I filled with black tea. I directed her to give the senator a spoonful three times a day, or as often as she pleased, until it worked on him — the more he took the more he would love her.

Laura told how Sarah Althea came back to her to complain that though she had put the aphrodisiac in the senator's whiskey, it had not worked. The seeress refused to refund the price, but she gave credit on a new talisman, a heady love philtre based on one of Sharon's socks, dipped in whiskey and worn around Sarah Althea's left knee "because the left leg is nearer the heart."

Tyler's cross-examination of Mrs. Scott elicited some of the richest testimony in the trial. He affected a deep interest in the methodology of the black witch. How did she determine what particular advice to give her patrons? "Easy," said Mrs. Scott:

> I goes into the oraculums [sic]. . . . After you gets in you [sic] oraculums, you examine them. . . . You asks the oraculum if it will have the desired effect. You get yes, or no, or so on. The oraculum said this charm would work, so I made it for her, but she said it didn't work.

Yet another black lady, one of Mammy's familiars, told of a love charm concocted by Mammy herself, the local Pythia:

> She [plaintiff] put it in the Senator's drink. I told her it was a mean dirty trick for anybody to do, but she wanted money, she said, and had to do it.

And one of Sarah Althea's lady friends described a love charm carried in a little red silk bag that the determined Allie kept in her bosom.

> She told me that she had taken a young pigeon, cut it open, took out its heart, stuck nine pins in it to dry, after which she wore it around her neck.

All these charms and blandishments failed to move the old senator. He no longer wanted any part of Sarah Althea Hill.

So ended "General" Barnes's "Magic Show." It was to be followed by Barnes's monumental folly. The trial was now in its sixth week. The interest of the press was beginning to wane. But things picked up a bit when Barnes called to the stand that prodigious rascal, William M. Nielson, a litigative decision that must have been fathered by a lawyer's death-wish. Barnes elicited that Nielson had been the plaintiff's principal advisor in bringing the divorce action. But the Australian was not a lawyer; how then could he have presumed to advise the lady? "Oh," said Nielson, "I was acting on the advice of one of the city's most prominent lawyers," the barrister he had himself selected to represent Sarah Althea in the contemplated legal proceedings.

Barnes: *Who selected the lawyer to make this fight?*

Nielson: *I did. Don't you want to know who I selected?*

Barnes: *You can state if you like.*

Nielson: *You.*

The newspapers record that Barnes reacted "as if struck with a hatchet." He sputtered and stammered. His normal courtroom aplomb dissolved.

An audible laugh followed a moment's silence after the answer, and everybody looked at the General, who perspired very freely, and blushed a rosy red. Then he flung down the documents he had in his hand.

Nielson went on to relate a street-corner conversation with Barnes in the early part of the year, before the commencement of any proceeding. First, he said, he had asked Barnes if he would be "available" to handle a divorce suit "for a friend." When Barnes, in the manner of lawyers through the ages, affirmed his availability, Nielson said he told him the whole story, including the names of the prospective parties and the substance of the contract. Barnes could not have foretold that before long he would be tapped by the great Choate for the lucrative professional task of defending Sharon. He was ready to grab the first client who came along, so he had opined that there was a good case against Sharon. There were two more meetings on the subject between Nielson and Barnes, during which Barnes, still unfeed by either party, examined the marriage contract, expressed the view that the case was a good one, should be brought promptly, and expressed his eagerness to lead Sarah Althea's crusade: "There is nothing would please me better than to go after the old rascal!" With this testimony, the gentlemen of the press discerned an exchange of cool glances between Barnes and his startled client. When court recessed, Barnes held a press conference in the corridor to announce that "there was not a word of truth in it as far as he was concerned or implicated." But the senator was observed in the corridor, talking to himself.

Sharon, at the time of the trial and shortly before his death

XXVII

THE DEFENSE: ACT TWO

Byblis in exemplo est, ut ament concessa puellae.
(Byblis is a warning that girls should not love unlawfully.)
Ovid, *Metamorphoses*

Henry C. Hyde, a local lawyer who made a specialty of examining questioned documents, was the principal handwriting expert for the defense. While Hyde examined Sarah Althea's written exhibits under a magnifying glass, Sarah Althea expressed her alarm lest the rays of light projected through powerful glass injure the surfaces of her "honor." Hyde now testified that the word "Wife" in the "Dear Wife" letters was not in Sharon's hand; that the words "Wm. Sharon, Nevada, August 25, 1880" were written by the senator, but that the body of the contract, admittedly in Sarah Althea's hand, was written at a much later time. Hyde's testimony was supported by a second expert, George C. Hickox. To the press, the trial slipped into the doldrums during the many days of handwriting testimony. There was no sensational copy in the maunderings of the experts.

Things again picked up a bit when Barnes started recalling for further cross-examination some of the plaintiff's early witnesses. Martha Wilson now admitted that her previous testimony was false. As she recanted, she "was seized with hysteria . . . that required the united efforts of her husband and other friends to check a flood of tears that threatened to swamp the courthouse." She confessed she had been promised $5,000 by Sarah Althea to say she had seen the contract in 1880. The story, she said, was "gotten up" by the plaintiff, Nellie Brackett and Vesta Snow. In a tone that forbade all trifling, Judge Sullivan asked, "Madam, did you expect a reward for your testimony?" "Yes, sir," answered the weeping witness.

The next penitent was Harry Wells who recanted the story about the meeting on Montgomery Street, when Sharon was supposed to have introduced Sarah Althea as "Mrs. Sharon." Tyler, he said, had told him "that there was enough in the case to make twenty men millionaires and he was going to have his share. . . . You and Mr. True, if we win this case, shall be placed beyond all possible want in this world." As he admitted his previous perjury, Wells "broke down and cried like a baby . . . burying his face in his hands he bowed his form over the table nearest and fairly howled out his grief at the shame of his sin."

"TIME! FOR THE WIND UP."

"Time! For the Wind Up."—from the Wasp

On May 13, the first day of the tenth week of the trial, the proceedings were animated by Sarah Althea's attack on Barnes with her trusty parasol. She threatened to "cowhide" him if he opened his mouth to her! At Sullivan's direction, Wells and Martha Wilson were formally charged with perjury and removed to the county jail.

The session of May 17 provided more high comedy. The plaintiff's "countenance was indicative of great good humour." She told reporters that she had heard a jolly story about her appealing to the court for an order allowing her to see her children once a week. By "her children," she explained, she meant Fred Sharon, son of the senator, and Frank Newlands, his son-in-law. Her merriment was stimulated because she was told that an acquaintance had asked Mr. Newlands if he wanted to see his "mamma" once a week and he replied that he would be damned if he did.

May 27 brought the "long-looked-for moment" when Sharon took the stand. His testimony stands out as straightforward and credible. When the stenographers had difficulty in hearing him the old man apologized. He was not wearing his teeth. Sly old Tyler observed loudly that "the prosecution could wait until the senator put his teeth in." This drew a sharp reprimand from the judge who directed Tyler to "refrain from insulting the witness."

Sharon began by describing that first vision of delight, when first he espied the plaintiff in the spring of 1880, seated in a buggy at the Belmont railroad station — a successful ambuscade laid by the master tactician, Mammy Pleasant, who even provided the buggy! There ensued a series of visits by Sarah Althea to his office "to seek financial advice." There were a few chaste dinners and soon Sharon visited her room at the Baldwin. After several meetings, he made her a proposal:

> *I offered her $250 a month to be my mistress. She refused, and in an instant I had offered her $500 a month . . . and she crawled into my bed.*

Sharon admitted the validity of the "Dear Wife" notes — all but the words "Dear Wife," which, he said, were forgeries. The marriage contract he denounced as a complete fabrication.

Barnes then led him through all the details of the intimacies. Sharon said that of course, he let her use his carriage a few times. He took her to Belmont, but there was always a chaperone. From the fall of 1880, she spent many nights with him at the Grand. Questioned about the "choking" episode, he said:

> *She climbed through the transom into my room, by breaking the iron catch. I was very ill at the time and she annoyed me and made me nervous by walking up and down, and I said to her: "I wish you would break your damned neck." I spoke calmly to her and told her to go out of the room. She would not, and I took hold of her and pushed her into an adjoining room. She lay on the floor and I told her not to carry on like that or I would send for the watchman. She still lay there and I took a pitcher of cold water and poured it over her and told her to get up and lie on the bed.*
>
> Barnes: *Did you ever say to Miss Hill that if she would let you live with her you would give her a thousand dollars a month and your daughter's white horse?*

Sharon: *Nothing of the kind ever occurred. I offered her five hundred dollars a month to live with me, and she accepted it.*

Barnes: *What about the offer of a settlement?*

Sharon: *She came into my room in November 1881 after we had had some talk of a settlement. I told her I wanted to settle with her, and did not want her to visit my rooms any more, as her conduct had been offensive to me. I offered to pay her $5,000, and she said that would not do; that she wanted $10,000. I said I would not give her $10,000 but would give her $7,500.*

Sharon next described how, after rejecting all of Sarah Althea's attempts to restore herself to her former position, he encountered the lady and her two champions, Nielson and young Rodney, in the lobby of the Palace. Nielson demanded money from him and the old man advanced on him and loudly told him to get out, and accused him of being a cheap blackmailer.

Barnes: *Was there anything said about her being your "lawful wedded wife?"*

Sharon: *Never at any time. That story is a pure fabrication. . . . The word "wife" was never mentioned between us.*

Sharon finished his direct testimony by describing how, after he discovered that Sarah Althea was picking his pockets as he slept, he determined to get rid of her. She told him that she had decided to "go East and study for the stage." It was then that Sharon offered her $5,000 "to go peacefully." She demanded $10,000 and they compromised on $7,500. She wrote out a receipt in full but he charged that she later stole the receipt. He had accused her of stealing the paper: "You dirty whore, you stole the receipt." At this, the lady fled.

With this, he was turned over to Tyler for cross-examination. Tyler played it hard for laughs:

Tyler: *Did you sing "Auld Lang Syne" to her?*

Sharon: *I don't think I did.*

Tyler: *You do sing "Auld Lang Syne," don't you?*

Sharon: *Sometimes I hum a few bars for my own amusement. I do not think I sang to her.*

Tyler: *How about "Maid of Athens, Ere We Part," — do you sing that?*

Sharon: *No sir, I sometimes quote "The Maid," but I don't sing it.*

The reporters agreed that this exchange "kept the courtroom perfectly convulsed."

The cross-examination reached new heights of entertainment when Tyler asked Sharon:

Mr. Sharon, have you in the past five or six years had any other mistress that you paid by the month or otherwise?

The chivalrous Barnes objected to this question on the ground that it would lead to "dragging the names of other women into the case and destroying them in the eyes of the world." Terry, always aroused by the subject of chivalry, explained to the court that the object of the inquiry was to show that Sharon "was a man who was habitually free with women, using his wealth to debauch them." This demonstration, he urged, would fortify the theory of the prosecution that "the defendant had found his gold useless in corrupting the plaintiff and had signed the marriage contract to overcome her scruples." A bitter wrangle among the lawyers was concluded with a stipulation that "the defendant had meretricious relations with many women" and that "he had not treated them with the consideration he had the plaintiff."

"That is all," said Tyler, to the relief of everybody concerned. At this, Judge Sullivan adjourned the trial for almost two months. There was "a general packing of pencils and papers and law books and everybody bade everybody else goodbye in high good humour."

There was one little hitch in the general *bonhomie:* Sharon had admitted that there was still $750 due on the promissory note he had given to dear Allie. On the day following the adjournment, she sued him for the $750.

THE WASP.

A FELLOW-FEELING MAKES THESE TWO OF A KIND.

"A Fellow-feeling Makes These Two of a Kind"—William Sharon and E. S. "Lucky" Baldwin at sea over marital woes, as seen by the Wasp

XXVIII

THE END OF THE TRIAL

In all the woes that curse our race
There is a woman in the case!

W. S. Gilbert, *Fallen Fairies*

With the trial adjourned for the summer, the gladiators of both sides rested from the struggle and made plans for its renewal. Sharon took advantage of the respite to journey to Chicago to attend the Republican National Convention. Now, the press of the nation enjoyed the privilege thus far confined to California journalists; they could personally interview the notorious old libertine. He regaled several press conferences with his observations on the lady and the trial, on the institution of marriage, the law and the state of the nation. He even recited "Maid of Athens" for the reporters. His declamations were so heavily larded with quotations from Byron, Pope, Burns and other bards, that the press pronounced him a combination of Lothario and Dean Swift. In an interview with a New York reporter he said that while he had been a steadfast Republican for many years, he had reservations about the candidacy of Blaine. "Now, if the Democrats had sense enough to nominate Justice Field," he said, "a man highly regarded in California, they might beat Blaine." Back in San Francisco, Sarah Althea gave her own interviews, replete with allusions to her "honor"; she adamantly rejected any thought of settlement; indeed, she would spurn any settlement that did not include a public acknowledgment that she was the lawful wedded wife of Senator Sharon.

When the trial resumed at the end of summer, there was more handwriting testimony and the superior mettle on the defense side began to be felt. Nellie Brackett's devotion to Sarah Althea grew dimmer, a process that everybody understood when it was learned her father had received a $3,000 check from Sharon through "General" Barnes; and Little Nell's testimony about the love philtre was seen as "very damaging" to Sarah Althea. One of Mammy Pleasant's erstwhile retainers admitted she had lied when she said the marriage contract was shown to her two years before the trial; she admitted that her first sight of the critical document was on the eve of the trial.

Tyler made a feeble effort to rebut the expert handwriting testimony adduced by the defendant. He brought on a seventy-seven-year-old dotard who professed to be a "handwriting expert," whose expertise derived from "experience": When a lad of seventeen, he had taken a counterfeit bill at a store where he was employed as a clerk and resolved never to be so taken in again. He studied counterfeits and handwriting with that idea in view and had never been taken in since. Sullivan accepted this as establishing his expertise, and permitted him to testify. He averred that to his practiced eye the marriage contract bore Sharon's signature.

Tyler's next handwriting witness, Max Gumpel, proved neither feeble nor naive. His appearance caused a murmur of surprise, as it was well known that Gumpel had been called and sworn for the defense. After several days' examination of the documents, Gumpel had announced that he was not ready to testify and had not been heard of in the case since. Gumpel was now in the position of testifying for the prosecution at the expense of the defense. Barnes had conceded that he was qualified; how could he not, since he had hired him? Later revelations would establish Gumpel as one of the most sinister characters in the whole drama. For the moment, he expressed the opinion that the signature on the marriage contract was indeed that of Sharon as were the words "Nevada, Aug. 25, 1880." He found the "Dear Wife" letters genuine. We shall hear more of Mr. Gumpel.

There was still more melodrama before the lawyers made their closing arguments. The defendant called one Gustav Nowitzki who described himself as Nielson's "bodyguard." He testified to a conversation with Sarah Althea in which she asked him, "Would you like to make $100,000 by killing Mr. Sharon for he does not treat me right?" This drew from Tyler the cynical comment:

> Does the defense wish to state that the plaintiff was such a fool as to kill the goose that laid the golden egg?

Nowitzki admitted he thought she was joking.

When both sides rested on August 5, one Oscar T. Shuck, "a lawyer and journalist," announced to the press that he had composed "a sensational comic drama founded on the Sharon divorce trial." Its title: "Wife or Mistress: or Althea's Dream." He had selected Sarah Althea to play the lead, but the piece was never produced. Some real-life drama was to come.

On August 16, 1884, while the lawyers were making their closing statements to Judge Sullivan, Nielson published a bombshell in both local gazettes, the *Chronicle* and the *Daily Alta*. He wrote letters to the editors that, with appropriate allowance for Nielson's reflexive mendacity, exposed some of the mysteries in the case. He had split with Sarah Althea, and now he revealed that she had confessed to him that the "Dear Wife" letters had been fraudulently altered. He told how Sarah Althea's living expenses and costs of litigation were being paid by Tyler and Mammy Pleasant; he described many scenes of bitter quarreling between Sarah Althea and her supporters; how Judge Terry had supplanted him as the court favorite. Terry had applied some strong words to Nielson. The Australian ended his letters with words that were tragically prophetic: "I have too great respect for Judge Terry to reply to him. He will one day better understand his present surroundings and will then be on a plane on which he can discuss the subject without blind bias." Sarah Althea promptly sued the *Alta* — this time for libel for printing Nielson's letter.

On August 13, the court began to hear closing arguments in an oratorical cascade that went on for weeks. Tyler spoke for eighteen hours. Somehow, the character of Mammy Pleasant fascinated all the lawyers, and they spoke of her almost as much as they did about the "Dear Wife" letters and the marriage contract.

Tyler saw her as a ministering angel:

They utterly failed in their threats to injure Mrs. Pleasant's character. I have known that colored woman for thirty years, and I would ten thousand times rather have her chance with St. Peter before the Pearly Gates than the chance of such a moral leper and debauchee as Mr. Sharon. If he should have his thirty millions buried with him it would have no effect on old St. Peter and I would not be surprised if one day I saw that good old colored lady . . . sending down a cup of cool water to the parched lips of the men who have tried to traduce her.

To Barnes, Mammy was a black Messalina:

It is a most remarkable circumstance that [Sarah Althea] should have selected Mrs. Pleasant for her confidence — quite as remarkable as that she should have selected Martha Wilson, the Negro woman. Will anybody tell me why it was that during all this time this unfortunate woman never confided the secret of her marriage to one single respectable person of her own color or class in life? . . . If we find her living in such associations, and bringing from that class of people the only support of this miserable and wretched claim, there is but one conclusion to come to, and that there had been in her behalf deliberate, wilful and corrupt perjury.

Barnes flayed Sarah Althea with his scorn. He described in detail her conduct as the "bride" of the old senator, gallivanting around with other men, going to "disreputable resorts" and returning in the small hours, comparing her to Mary Magdalene. He concluded with a cruel shaft at Terry:

Why that woman had just as much, in fact just the same idea of being the wife of Senator Sharon at that time, as she has of now being married to Judge Terry [laughter]. There never was such a creature on the face of the earth. I know Judge Terry laughs and shakes with mirth at my idea of her. He has been laughing and playing with her during the whole progress of this trial. He probably knows her better than I do, but my impression is what I state, and underneath that smile of hers is the consciousness of guilt, and there it will remain, divorce or no divorce, as long as her wretched life is spared.

Terry needed only a few hours for his reply to Barnes. He found in Mammy Pleasant's devotion to the plaintiff an occasion to proclaim his special love and affection for the entire Negro race. He pointed out that Sarah Althea had spent her entire childhood in a slave state. What then was so unnatural about her intimacy with Mammy Pleasant? The old champion of Negro slavery, the advocate of the revival of the slave trade brought tears to the eyes of some of his hearers (and a sneer to the lips of others) when he explained:

We who have drawn our sustenance from black breasts, we who have gone to our colored nurses for relief from every childish affliction,

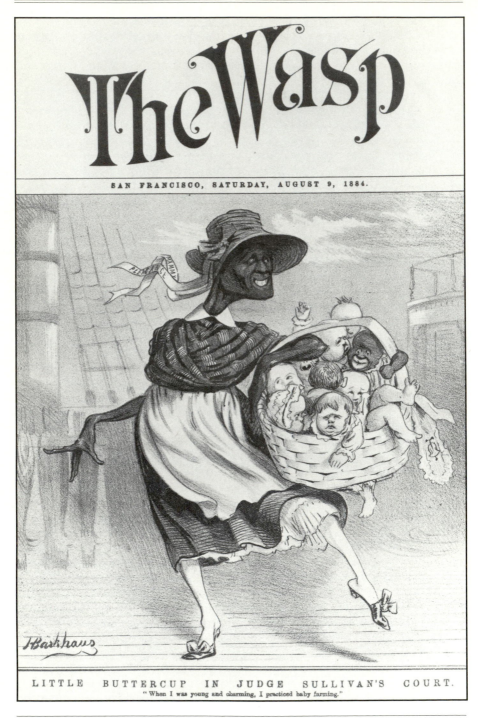

"Little Buttercup in Judge Sullivan's Court," from the Wasp

we who have looked upon them as second parents, know that the friendship and respect for them continues. . . . We know how staunch and true they are — faithful even to death. I am one who possesses this knowledge of the character of the colored "mammies" of my youth, and the plaintiff is another.

Terry closed the arguments of counsel with a stirring peroration: "She goes from this courtroom either vindicated as an honest and virtuous wife or branded as an adventuress, a blackmailer, a perjurer and a harlot."

To objective observers the case against Sharon seemed fragile. It looked like a blackmail attempt that had fallen apart. Most of the city's quidnuncs expected Judge Sullivan to throw it out of court. And on Christmas Eve, Judge Sullivan presented Sarah Althea with the richest of presents!

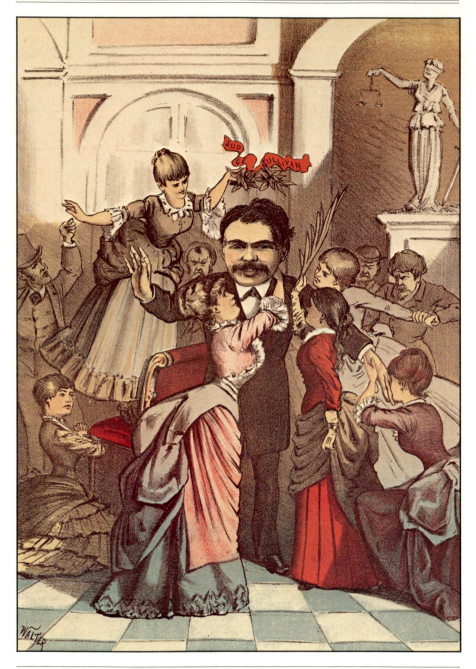

Judge Sullivan as ''The Pet of the Sex,'' from the Wasp

XXIX

MADAM SENATOR SHARON

Widowed wife and married maid,
Betrothed, betrayer, and betrayed.
Sir Walter Scott, *The Betrothed*

On the day before Christmas, 1884, combatants and commentators gathered in Sullivan's courtroom to hear him pronounce his judgment. First Judge Sullivan announced that to him the case was "disgusting beyond description . . . a mess of perjury." He rejected all the oral testimony on both sides. But by some feat of judicial sortilege he accepted the "Dear Wife" letters as genuine and concluded that the marriage contract was valid. Sarah Althea, he found, was "entitled to a decree of divorce on the grounds of wilful desertion and a division of the common property." He awarded $2,500 per month as alimony and $55,000 for counsel fees.

Sullivan's opinion is a masterpiece of contradictions. To find for Sarah Althea, as he did, he had to accept her testimony as credible. Yet he unequivocally brands her as a perjurer, a suborner of perjury and a forger of critical documents. Of Sarah Althea's testimony that Sharon had introduced her to social acquaintances as his wife, he found this testimony to be directly contradicted and "in my judgment her testimony is wilfully false." Of her testimony that shortly after she became Sharon's "wife," the old man gave her $7,500, the judge says: "False. No such advance was ever made." Of the most critical document, the alleged marriage contract, he says:

> Among the objections suggested to this paper as appearing on its face, was one made by counsel that the signature was evidently a forgery. The matters recited in the paper are, in my judgment, at variance with the facts it purports to recite. Considering the stubborn manner in which the production of this paper was at first resisted and the mysterious manner of its disappearance, I am inclined to regard it in the light of one of the fabrications for the purpose of bolstering up plaintiff's case. I can view the paper in no other light than as a fabrication.

Indeed, he made a general charge of perjury against the plaintiff, that her testimony was fabricated:

> I am of the opinion that to some extent plaintiff has availed herself of the aid of false testimony for the purpose of giving her case a better

appearance in the eyes of the court, but sometimes parties have been known to resort to false testimony, where in their judgment it would assist them in prosecuting a lawful claim. As I understand the facts of this case, that was done in this instance.

But by some bizarre process Sullivan found that the perjury pervading the plaintiff's case was offset because Sharon was a "malevolent," a "libertine" . . . possessed of strong animal passions that from excessive indulgence, had become unaccustomed to restraint. He may have regarded as a "trifle, light as air, the miserable bit of paper behind which a weak woman could shelter her virginity and her claim to a standing in the community." So, in a case that depended uniquely on the quality and credibility of the plaintiff's oral testimony, he found in favor of the perjurer.

Sullivan placed great reliance on the testimony of Gumpel: he was a witness called first by the defendant, "he came into court fully accredited; his competence is unquestioned . . . entitled to great weight." When the judge concluded with the pronouncement that the marriage contract was genuine, Sarah Althea "almost exploded with joy. There came a little smile and then she leaned over the green plaid shawl and gave a single sob." Sullivan found her to be the lawful wife of Sharon, granted her a divorce and ordered the appointment of a referee to supervise the division of Sharon's property.

Judge Sullivan's attitude throughout the trial made it manifest that he loathed both parties and the task of being the arbiter of their sordid differences. He tried manfully to preserve a judicial mien, but the cognoscenti in the courtroom understood he was seeking the easiest way out. When the little judge finished reading his opinion, which ruled "that William Sharon by virtue of his secret contract of marriage has become and now is the husband of Sarah Althea, that he has been guilty of wilfully abandoning his wife" and awarded alimony and a division of the common property, the city was shocked.

Before the last words had passed the judge's lips, there was a scene of wild rejoicing in the courtroom! Congratulatory embraces were exchanged between client and lawyers, between Sarah Althea and her faithful retinue! The air was filled with exultation! Sarah Althea Hill or — by the grace of God and of the Superior Court of the County of San Francisco — Mrs. William Sharon, was transported from the scene on the perfumed zephyrs of victory. Of course, the victory was enormously popular with sections of the press and public. The lovely forlorn girl, a bit shopworn, a bit shabby to be sure, had bested the Bonanza King, with all his millions, all his legions of lawyers. King Cophetua had booted the beggar maid from his bed, and she had made him pay a heavy price. All over the land, the decision was hailed as a triumph for underdogs, as proof that in America, at least, wealth and rank did not always prevail over virtue and justice. There was wide editorial comment that only in the land of the free and the brave could a lady so vilely used get her just deserts from a rich voluptuary. No longer was she a *poule de luxe;* she was a Bonanza Queen, duly certified by California's courts! Some sympathetic journalists remarked on the judge's propitious timing. How fitting to bestow this richly-earned gift on the very eve of Christmas!

But there were some important happenings in 1885 that kept Sarah Althea from enjoying the fruits of Judge Sullivan's Christmas present. The old senator had been in failing health at the trial; now, under the hammer blows

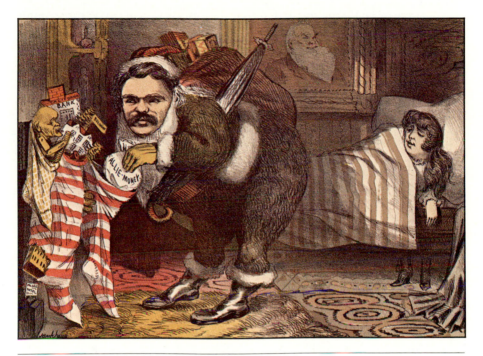

"Mrs. Sharon's Santa Claus," from the Wasp

of defeat and humiliation, he began to show signs of final senescence. He had suffered his share of "litigious terms, fat contentions and flowing fees." He immured himself in his room at the Palace — no poker, no girls and very little business. Only the faithful Chinese, Ki, was in constant attendance; even son Fred and son-in-law Francis Newlands found it hard to see him. Those who did penetrate the sanctum saw a hollow man — a man consumed by ill health, the loss of his daughter and the ravages of Sarah Althea's lawsuit. Ambrose Bierce had the Sharon-Hill litigation in mind when, in his *Devil's Dictionary*, he defined a lawsuit as "a machine which you go into as a pig and come out as a sausage." The old man sensed that the end was near. Even more bitter than the medicine Ki poured into him was the realization that, unless the federal courts stripped Allie of her disguises and threw out the contract, half of the millions he had amassed would go to the tart! And half of that would go to her jackal lawyers! Wryly, the dying man would relate to the few reporters who gained access to him that Miss Hill was "the highest-paid whore in history." "Why," he said, "the *grandes horizontales* of Paris are cheapskates compared to her. I hear they charge a thousand francs a night. That's chicken feed! If Allie wins out, she'll be netting about a hundred and fifty thousand for every roll in the hay. That's better than Cleopatra did!" But the drollery disappeared as the old man sensed the approach of death. He became deadly serious. On November 5, 1885, he issued a release to the press, a Parthian shaft that found its target only after he was gone:

> *I am exceedingly weak in body and suffer great physical pain, but my mind is perfectly clear. In this condition I declare that I never proposed or offered marriage to Sarah Althea Hill at any time or in any form. . . . The alleged contract of marriage . . . is a forgery. I never signed it or any other document of that nature or import. I never addressed her as my wife in any communication, and the letters produced by Miss Hill, which so address her, are, so far as the word wife is concerned, one and all willful forgeries. Her declarations under oath that I ever married her, ever signed the pretended marriage contract, or wrote her the "Dear Wife" letters . . . are all and singly willful perjuries. I have resisted her false claim to wifehood as in duty bound to myself, my family and society. . . . I have directed those upon whom representation of me or of my estate devolves to contest her pretension in every legal and proper manner.*

Ten days later he was dead, at sixty-four. On the news of his death, Ambrose Bierce is reported to have said: "Death is not the end; there remains the litigation over the Estate."

But before the old senator died, there was some heavy skirmishing. Barnes and his battalions moved for a new trial. They filed affidavits of bellboys, porters and chambermaids of the Baldwin Hotel — where Sarah Althea lived before moving into the Grand — "reflecting on [her] virtue and morality," trying to brand her as "an unchaste and immoral woman." Some of the affidavits referred to frequent visits from Reuben Lloyd, leading to "the inference that improper relations existed between him and me." Sarah Althea met these "vile, wicked and most infamous falsehoods" in her most furious style. She had poor Terry, by now hopelessly under her spell, address a letter to Lloyd imploring him to refute these "slanders." "You are a Mason, Mrs.

Sharon is the daughter of a Mason. Are you not obliged to protect a Mason's daughter from slander?" Lloyd ignored both letters, and on May 23, 1885, Sarah aimed a broadside at her old lover. She published a document entitled "Mrs. Wm. Sharon vs. Reuben H. Lloyd." It was addressed to "the members of the Masonic Fraternity and I.O.O.F. in San Francisco, Cal. and throughout the State." She recounts Lloyd's reluctance to certify her respectability and implores their aid in "inducing Mr. Lloyd to do his duty." She does not furnish any instructions as to how this was to be done.

Sharon's will divided his estate one-third to son Fred, one-third to his surviving daughter, Lady Fermor-Hesketh, and one-third to be divided among Newlands and his three daughters. Fred Sharon and Francis Newlands were named executors, but Newlands renounced and Fred took charge, with Newlands as chief counsel for the estate. Too late for Sharon, but within weeks of his death, the federal cavalry came charging over the hill! On December 26, 1885, the United States Circuit Court handed down a decision that changed everything. For Sarah Althea, for Terry and Tyler and all their supporters, things would never be the same after the sounding of the federal trumpets.

However, on Christmas Eve, 1884, Sarah Althea rushed from the courthouse with her cortege of well-wishers; gifts must be purchased for those who had sustained her, who had stood with her through the fiery ordeal. She went from shop to shop, purchasing little tokens of gratitude. She played to the hilt her new role of Lady Bountiful. When one shopkeeper inquired about the manner of payment, she regarded him with the special hauteur of the half-mad, the indignation of the manic. "Charge it!" she said, "Charge it to Mrs. William Sharon! That's the senator, you know!" And since most of them did know of her good fortune, the gifts were charged and delivered in time for Christmas. In Allie's mind, all was well. She was Queen of the Land of Ophir, and all its gold and silver, the ivory, the apes and peacocks were hers. She could forget now the groveling, the humiliations and the indignities, the terror of poverty and need that drove her to fabricating the marriage contract, the felonious alteration of the "Dear Wife" letters. Until the old man died, she would somehow manage on a mere $2,500 a month, and then his millions would pour in on her.

Immediately after the decision Tyler filed with the court his written "fee" agreement with the plaintiff. Its terms gave some pause to the journalists. Under the agreement Tyler was to advance all the costs of the litigation — "and as compensation he is to receive one-half of all sums realized or secured to her by such litigation." The agreement also recognized W. M. Nielson as Sarah Althea's "agent."

Even the journalists saw in this document a most troublesome point. It states that Tyler was hired to "litigate a marriage contract entered into about three years ago." The "marriage contract," the celebrated Plaintiff's Exhibit Number One in the trial before Judge Sullivan, gives the precise date "August 25, 1880" in four different places. Was it possible that when Sarah Althea hired Tyler she had not even shown him the marriage contract with that precise date? Or that when she signed the retainer agreement she could not remember the most momentous date in her life? Why "about three years ago" when the document gives the exact date? Or that when she finally did hire Tyler (Mammy Pleasant's lawyer) for the job, she was not certain enough

Mrs. Wm. Sharon
— v s. —
Reuben H. Lloyd.

Political Record, May 23d, 1885.

ALTHEA'S APPEAL.

An Open Letter to the Masonic Fraternity.

R. H. LLOYD REFUSES TO GIVE TESTIMONY.

Manly Courage at a Discount — A Woman's Virtue Treated Lightly —More Homage to Wealth.

To the members of the Masonic Fraternity and I. O. O. F. in San Francisco, Cal., and throughout the State :

Gentlemen,—

I am a woman. the daughter of a Mason. For more than a year past I have been engaged in litigation with Ex-Senator William Sharon, who was my husband, but denied the fact, and tried to brand me as an unchaste and immoral woman.

After a long, tedious, and bitter struggle in the Courts, during which no witness testified to any act reflecting on my character for chastity, I was pronounced by the Court to be the wife of Wm. Sharon.

After a judgment was given in my favor, Mr. Sharon moved for a new trial and has filed affidavits of bell-boys, porters and chambermaids of the Baldwin Hôtel, reflecting on my virtue and morality. These affidavits were procured by the unscrupulous use of money, and are false. None of the persons who have been hired to make them, dared to take the stand as a witness on the trial, and submit to a cross examination.

Some of these affidavits connect my name with that of Mr. Reuben H. Lloyd, a member of your Order, in such a manner as without pointedly charging, would lead to the inference that improper relations existed between him and me. Mr. Lloyd knows well how utterly false such charges are.

Any right thinking man

Sarah's appeal to the Masons

of the date of the marriage contract to refer to it specifically in Tyler's retainer? Efforts to discuss these gnawing little points were airily dismissed by Sarah Althea as "pettifogging trifles."

Barnes routinely filed an appeal from Sullivan's opinion, and parties and lawyers settled in for the tedious siege-warfare of appellate litigation. Terry joined with Tyler to sue Sharon in superior court on Sarah Althea's behalf on the unpaid promissory note to pay her $2,500 "for each and every month of the year A.D. 1883." Sharon admitted making the note, but defended on the ground that the note represented payment for "past illicit cohabitation" and should not be enforced. The defense was not properly pleaded and the California Supreme Court enforced payment. Next, Tyler and Terry made a futile motion to dismiss Sharon's appeal from Judge Sullivan's decree on technical grounds.

The first real battle of the siege came when the lawyers for the new Madam Senator challenged on constitutional grounds the right of the California Supreme Court even to hear an appeal in a divorce case. In a long opinion that reached back to Justinian, the case of *Praemunire,* decisions in the reign of Richard II, and a legal text published in 1649, a split court arrived at a pragmatic Solomonic decision. The most harmful part of the decision, to Sarah Althea and her lawyers, was that the court stayed all proceedings in the case until the appeal could be determined. That meant that neither she nor her lawyers would get any money . . . yet. Not yet would the quinqueremes of Nineveh row home from Sarah Althea's Ophir with their rich cargoes.

Tyler, Jr. faces the redoubtable Field

XXX

SHARON v. HILL: THE FEDERAL CASE

*A community which allows the integrity of the family, the
cornerstone of society, to rest on no better foundation than
a union of the sexes, evidenced only by a secret writing, and
unaccompanied by any public recognition or assumption of marital
duties except furtive intercourse befitting a brothel, ought to
remove the cross from its banner and symbols and replace it with
a crescent.*

Judge Matthew Deady, in *Sharon* v. *Hill,* 36 Fed. 337

To understand the bombshell that the federal court would now drop into Sarah Althea's dream world, we must go back to the beginning of the litigation. Almost as Tyler filed his complaint for divorce in the California state court on October 3, 1883, Barnes sued for Sharon in the federal court in San Francisco to have the marriage contract declared false and fraudulent, to cancel and annul it, and to enjoin Sarah Althea from using it.

As we have seen, when the state court action began, Sharon rushed East to get some legal help. He first consulted his friend, Senator Stewart of Nevada, whose legal talents he esteemed highly. Then he discussed the matter with his friend (and tenant at the Palace Hotel) Stephen J. Field, who sent him to Choate, who sent him to Barnes. It has been said, without any attribution of authority, that "Field had told Sharon to bring an action in the federal court in San Francisco *where the troublesome young woman would be taken care of.*" (The italics are mine.) No reliable evidence to support this startling averral can be found, but the probabilities that it occurred are impressive. Even by the flexible standards of that time, Field was as lax and perfunctory as his colleague Sawyer in assessing his qualification to judge particular cases where he had relationships with interested parties. When we consider that a federal case in San Francisco would almost certainly come before Field, *qua* circuit judge — as indeed it did — the allegation that Sharon discussed his case with Field is startling. Field seldom shrank from judging cases in which some of the interested parties and their counsel were personal intimates. But to judge a case he had himself nurtured and in which he had helped to select counsel would be the ultimate in judicial arrogance. In a sense, it would have made Sharon's case his own. Even the most flexible interpretation of Coke's maxim, *Nemo debet esse judex in propria causa,* should have moved Field later to disqualify himself, to "recuse." Instead, when *Sharon* v. *Hill* came to his court, he reached for it with eagerness.

Whether or not Field advised Sharon as to the institution of the federal action, his personal relations with Sharon, with Newlands and members of their families, and his long-time occupancy of a suite at the Palace should have impelled him to keep his hands off the case. But then, through his life Field demonstrated that rules applicable to other men — even other judges — did not reach to him. He saw himself as an Olympian who made his own rules.

Federal jurisdiction over *Sharon* v. *Hill* derived from diversity of citizenship, i.e., Sharon, a citizen of Nevada, sued Hill, a citizen of California. When the federal action was brought, Tyler moved promptly but unsuccessfully to dismiss it on the ground that Sharon's averral of Nevada citizenship was false. His motion was denied by Sawyer, and on January 9, 1885, the federal court designated an "Examiner in Chancery" to hear the evidence and report to the court. The examiner was S. C. Houghton, a San Francisco lawyer, colorless but thorough, diffident but firm. Houghton toiled assiduously from February 5, 1885, to August 11, 1885, to get all the facts. Poor Houghton! His task was not easy. When he directed Sarah Althea to produce the marriage contract and the "Dear Wife" letters for inspection by Sharon's experts, she defied him. These precious documents — exemplifying her "honor" — had already been too much handled. Further examination might damage them irreparably and she could not "trust" the federal court.

For this contumacy, Judge Sawyer ordered her to jail. After enjoying a day's sojourn in the local lockup, the lady capitulated. She complied with Houghton's order, produced the papers, and was permitted to depart the Broadway jail in a splendid barouche provided by Mammy Pleasant. As she left the jail, she threw flowers to the little crowd that witnessed her departure and utilized the occasion for a touching speech to her admirers in which she modestly compared herself to Joan of Arc, Mary Queen of Scots, Molly Pitcher and other heroic females. She admonished the "Good People of California" to stand up for their rights, as she had done, "no matter what you may suffer."

The evidence adduced before Houghton covered 1,731 pages of legal cap written, as the court later noted, "with a typewriter." There were hundreds of exhibits. Of course, Sarah Althea transformed the proceedings into a combination of harlequinade and passion play.

But as the federal case got started, there was a characteristically comic interlude in Judge Sullivan's court. It was no secret that Sharon had empowered Barnes to spend large sums for investigators to try to establish the perjuries in Sarah Althea's case. Chief of the investigators was Police Captain W. I. Lees, who saw himself as the relentless Javert of Barnes's staff, but acted more like the bumbling police detectives of the Sherlock Holmes stories. Even to the laity, it was plain that Sarah Althea's victory in the state court reposed squarely on Gumpel's testimony that the marriage contract had been signed by Sharon. Gumpel had presented himself to Judge Sullivan as an expert witness first selected by Barnes, but whose inexorable probity required him to reject employment on Sharon's side and to come forward as a witness for the prosecution. Gumpel fortified his apparent integrity with Sullivan when he denied under oath that he had even discussed his testimony with Tyler; he had recoiled in indignant horror from the suggestion that he had any monetary interest in the plaintiff's case. Now Captain Lees had uncovered a piece of paper signed "M. Gumpel" and "George W. Tyler" dated months before

Gumpel gave testimony favorable to Sarah Althea, that he would be paid $25,000 by Tyler out of the proceeds of the case.

Such a document, if genuine, would brand both Gumpel and Tyler as perjurers; it would require immediate reversal of Judge Sullivan's decision and the inevitable disbarment of Tyler. Barnes could not wait to put this petard into the air. His chance came in early 1885, as the Christmas festivities ended and the echoes of the victory celebration were dying down. Sullivan had ordered a hearing during the first week of January to deal with the application of the triumphant heroine for alimony and counsel fees. When court opened, Tyler had hardly uttered a word in support of the application when Barnes leaped to his feet:

"Your Honor," he shouted (with what was recorded as "a demonic gleam" in his eye),

I interrupt to advise this Court that it has been the victim of an infernal villainy! I hold in my hand (brandishing a paper) documentary evidence of perjury and collusion not only countenanced by but actively participated in by Mr. Tyler.

He read to the court the paper discovered by Lees. To the astonishment of the press, Tyler gave no appearance of fright or consternation; he was amused by the charge; indeed, he was convulsed with laughter! For good reason: Lees and Barnes had been tricked into paying $25,000 of Sharon's money to one John McLaughlin, a clerk in Tyler's office, to turn over to them a faked document, actually manufactured by the ineffable Mr. Gumpel. Sharon was so furious that his aides should prove so gullible, that he deducted the $25,000 from Barnes's fee. In the end it was clear to all that the McLaughlin paper was a hoax, intended — impishly or maliciously — to humiliate Barnes. The local bar association appointed a committee to study and report on the conduct of the lawyers in the case. The lucky McLaughlin disappeared, taking Sharon's $25,000 with him. From this moment Barnes lost the confidence of his client. But for his humiliation he would soon exact a heavy price from Tyler.

By February, the hullabaloo over the spurious contract had subsided; Judge Sullivan awarded alimony of $2,500 per month to Sarah Althea, and $55,000 in counsel fees to her battery of lawyers. He also appointed a referee to fix the amount of community property that would be apportioned between Sarah Althea and the senator. The season of comedy ended with an indictment of Gumpel, Tyler and McLaughlin for obtaining money under false pretenses from Barnes and Lees. Local newspapers revealed that McLaughlin had been seen in Hawaii, disporting himself with the local belles and booze and Sharon's money. They also reported that when arraigned on their indictment, Tyler and Gumpel were released on bail provided by the ubiquitous Mammy Pleasant. Things became more serious as the parties settled down to the taking of testimony before Mr. Examiner Houghton. It must be understood that this was a proceeding *de novo,* i.e., as if there had never been a trial in the state court. Of course, the hearing was a replay of the trial before Judge Sullivan.

While Houghton was more skillful than Sullivan in controlling the lawyers and witnesses, no jurist was proof against Sarah Althea's obstreperous antics. On August 3, one R. W. Piper was testifying in Sharon's behalf at a session before Houghton. Piper was another handwriting expert, originally imported from Chicago by the *Alta* to testify in the libel suit brought against the newspaper by Nielson. Now he was Sharon's witness. Sarah Althea, present in the courtroom, paid no heed to the witness; she occupied herself in reading a deposition of one Susan Elizabeth Smith that contained material derogatory of Sarah Althea's character. (By now, the old senator had understandably lost confidence in Barnes; for the moment litigative strategy was in the hands of William M. Stewart. Barnes's former assistant, Evans, remained in the case as Stewart's associate counsel.) Sarah Althea interrupted the testimony of the witness, shouting loudly:

> *When I see this testimony, I feel like taking that man Stewart out and cowhiding him. I will shoot him yet; that very man sitting there. To think he would put up a woman to come here and deliberately lie about me like that. I will shoot him. They know when I say I will do it, that I will do it. I shall shoot him as sure as you live; the man that is sitting right there; and I shall have that woman, Mrs. Smith, arrested for this, and make her prove it.*

The examiner had developed some experience in dealing with Sarah Althea; he knew it needed ironbound patience. So with ironbound patience he explained: "Those are not matters which should be brought up now. Don't talk in this way when a witness is under examination."

Houghton appealed to Tyler, who, as usual, could not restrain his ebullient client.

> Sarah Althea: *I know the woman he [Stewart] is living with, and he brought his wife out here to cover up. I will expose the whole thing; about the child and all.*
>
> The Examiner: *Will you remain quiet until this examination is completed?*
>
> Sarah Althea: *I don't know whether I will remain quiet without I get that man's life. I get so worked up when I read this testimony of Mrs. Smith. . . . I can hit a four-bit piece nine times out of ten.*
>
> The Examiner: *If you interrupt the proceedings any further, I shall adjourn the examination and call the attention of the court to this matter, and it won't be my fault if the court does not take such measures as will put a stop to such interruptions.*
>
> Sarah Althea: *That is enough; you needn't say anything more.*
>
> The Examiner: *But I propose to say something more.*
>
> Sarah Althea: *All right; then I'll talk.*

And she did. She also acted. What happened next is related in the words of Houghton, reporting the incident to the court:

> *The respondent ceased speaking at this point, and the examination proceeded. In addition to the above-quoted remarks of respondent, she made further statements defamatory of the character of people not connected with the case, which remarks are deemed not necessary to be repeated in this report. The examination of the witness Piper having been concluded, Victor Craig was recalled as a witness on behalf of the complainant in rebuttal. Pending his examination, the respondent drew a pistol from her satchel and held it in her right hand, the hand resting for a moment on the table, with the weapon*

> *pointed in the direction of Judge Evans, the hand and weapon being*
> *then dropped to her lap, beneath the table. At this time Mr. Stewart*
> *had left the room. Judge Evans, noticing the action of the respondent,*
> *said: "What do you want? Do you want to shoot anybody?"*
> Sarah Althea: *I am not going to shoot you just now, unless you would*
> *like to be shot, and think you deserve it.*
> Evans: *No; I would rather not be.*
> The Examiner: *Unless you give that pistol into my custody, I shall*
> *adjourn the examination and report this matter to the court.*

Mr. Houghton thought it "proper to add that upon previous occasions respondent has brought to the examiner's room, during the examination, a pistol, and has sat for some length of time holding it in her hand, to the knowledge of all persons present at the time."

These goings-on were reported to a court that consisted of Mr. Justice Field and Judge Sawyer. Field expressed the outrage both judges felt; he directed the marshal "to disarm the defendant whenever she comes before the examiner, or into court, in any future proceedings, and to appoint an officer to keep strict surveillance over her." He then observed

> *that the block embracing this building and the custom-house is under*
> *the exclusive jurisdiction of the United States. Every offense commit-*
> *ted within it is an offense against the United States, and here the state*
> *has no jurisdiction whatever. This fact seems to have been forgotten*
> *by parties.*

Prophetic words! Mark them well.

But W. B. Tyler, son and partner of the ineffable George W. Tyler, was not satisfied to get his client off with the punishment for contempt that her conduct deserved. During the state court trial, when it was learned that arms were being brought into the courtroom, Judge Sullivan had interrupted the proceeding while lawyers, witnesses and spectators were searched for arms. At that time the press quoted Terry as saying: "I have carried no weapons since the war. I carry no weapons now, nor have I for many years."

Now, in the federal court, Tyler, Jr. persisted in forcing a colloquy that seemed trifling and silly at the time, but evoked from Field some observations that would be remembered vividly on a later day:

> *I may add here, further, that any lawyer who so far forgets his pro-*
> *fession as to come into a court of justice armed ought to be disbarred*
> *from practice. . . . Any man, counsel or witness, who comes into a*
> *court of justice armed, ought to be punished, and if he is a member*
> *of the bar, he ought to be suspended or removed permanently. . . . I*
> *trust I shall never be called to preside over a federal court where any*
> *lawyer will presume to come into it armed, and if he does, I shall*
> *exercise such authority as is vested in me to prevent it.*

Houghton's report on the evidence adduced before him was submitted to a circuit court consisting of Judges Sawyer and Matthew P. Deady. They listened to a month of argument by counsel for both sides, including extensive readings from the testimony taken before the examiner. By this time, there were some changes in the legal battalions. Only Tyler and Terry appeared for Sarah Althea. Barnes was out of things; Sharon's cohorts were now led by his first counselor, Stewart, and included son-in-law Frank

Newlands, who plainly had a large voice in the campaign.

The lull in activity was spiced by a controversy between Sarah Althea and her stalwart knight, Tyler. The temporary Madam Senator criticized Tyler for revealing the terms of his fee contract; specifically, she accused him of acting as if he would keep fifty percent of the booty, when in fact he was bound to divide it with "another person," whom the press immediately identified as Mammy Pleasant. Meanwhile, nobody was getting any of the senator's money because the Supreme Court of California had stayed all proceedings to enforce Sullivan's decree. The state court had also denied an application to interfere with the prosecution of the action in the federal court.

On December 26, 1885, that court acted through a decision written by Judge Deady, which marshaled all the evidence and destroyed Sarah Althea's hopes; it was veritable judicial Cannae. It mattered not to the court that the victor, the old senator, had been in his grave for almost two months. The newspapers observed that the old man's shouts of jubilation could be heard from the shades.

Judge Deady's opinion was a sharply-detailed and scholarly review of the evidence. It contrasts starkly with Judge Sullivan's confused and bumbling state court opinion. Deady begins with a clear announcement of the relationship between Sarah Althea and Sharon: she was his hired mistress, not his wife; her claims were rooted in perjury; her "documentary evidence" was damned as crudely fabricated and forged. Before dealing with the "Dear Wife" letters and other documents, Judge Deady commented on some of the peculiar problems of dealing with Sarah Althea as a litigant:

Item: *She refused to produce the "Dear Wife" letters until directed by court order.*

Item: *She produced only three of the five letters.*

Item: *The defendant in disregard of the order of the court, and on contumacious, frivolous and contradictory pretexts, refused to allow a particle of ink to be taken from them for examination by the expert under the microscope.*

Item: *After March 19, while study of the letters was still in progress, she refused to produce them.*

"This singular conduct," said His Honor, "can only be interpreted as an admission that such inspection would tend to prove their falsity."

The judge next turned his attention to the quality of the documentary "proof." The most important document was the alleged "marriage contract." The court reviewed in detail the expert testimony on both sides, and came to some firm conclusions:

1. *The signature was not written by Sharon.*

2. *It may have been written by Sarah Althea's "expert," Gumpel.*

3. *So far as the genuineness of the disputed writings depends on the testimony of the parties, the preponderance of the evidence is with the plaintiff (Sharon).*

On the subject of Sharon's testimony, Deady made some observations that should startle readers of our time:

Whatever deductions may be made from his credibility, on account of his participation in this transaction and interest in the result, must also be made from hers; and even more; for, in the very nature

Judge Matthew Deady

of things, this is a game in which the woman has more at stake than the man. And, however unfavorably the plaintiff's general character for chastity may be affected by the evidence in this case, it must not be forgotten that, as the world goes and is, the sin of incontinence in a man is compatible with the virtue of veracity, while in the case of a woman, common opinion is otherwise. Nor is it intended by this suggestion to palliate the conduct of the plaintiff or excuse the want of chastity in the one sex more than the other, but only, in estimating the relative value of the oath of these parties, to give the proper weight to the fact founded on common experience, that incontinence in a man does not usually imply the moral degradation and insensibility that it does in a woman.

The reader is reminded that these words were written about a century ago, and there were few in that age, men or women, who would have disputed the moral judgments or the evidentiary principles they expressed. None of the reporters commented on these reflections of the judge. He was right; as that world went and was, he was propounding views universally accepted. A man could be unchaste, a Don Juan, a voluptuary, but his veracity was unaffected by these qualities. A loose woman was another story! The word of a woman who had lapsed into any kind of sexual immorality had no worth. Here is the standard Deady applied to Sarah Althea's yarn about entrusting money to the senator for investment:

The story that some time in 1880, and prior to the date of the alleged marriage, she gave the plaintiff $7,500 to invest in stocks for her, is undoubtedly false; and she has attempted to support it, not only by perjury, but by forgery. Perceiving that the payment to her under the circumstances, of that large sum, shortly before she left the plaintiff's hotel, bore upon its face the evidence that it was given to a discarded mistress rather than a deserted wife, she deliberately swore, both in Sharon v. Sharon *and in this case, that the transaction was a return to her of that amount which she had put into the plaintiff's hands some 18 months before for investment; and not only that, but she produced on the trial in the former case, to support her statement, a writing to the effect, purporting to be signed by the plaintiff and witnessed by Nellie Brackett. But when asked, on cross-examination, to produce that paper here, she declined to do so or to answer any question about it. And Nellie Brackett swears that the writing was manufactured by defendant; that she copied the signature of the plaintiff from one in an autograph album, and that she witnessed it at the defendant's request, upon an understanding that it was only to be used to influence her lawyers.*

Judge Deady next addressed himself with surgical precision to the testimony of Sarah Althea's so-called "experts" on the authenticity of the "Dear Wife" salutation. Only Mr. Gumpel, the shifty lithographer, merited serious attention. But "his relation to the case, and his conduct as a witness therein, are both suspicious and unsatisfactory and lead [the court] to regard him and his testimony with distrust." The court found a distinct possibility that "in some respects a remarkable penman" helped fabricate the "Dear Wife" documents. The judge was impressed with the testimony of Sharon's experts, and concluded with them that Sharon's signature was probably written by Gumpel, and that the "Dear Wife" salutations were forgeries. Sarah Althea's testimony was rejected as palpably false.

On the subject of the "Dear Wife" letters, Deady wrote:

The "Dear Wife" letters have nothing wifely about them except the word "wife."... [They] are short, curt scrawls, announcing the sending of money, presumably on account of her monthly stipend of $500. ... There is not a particle of love or affection in the letters; not even enough to suggest that she was his mistress.

Judge Deady's analysis of the "marriage contract" itself was equally devastating:

It begins at the top line of the second page instead of the first one, and is finished back on the unruled space at the top of the latter. The signature of the plaintiff is on the top line of the first page, where it might have been written as an autograph or imitation, or even without any purpose; and, considered as a signature to a legal instrument, has the unusual and unmeaning appendage, "Nevada, Aug. 25, 1880"; and this, although that date, and the fact that the alleged signer was of Nevada, was already stated three times in the body of the writing. It is full of verbose formalisms and useless repetitions, and in structure and verbiage is just what might be expected from a stylish, half-educated woman, and is altogether unlike what might be expected from the dictation of a person of experience, brevity, and directness, such as the plaintiff appears to be. The last four lines are written much closer than the others, and the words contained in them are crowded together, and two of them abbreviated; and even then there was barely room for the matter without trenching on the signature after omitting certain words and parts there of — 19 in number — which were used in corresponding and foregoing parts of the instrument. ... Taking common experience and observation in such matters as a guide, the most satisfactory inference from the facts on the face of the declaration is that the body of it was written after and over the signature. ... This is not the first time in which persons engaged in an illegal or criminal transaction have strangely or foolishly, as it appears to others after the fact, omitted to take some very simple precaution to prevent the detection or failure.

Nellie Brackett swears that the soiling and crumpling process was a part of their manufacture; that the defendant wet them with coffee grounds, and ironed them, and held them over the gas, and the like, to give the new smooth paper the appearance of age and use. Ah Sam, the defendant's Chinese servant, at Laurel place, gives a very graphic account of the process. He says he lived with her "two Christmases ago," and saw her with papers in the kitchen, which she put dirt and coffee on to make them look old and yellow, and that he ironed them for her.

The defendant's answer to this evidence is that she buried the documents for safety in a tin can in the cellar, where, strange to say, they got wet, but whether from the sprinkling of the street or a shower does not appear, and she afterwards ironed them to dry and smooth

*them. But this does not account for the corners of some of them, and
particularly the upper ones of the ink letter, having the appearance
of being burned off, as though they had got singed in the gas. And the
story indicates that she then had a great deal more concern for the
safety of her "papers" than when she left them in a loose roll on the
wall behind a picture at Martha Wilson's; and, taken altogether, it
is evidently a weak invention of the defendant's in support of what
she knows to be false and forged writings. And thus one falsehood
begets another from the beginning to the end of this case.*

Most telling and impressive were the judge's inferences from the language of the letters:

*When compared with the usual and ordinary conduct of married
men and women under the circumstances, there is such incongruity
and want of harmony between the "Dear Wife" address of these letters, and the general tone and subject matter of them, that they must
be, as the plaintiff insists, and the evidence already considered is sufficient to show, at least in the one instance, the tracings of a genuine
letter, with the word "wife" substituted for "Miss Hill" or "Allie,"
and in the other genuine letters in which a like substitution has been
made.*

In the federal hearing, the same witnesses who had persuaded Sullivan
to find in favor of Sarah Althea not only fell apart — they became witnesses
for Sharon. Nellie Brackett proved to be one of Allie's worst investments.
She repudiated *in toto* the testimony she had given before Judge Sullivan,
explaining that Sarah Althea "concocted [it] in the fall of 1883, and had her
learn it by heart, and go on the stand in *Sharon v. Sharon* and swear to it."
Martha Wilson, "the poor nervous little Negro woman, born a slave, who can
neither read nor write," whose testimony at the trial before Judge Sullivan
had been so helpful to Sarah Althea, admitted in the federal case that this
testimony was false; that she saw the marriage declaration only in the fall of
1883; that Sarah Althea had induced her to swear to the falsehood "out of
sympathy and a promise of $5,000."

Judge Deady gave special attention to Mammy Pleasant:

*Mary E. Pleasant, known as Mammie Pleasant, is a conspicuous and
important figure in this affair, without whom it would probably never
have been brought before the public. She appears to be a shrewd old
negress of considerable means, who has lived in San Francisco many
years, and is engaged in furnishing and fitting up houses and rooms,
and caring for women and girls who need a mammie or a manager,
as the case may be.*

> *Mammie Pleasant has taken charge of this case from the begin-
ning and, to use her own phrase, is making the defendant's "fight,"
whom she supports, and to whom she was forced to admit, after
much evasion, she has advanced more than $5,000, and how much
more she would not tell. In my judgment, this case, and the forgeries
and perjuries committed in its support, have their origin largely in
the brain of this scheming, trafficking, crafty old woman. She states
that as early as 1881 the defendant wanted her to furnish her house
at a cost of $5,000 or $6,000 on the strength of her relations with the*

*plaintiff. But it seems that Mammie was not certain that the plaintiff
could be held liable for the expense, and so she called on her counsel,
Mr. Tyler, and stated the case to him, without as she is careful to say,
mentioning any names; but said that the man owned two hotels, and
was living in one of them, and the woman in the other, which, under
the circumstances, is equivalent to saying "the party of the other
part" is William Sharon. After due deliberation, Mr. Tyler gave her
a written opinion, which she says cannot now be found, to the effect
that such a contract as she mentioned and he suggested was a lawful
marriage, under the Code, and the supposed man who owned two
hotels (the Palace and the Grand) would be legally liable for the expense of furnishing his "Code" or "contract" wife with a suitable
residence, although he was then maintaining her at a cost of $500
a month at the Grand.*

When Deady turns to the remarkable letter that the press had dubbed
the "Us Girls" or "Egg in Champagne" letter, he asks, "How could anyone
have the hardihood to claim this document was written by a wife to a cruel
and unfathful husband?" No chance!

*It is apparently the work of an artful woman who is anxious to get
her net over the head of a wayward old millionaire again, and recall
him to her side once more, not so much for love as moonlight drives,
visits to the springs; lovely days in the country, egg in champagne,
and the like; and distrusting the power of her own familiar charms,
in honeyed phrases she adroitly contrives to put young "Nell" in the
foreground, as a fresh lure to the wary old bird.*

In plain English, the judge recognizes Sarah Althea for what she had become:
a discarded mistress, turned desperate procuress, engaged in a transparent
conspiracy to extort money from an elderly millionaire. The highest Court
in the land would later comment that Deady's opinion was very full in its
statement of the forgery practiced by Miss Hill, and that the forgery "was also
accompanied by perjury."

Judge Sawyer concurred with Deady in a separate opinion, much of
it given to consideration of technical legal points. But, on the facts he concludes:

*I am satisfied, after a most laborious and careful consideration of
the evidence, that the instrument in question, the so-called "Dear
Wife" letter in ink, and the other "Dear Wife" letters, the latter at
least as to the word "wife," are not genuine; that they are forged and
fraudulent; and that the alleged declaration of marriage set out in
the bill ought to be canceled and annulled as a forgery and a fraud.*

With this decision the Sharon-Hill controversy rested in a kind of legal
limbo. The state courts had found that Sarah Althea was a respectable lady,
the lawful wife of the recently-deceased senator and entitled to share his fortune as she had his couch. The federal court said the lady was a whore, a
perjurer, a forger, an extortionist entitled only to the scorn of all decent men
and women. Plainly, great legal battles remained to be fought. The gladiators
would be different. Barnes was succeeded by Stewart and Newlands. On Sarah Althea's side, Tyler had been relieved of his command and replaced with
Terry. But Terry had an additional role: lawyer and consort!

*This is the house in Stockton in which Sarah Althea and Terry lived
after their marriage.*

XXXI

"JUDGE AND MRS. DAVID S. TERRY HAVE THE HONOR TO ANNOUNCE . . ."

You know, my Friends, with what a brave Carouse
I made a Second Marriage in my house;
Divorced old barren Reason from my Bed,
And took the Daughter of the Vine to Spouse.

Edward Fitzgerald, *The Rubáiyát of Omar Khayyám*

As we have seen, during the state court trial, there were many waggish comments in the press about Terry's "gallant and unceasing attentions" to the vivacious plaintiff. In June 1884, an alert reporter for the *Alta* remarked on the coy interplay between Sarah Althea and Terry. Their courtroom flirtations, he wrote, were so flagrant as to be "noticed by spectators." But they were "as oblivious to criticizing spectators as a pair of freshly betrothed lovers." From February 1885 on, Sarah Althea was seen several times in Stockton with Terry, and there was local gossip about her relationship with the old judge. On January 7, 1886, twelve days after the federal court had sent its torpedo into Sarah Althea's dream-barque, the *Daily Alta* carried an item that caused much snickering in San Francisco's legal circles, and consternation in Stockton "society":

> *Stockton. January 7: This quiet little city had a tremendous social sensation today when two of the most conspicuous residents of California were married. . . . The groom, David S. Terry, has resided here for years, and is both feared and respected throughout the entire San Joaquin Valley. His bride, Miss Sarah Althea Hill, is also pretty well known here . . . but is regarded in an entirely different light from Terry. The latter's motives in contracting an alliance with so oppositely constituted a mate have been under discussion all day yesterday and today. . . . All that is definitely settled is that Miss Hill has become Mrs. David Terry, and that she clung to the name of Sharon up to the moment of the transformation, as is shown by the name in the marriage license procured this morning. ,*

Even the *Daily Democrat* in Terry's home town of Stockton, normally friendly to him, could not avoid a leering note. It announced:

> *After many months of severe struggling unaided and alone, with the numerous Minions of Mammon, Sarah Althea at last decided to let her head rest upon the bosom of her stalwart legal friend and defender and to be henceforth protected by him. Judge Terry has stood by her nobly in all her troubles since he became acquainted with her and*

the lady should be well satisfied with the kind fate that has landed her in such a safe harbor.

Terry's family and friends were horrified by the marriage. Son Clint, who lived in Terry's Stockton home, refused to attend the wedding. He told everyone that his father should have had more respect for the memory of Cornelia Terry than to replace her with a common slut. "What do you think of Terry and Sarah A.?" asked one prominent Californian of another. "Oh, Terry is just about old enough now to get weak on the fair sex. These venerable mashes do funny things now and then."

To one friend who timidly questioned the wisdom of marrying Sarah Althea, Terry remarked "I adore her — she is the smartest woman I ever saw." Wagstaff observes that the union with Sarah Althea "seriously disturbed" Terry's social relations, that "the social avenues that had been open to his former wife were closed to her, and his manly spirit was stung to the quick. . . . Samson had his Delilah." Whether or not the happy couple were ostracized, as some reports suggest, they gave every outward sign of felicity. The union was, as Johnson said of a widowed friend's remarriage, "a triumph of hope over experience." And they were both engrossed in their holy war against the wicked Sharon-Newlands interests. On the day after the wedding, they announced that their marriage in no way signified the end of the crusade. It would go on to the end, and Terry had a new incentive to clear his wife's name. How better to attest her moral probity than to take her in marriage? How better to erase the ugly slurs on her character?

Terry's friends and supporters were deeply troubled by his marriage to "the heroine of the great Sharon scandal." Later, one of them wrote: "His friends will not have the hardihood to deny his marriage with Miss Hill was an insult to them and to the memory of the mother of his children, and a menace to society. The marriage compassed the judge's ruin." To be sure, the social life of the Terrys was curtailed because of the provincial prudery of the time. Men treated Terry as usual, but their womenfolk would have only the most guarded relations with Sarah Althea. She was not ostracized in Stockton, but clearly she was not embraced by Cornelia's friends. Terry did his best, but she was not accepted.

At the beginning of 1886, the state and federal courts seemed to be at war with each other over the Sharon-Hill litigation. The state court, per Judge Sullivan, had granted a divorce in a marriage that the federal court said did not exist. It would be enlightening to learn what California's highest court had to say. Appeals to that court by Sharon's heirs were pending. But the first and most exigent step facing Terry was to perfect the appeal from the fatal decision of Judges Deady and Sawyer in the federal court.

In July 1886, during the pendency of the appeal in the state court, Terry took a step so ill-conceived that some lawyers sneered that his marriage to Sarah Althea had "unhinged his mind." He actually charged in the state legislature that two judges of the state supreme court that would normally hear the appeal from the Sullivan judgment were "totally incompetent by reason of physical and mental infirmity to discharge the duties of [their] office" and demanded their removal from the bench. A legislative committee was convened to investigate. Terry wasted weeks in a full hearing. The committee recommended that the charges be dismissed, and the matter died.

Terry's law office, Stockton. Terry's name appears at the top of the sign on the right.

In any case, neither of the challenged judges was on the supreme court panel that on January 31, 1888, came down with a decision that affirmed Judge Sullivan in finding that there was a valid marriage and in awarding a divorce. But the elation the Terrys felt over this victory was diluted by the court's action in reducing alimony from $2,500 per month to $500 and in eliminating counsel fees of $55,000. One judge dissented vigorously. He argued that, giving Sarah Althea the benefit of every doubt, "the facts found in this case did not, under the law of this state, constitute marriage."

In 1888, the local social coolness toward Sarah Althea began to generate much discomfort and friction. Terry bitterly resented the refusal of Stockton's citizenry to accept his new young wife. They decided to move to Fresno. The move was promptly attended with misfortune. The building to which Terry moved his office burned down and his valuable law library was lost. Among the records destroyed in the fire, it was later claimed, was Sarah Althea's marriage contract, her "honor." The couple's move from Stockton to Fresno was remembered for a dinner that Sarah Althea gave for the Fresno press. An enthusiastic reporter wrote that she "reached the pinnacle of perfection [as a hostess]. Through her natural grace of manner, she makes every person feel at home, and unconstrained by conventionality."

In that summer of 1888, Sarah Althea accompanied Terry around the state on his professional tasks. On one of these errands the Terrys encountered Judge Sawyer and committed a folly that undermined the federal appeal, forfeited the support of their dwindling well-wishers and started them on the final stage of self-destruction.

At that point, the decree issued by Judge Deady held the "marriage contract" to be "a false, fabricated, forged and counterfeit instrument," and as such, null and void. But under federal law, the decree had "abated" when Sharon died. To enforce the decree Sharon's heirs brought a "Bill of Revivor." If it was granted, Deady's decree would be restored. The Bill of Revivor was argued in June 1888 before a court which included Field, Sawyer and Judge Sabin, a federal district judge from Nevada. Terry was eloquent in behalf of his wife's cause. But before the court could decide, the Terrys committed an act of incredible imbecility.

On August 14, 1888, the Terrys found themselves passengers with Judge Lorenzo Sawyer on the same Southern Pacific train from Los Angeles to San Francisco. The parties had been informed that the court would announce its decision on the Bill of Revivor on September 3, and all three were scheduled to attend that event. Not only had Judge Sawyer joined with Deady in the decision so adverse to the interests of Sarah Althea, he was included in the court before which the Bill of Revivor was pending. Anyone with a grain of sense, seeing Sawyer on the train, would have moved to another car or would have ignored the old judge. Not Sarah Althea! Not David S. Terry! When they spotted Sawyer, Sarah Althea strutted up and down the aisle, leering at the judge, uttering threats and insults. When the old judge refused to respond, she became infuriated, seized his gray hair and shook his head from side to side. Terry stood by, encouraging her and "laughing gleefully at her exploit." The two finally took seats in the car, and Sarah Althea stood up to address the other passengers: "Well," she said, "I gave that old bastard a good wooling!" Then she sat down beside her husband, and in the hearing of Judge Sawyer (and others) she said: "I will give him a taste of what he will get by and by. Let him render this decision if he dares." Terry made no effort to deter Sarah Althea; witnesses would say later that he "encouraged" her, and that he made his own fateful comment about Judge Sawyer: "The best thing to do with him would be to take him down to the Bay and drown him."

Judge Sawyer took no action, but as he returned to San Francisco the "wooling" incident had the effect of stirring within him apprehensions about the Terrys that would have appalling consequences. He called J. C. Franks, the United States marshal in San Francisco, to his chambers to request that he have a number of deputies in the courtroom on September 3 "to prevent violence." Franks agreed and made his arrangements. A number of trusted men were specially deputized for the occasion, including one David Neagle.

There was some muttering among Terry's friends that because of his intimacies with Sharon's friends and family and of the old relationship between Terry and Field, Field should have "recused" himself from any participation in the case. Under today's standards, Field's prior relationship with Newlands would, standing alone, have justified the judge's withdrawal from the case. Francis Newlands had been one of Field's "managers" in the judge's effort to obtain the Democratic nomination for president in 1884. Eleazar Lipsky — an open partisan of Terry and an equally open critic of Field — points out that

> Field seems never to have disqualified himself for conflict of interest. He sat in at least three important constitutional cases argued by his brother, the renowned New York lawyer, David Dudley Field — In re Milligan, In re Garland and Cummins v. Missouri.

It is far from clear that under the standards of the age, the fraternal relationship with David Dudley Field was disqualifying, but the connection with Newlands, an actual litigant, a party in interest, is far more troublesome. Strangely, there is no evidence that Terry ever suggested that Field "recuse" himself.

As usual, Terry exacerbated the situation by making a public charge that Sawyer "was a bribe-taking judge who had taken his orders from Field." As if the "wooling" incident were not enough, the Terrys had said and done enough to convince press and public that their next appearance before Field and Sawyer would be a notable event. It was!

The Appraisers' Building, Washington and Sansome streets, San Francisco,
where the federal circuit court sat

XXXII

THE APPRAISERS' BUILDING,
SAN FRANCISCO

*Justice Field and his associates on the Bench are to be
congratulated on the firmness with which they asserted the dignity
of the Court.*
Daily Alta California, September 4, 1888

On Monday, September 3, 1888, the United States Circuit Court, over which Mr. Justice Field presided, convened to announce its decision on plaintiff's Bill of Revivor. The atmosphere in the courtroom was one of "great tenseness and expectancy." San Francisco's lawyers, journalists and court buffs recognized that if Newlands's motion for Revivor were to be granted, the Deady-Sawyer decree would become operative, and it would be the end of the road for Sarah Althea and her allies. The courtroom in the Federal Appraisers' Building was thronged with observers and the press.

Before the court convened, there was a conference in Judge Sawyer's chambers, attended by Field and Marshal Franks. Both judges again told the marshal of their concern that the Terrys might create a disturbance when their decision was announced, and inquired if he had a sufficient force on hand to preserve order. Franks assured them that he had made suitable plans in anticipation of some violent outburst by Sarah Althea or Terry. A number of deputy marshals and San Francisco police officers would be spotted around the courtroom.

The legal batteries that had supported Sarah Althea in the trials before Sullivan and Houghton had melted away, and of all the lawyers, only Terry remained at her side. Porter Ashe, Terry's *fidus Achates,* accompanied the Terrys, "for moral support," carrying some books, papers and Sarah Althea's parasol. The Terrys sat at a table reserved for lawyers within the railing that separated spectators and press from lawyers and litigants, about twelve feet from the judges' bench. Terry had a few books and papers under his arm; Sarah Althea carried only a "small satchel." The court filed in: Field, Sawyer, George Sabin and a fourth jurist, Judge Hoffman, who had taken no part in the case but was invited by Field to sit on the bench as an "observer." My account of the events that followed is based on the sworn testimony of the principal participants.

The judges took their seats at 11:00 a.m. Without a preliminary word, Field began to read the court's opinion from a bulky manuscript; he spoke in low, moderate tones which required some of the spectators behind the rail to strain to hear. Within five or ten minutes, the trend of the opinion was unmistakable. Those close to Sarah Althea heard angry, but unintelligible mutterings. Terry was observed to urge her to silence. After about twenty minutes, Field had read enough to convey to all that his decision was fatally adverse to Sarah Althea's interests, and she began "to move about in a restless manner." Again, Terry leaned over and spoke a few words to her, evidently to quiet her down.

Just then, C. W. Cross, a San Francisco lawyer and friend of Field, finding it difficult to hear, moved to the front of the courtroom and sat in a chair beside Sarah Althea. He observed that she was fingering the clasp of her satchel. Since he knew of her disposition to brandish a pistol in court, Cross determined to bring her action to the notice of Marshal Franks, who was standing about ten feet away. As Cross sought to get the marshal's attention, Sarah Althea leaped to her feet and pointed a finger at Field. Her voice was shrill and loud enough to be heard at the back of the room. She screamed:

> *Judge, are you going to take the responsibility of ordering me to deliver up that marriage contract?*
>
> Field *(in a calm and level voice): Take your seat, madam.*
>
> Sarah Althea: *How much did you get for that decision? You have been bought by Newlands. How big was the sack?*
>
> Field *(still calm): Madam, be still and take your seat!*
>
> Sarah Althea: *Justice Field, we hear you have been bought . . . no one can get justice in this court unless he has a sack. . . . What have you been paid by the Sharon people? You have been bought by Newlands's coin. How much did Newlands pay you?*
>
> Field: *Mr. Marshal, remove that woman from the courtroom. The court will deal with her later.*
>
> Sarah Althea *(in a loud voice and insulting mannner): I won't go out and you can't put me out!*

Sarah Althea continued "to revile the judge in the most vulgar manner, and becoming wild with rage, her voice attracted people from all parts of the Appraisers' Building." As Marshal Franks stepped toward her, she handed her satchel to Porter Ashe and struck the marshal in the face with both hands, shrieking: "You dirty scrub, you dare not remove me from this courtroom!"

The marshal raised his arms to shield his face from the hysterical woman, and his elbow struck Sarah Althea's shoulder. Now Terry rose to his feet and roared "with an oath": "No living man shall touch her. . . . Don't touch my wife; get a written order." The marshal responded: "Judge, stand back; no written order is required."

According to the later testimony of Marshal Franks, corroborated by other witnesses, Terry then struck him a hard blow in the mouth, with his right fist, breaking one of his teeth. The marshal immediately released Sarah Althea and sought to protect himself from Terry who then "put his right hand in his bosom" and two of the deputies caught him by the arms and forced him down in his chair.

With Terry thus restrained for the moment, two of the deputy marshals forcibly took Sarah Althea out of the courtroom into the adjoining marshal's

Terry's ejection from Field's Courtroom, from the San Francisco Examiner

office. She resisted, "scratching and striking [the marshals] all the time, using violent language, denouncing and threatening the judges and [the marshals]." In the corridor, she charged that the marshals had stolen her diamonds and bracelets from her wrists. Porter Ashe picked up her satchel which had fallen to the floor and followed her out of the courtroom. Sarah Althea saw Ashe close by and screamed that he should give the satchel to her.

Terry did not witness Sarah Althea's outburst in the corridor and the marshal's private office. He was still pinioned by the marshals in a chair in the courtroom. He was "swearing all the time, saying, 'God damn you, let me up; you sons of bitches, let me up'; and other exclamations of that character." As the scene was played out in the courtroom, the judges sat in silence, observing the struggle between the Terrys and the court officers. As the Terrys were forced into the corridor, the judges still sat in stony silence, listening to the sounds of combat without.

After Franks and Deputy Marshal Harris had taken Sarah Althea out of the courtroom, Terry was released from his chair and "forcibly" led to the courtroom exit. The events are best told in the words of Officer Finnegas:

> *Then we let Terry up, and I went up with him to near the swinging doors connecting the court-room with the passage-way leading into the corridor. About five feet from the swinging doors, and in the court-room, I released my hold of Judge Terry's right arm, and let go of him, and he went through the door, and I held one side of the door open with my left hand, and this door was not closed until Judge Terry had drawn his bowie-knife, and was brandishing it in the passage-way leading to the corridor. When he got a few feet from the swinging doors into the passage-way, I heard someone say, "Look out, he's got a knife." I let go the swinging door and ran out, and caught him in the said passage-way by the right arm, in which he held*

his knife, and at the same instant a deputy-marshal by the name of Farish caught hold of Judge Terry.

Terry was engaged in a violent contest with the marshals. One of them held the arm that brandished the knife. Another had his arms around Terry's torso. Finnegas goes on:

During this time Judge Terry shouted loudly, using such exclamations as "Let go, let go, you sons of bitches; I will cut you into pieces; I will go to my wife." We struggled into the space before the counter in the marshal's office, where we took Judge Terry's knife from him. I loosed some of his fingers, and Deputy-Marshal Farish loosed some, and a man standing by pulled the knife from Judge Terry's hand.

When Terry was subdued and his knife taken from him, he was permitted to enter the marshal's office, where Sarah Althea was still struggling with the deputies. According to Finnegas,

Terry's conduct throughout this affair was most violent. He acted like a demon; and all the time while in the corridor, and before the counter of the marshal's office, he used loud and violent language, which could be plainly heard in the courtroom, and, in fact, throughout the building.

Deputy Marshal Farish testified that as Terry was escorted from the courtroom he drew his Bowie knife and shouted, "I will cut you to pieces! . . . I am going to my wife." As Terry was permitted to join Sarah Althea in the marshal's office, Porter Ashe, still carrying Sarah Althea's satchel, also entered the room. Marshal Franks took Sarah Althea's satchel from Porter Ashe, and opened it. He found in it a forty-one-caliber revolver, five of the six chambers loaded. The marshal locked the pistol in his safe, along with Terry's Bowie knife. The witnesses were unanimous that the knife was indeed a Bowie knife, nine and one-quarter inches long, with a five-inch blade, pointed and sharpened to a fine edge.

Once the Terrys were removed from the courtroom, Field continued reading his opinion, "unperturbably, as if nothing had happened." He concluded about noon. Then a tight-lipped, white-faced Field, visibly enraged, assembled the other judges in his chambers, to deal with the outrage. Written orders were prepared adjudging Terry and Sarah Althea "guilty of a contempt of this court by misbehavior in its presence and by a forcible resistance in the presence of the court to a lawful order thereof." There was a brief discussion as to the need for a hearing; it was concluded that no hearing was required and written orders were issued to the marshal. Terry was sentenced to six months' imprisonment, Sarah Althea to thirty days', both sentences to be served in the Alameda County jail, across the Bay in Oakland.

While the Terrys were detained in the marshal's office awaiting the court's action, Terry made a number of loud and derogatory remarks about the judges, all duly noted by the marshals. Sawyer, he said, was "a damned old scoundrel"; Field was "the crookedest judge that ever sat on the bench!" The noon hour passed and the pair were still detained, when Terry said to Marshal Franks, "Tell that old bald-headed son of a bitch, Field, that I want to go to lunch." Then, ever the cavalier, he turned and gently placed his arm around his wife's shoulder. "My dear," he said, "you have done all this."

Sarah Althea, now in her role as the martyred heroine, responded,

Field at the time of the decision in Sharon *v.* Sharon

My dear, I could not help it. I had to do it. I have got this now just where I wanted it. I want to keep this matter before the public. I don't want the public to lose sight of our case. I know they will send me to jail. I don't care. I want that old villain to send me to jail, and I have no doubt he will.

Then with chin in the air and eyes flashing, she addressed the marshals guarding the room:

I could have killed old Field from where I stood in the courtroom, but I was not ready then to kill the old villain.

For Sarah Althea, everything that happened on that terrible day was an occasion for histrionics. That evening, en route to the ferry, Terry remarked to Marshal Franks that "the scene which had transpired was but a faint expression of the contempt which he entertained for the court." Both he and Sarah Althea made other useful remarks, all duly recorded. One of Terry's angry statements would have far-reaching consequences. He said, "Field thinks that when I get out, he will be away, but I will meet him when he comes back next year, and it will not be a very pleasant meeting for him."

In the early evening, as the hack drove on to the Oakland Ferry, Sarah Althea, who could never resist the presence of an audience, made an impromptu speech to the passengers on the boat. She explained that she could have killed Field and Sawyer, and no jury would have convicted her. Deputy Marshal Harris reported that Terry then said, "No, you could not find a jury that would convict anyone for killing that old villain."

Their incarceration in the Oakland jail was a bitter humiliation to the Terrys, but they endured no physical hardship. The more erudite among the reporters likened their imprisonment to that of Galileo by the Inquisition and to Leigh Hunt's luxurious "cell" in Surrey Gaol for libeling the Prince Regent, surrounded by flowers, books, magazines and newspapers. It is not recorded whether, like Leigh Hunt, they were provided with a pianoforte. The jailer and his wife gave up their own living quarters to their distinguished prisoners. The prisoners received many visitors and were allowed to hold press conferences almost daily. In October, it was reported that Sarah Althea was ill. At this time, she probably suffered the miscarriage which became known to her public on January 4, 1889, when she sued Marshal Franks, alleging that at the time of the courtroom incident she was "gravid," and that it was his brutal treatment of her that caused the miscarriage. She asked damages of $50,000. The case was not prosecuted.

When her sentence expired, Sarah Althea insisted on remaining with Terry in the Oakland jail until his sentence was completed. She was at his side during all the boasting and threatening, all the ill-advised gasconades that were to prepare his doom. She fanned the flames with her own twittering rhetoric of vengeance and violence.

Terry was in jail only forty-eight hours when he began his efforts to be released. He drafted a petition to the circuit court couched in characteristically arrogant and defiant terms, seeking revocation of the six-month sentence. Friends urged that he present an apologetic and conciliatory address to the court, explaining that he was the victim of his wife's wild and extravagant conduct. Indeed, a petition expressed in such tones was prepared for Terry by one of his well-wishers, John A. Stanley. It concluded with the phrases that have from time immemorial been the stereotyped but indispensable ingredients of a petition for judicial clemency: words of penitence and regret, assurances that he had intended no disrespect to the court, that he had been driven to uncontrollable rage when he saw his pregnant wife manhandled by the marshals. But oppression makes even wise men mad, and the belief that he was unjustly prosecuted by Field drove Terry to the edge of sanity.

Terry refused to sign Stanley's irenic paper. His friends persisted, and he agreed to sign another version, prepared by Stanley and modified better to suit Terry's sense of outrage. Old Judge Solomon Heydenfeldt, once a colleague on the California Supreme Court with both Terry and Field, undertook to show the paper to Field. It was agreed that only if he received encouragement from Field would he file the petition formally for action by the court. On September 12, Heydenfeldt and Field met in Field's suite at the Palace Hotel. Heydenfeldt had written Terry about the impending meeting that "if it seems advisable, will present your petition." He besought Terry's assurance that "in case of a favorable issue, it will not be followed by any attempt on your part to break the peace, either by violence or denunciation."

Terry's reply is the characteristic effusion of a man in the grip of a suicidal obsession. He wrote:

> I do not expect a favorable decision from any application to the court, and have very reluctantly consented that an application be made. Field probably wishes to pay me back for my refusal to aid his presidential aspirations four years ago.... If I was released I would seek no personal satisfaction for what is past.... I will not commit any breach of the peace.... I will not avoid meeting any of the parties concerned; but I will not promise that I will refrain from denouncing the decision and its authors. I believe that the decision was purchased and paid for with the coin of the Sharon estate, and I would stay here ten years before I would say what I did not believe.

The allusion to Field wanting to "pay him back" is probably to Terry's oft-repeated story about the circumstances in which he had opposed Field's candidacy for the Democratic presidential nomination in 1884. At that time, it was said, Terry compared Field with Francis Bacon "in ability and corruption." That a seasoned lawyer, an ex-judge, should ask clemency from a court in the same petition in which he charges it with infamous corruption is incomprehensible. But Terry's mind was beyond professional objectivity; it belonged now to his rage and self-pity. Heydenfeldt must have understood this, but he was a good friend and he tried.

When the two old judges met in Field's suite at the Palace, Heydenfeldt emphasized Terry's personal tragedies, his infatuation with a young woman whose very sanity was in question, and begged Field to be merciful to an old colleague now fallen into calamity. He showed Field the proposed petition, and Field "put it in his pocket." Heydenfeldt thought Field pocketed the petition to examine it more closely at his leisure. If Heydenfeldt believed he had touched a spot of compassion in Field, he was mistaken.

When Field's handling of Terry's petition became known, it would gain much sympathy for the luckless Samson imprisoned in Gaza-across-the-Bay with his dotty Delilah. Heydenfeldt left Field believing that Field would give him his comments on the petition informally, that changes could be made, and that a final version would then be lodged formally with the court. Through misunderstanding or mischief, Field acted as if delivery of the petition to him constituted formal filing with his court. He sent no message to Heydenfeldt, but went to work assiduously preparing his case against Terry. He spent the next few days calling into his chambers the marshals and the other witnesses of the scenes in the courtroom, the corridor and the marshal's office. He obtained their affidavits refuting Terry's statements in the petition. Terry's petition, prepared for him by Stanley and presented to Field by Heydenfeldt, reads:

> *To the Honorable Circuit Court aforesaid: The petition of David S. Terry respectfully represents: That in all the matters and transactions, occurring in the said court on the 3d day of September, inst., upon which the order in this matter was based, your petitioner did not intend to say or do anything disrespectful to said court, or to the judges thereof, or to any one of them. That when petitioner's wife, the said Sarah A. Terry, first arose from her seat, and before she uttered a word, your petitioner used every effort in his power to cause her to resume her seat, and remain quiet, and he did nothing to encourage her in her acts of indiscretion; when this court made the order that petitioner's wife be removed from the court-room, your petitioner arose from his seat with the purpose and intention of himself removing her from the court-room quietly and peaceably, and he had no intention or design of obstructing or preventing the execution of the said order of the court.*

This much of the petition is true, and had the petition continued in this vein, it might have gotten a hearing. But Terry goes on to say:

> *He never struck or offered to strike the United States marshal until the said marshal had assaulted himself, and he had in his presence violently, and, as he believed, unnecessarily, assaulted petitioner's wife. Your petitioner most solemnly avers that he neither drew or attempted to draw any deadly weapon of any kind whatever in said court-room, and that he did not assault or attempt to assault the United States marshal, with any deadly weapon in said court-room or elsewhere.*

This part is certainly false. Every witness agrees that Terry struck Marshal Franks the first blow, that it was struck in the courtroom, and that the Bowie knife was flashed in the courtroom. The petition goes on:

> *In this connecton he respectfully represents that after he had left said court-room he heard loud talking in one of the rooms of the United States marshal, and among the voices proceeding therefrom he recognized that of his wife, and he thereupon attempted to force his way to said room through the main office of the United States marshal; the door of this room was blocked with such a crowd of men that the door could not be closed; that your petitioner then for the first time drew from inside his vest a small sheath-knife, at the same time saying to those standing in his way in said door that he did not want to hurt any one; that all he wanted was to get in the room where his wife was. The crowd then parted, and your petitioner entered the*

doorway, and there saw a United States deputy-marshal with a revolver in his hand pointed to the ceiling of the room. Some one then said "Let him in, if he will give up his knife," and your petitioner immediately released hold of the knife to someone standing by.

Again, false. The "small sheath-knife" was certainly his lifelong companion, the Texas Bowie knife, and it was taken from him by force before he even entered the corridor. The petition goes on:

In none of these transactions, did your petitioner have the slightest idea of showing any disrespect to this honorable court, or any of the judges thereof. That he lost his temper, he respectfully submits was a natural consequence of himself being assaulted when he was making an honest effort to peaceably and quietly enforce the order of the court so as to avoid a scandalous scene, and of his seeing his wife so unnecessarily assaulted in his presence. Wherefore your petitioner respectfully requests that this honorable court may in the light of the facts herein stated, revoke the order made herein committing him to prison for six months. And your petitioner will ever pray, etc.

If we accept the virtually uncontradicted testimony of witnesses, Terry's petition is a self-serving and audacious profanation of the truth. The document is singularly lacking in those professions of regret and apology that any court, so affronted, must expect. Such expressions were in Stanley's earlier draft, but the unbending Terry would have none of it. Of course, any court that had endured the conduct of the Terrys would be enraged by the very tone of the document, its adamantine insistence that Terry was a man persecuted and abused. But incarceration had not allayed Samson's blindness. The offense of the Terrys was grievous, but a fitting petition with appropriate expressions of contrition addressed to a compassionate judge would usually have drawn a reduction in the sentence.

Field was no more compassionate than Terry was contrite. If there was any pity in Field, Terry's petition swamped it, and there remained only renewed outrage and fury, to which the old man surrendered. Field filed the affidavits of the marshals and the other witnesses with the pitifully lame petition. It is manifest that these witnesses had been sharply examined, their testimony sorted out with professional skill. The result was a devastating refutation of Terry's petition by an artful and cunning lawyer, and a flat rejection of any vestige of mercy.

On September 17, Field, flanked by Judges Sawyer and Sabin, without notice or warning to Terry, Heydenfeldt or Stanley (but with ample notice to the local press), read in open court his opinion denying the petition in all respects. After some formal recitals the opinion avers, "On September 12, 1888, D. S. Terry presented the following petition." Then comes the hapless document, a recital of affidavits of five court officers, seven other eye-witnesses, and a scathing denunciation of Terry:

The misbehavior of the defendant David S. Terry, in the presence of the court, in the court-room, and in the corridor, which was near thereto, and in one of which (and it matters not which) he drew his bowie knife, and brandished it, with threats against the deputy of the marshal and others aiding him, is sufficient of itself to justify the punishment imposed. But, great as this offense was, the forcible resistance offered to the marshal in his attempt to execute the order of the court, and beating him, was a far greater and more serious affair.

Field knew how to gain public sympathy and acclaim for himself, as well as public contempt for Terry. The affront was not merely to him and his fellow judges. It was to the Grand Old Flag! He writes:

This resistance was the highest possible indignity to the government. When the flag of the country is fired upon and insulted, it is not the injury to the bunting, the linen, or silk on which the stars and stripes are stamped which startles and arouses the country. It is the indignity and insult to the emblem of the nation's majesty which stirs every heart, and makes every patriot eager to resent them. So the forcible resistance to an officer of the United States in the execution of the process, orders, and judgments of their courts is in like manner an indignity and insult to the power and authority of the government, which can neither be overlooked nor extenuated.

Field was infuriated by Terry's reference to the deadly Bowie knife he drew as "a small sheath-knife." Field says it was a Bowie knife; Farish calls it a Bowie knife; Finnegas describes it as a Bowie knife; it must have been a Bowie knife! The press, the public and history adjudge that it was a Bowie knife. Field was understandably offended by Terry's total lack of contrition:

He offers no apology for his conduct, expressed no regret for what he did, and makes no reference to his violent and vituperative language against the judges and officers of the court.

At this point Field could not have known that Terry was actually engaged in preparing charges of darkest corruption against Field, Sawyer and the other federal judges. We can only speculate to what height Field's virulence would have reached had he known that Terry now adopted and associated himself with Sarah Althea's accusation that the Terrys were the victims of a corrupt court, bought with Sharon's gold. Of course, Field had heard it from Sarah Althea, but he did not yet know that Terry, an ex-judge, an officer of the court, was loudly trumpeting this most terrible of accusations against a judge to every visitor who saw him in the Alameda jail.

Judges Sawyer and Sabin concurred in the denial of Terry's stiff-necked plea. Terry's prompt application to the United States Supreme Court for leave to petition for *habeas corpus* was just as promptly denied. The high Court, through Mr. Justice Harlan, opined on the basis of Terry's own account of the facts that he belonged in jail. An application to President Cleveland for a pardon was swiftly rejected.

To all this, Terry reacted with a splenetic stupidity which occluded the remnants of his professional vision and good sense. He lashed out at his "persecutors." He abandoned himself to self-pity and revenge. He brought a groundless action in the state court in San Francisco against Marshal Franks, and sought therein to examine Field as a witness. The action was immediately transferred to the federal circuit court where it died a quiet death. Terry and Sarah were indicted by the federal grand jury in San Francisco for criminal contempt. From his jailhouse law office Terry unsuccessfully attacked the indictments. The indictments were still pending at the time of his death. Lipsky's search of the archives in Washington turns up the significant fact that when the contempt indictments were returned, United States Attorney Carey asked the attorney general to appoint a special prosecutor. The lawyer he chose was David Louderback, a San Franciscan recommended to the attorney general by Field's friend and patron, Leland Stanford. The letter of recommendation is actually on the letterhead of the Central Pacific Railroad. In truth, as Terry believed, the local establishment was closing ranks against him, its old enemy, to protect its ally, Field.

During his incarceration, Terry's pathetic gasconades against Field increased in volume and folly. He told one visitor that after he got out of jail "[H]e would horsewhip Judge Field. . . . This earth was not large enough to keep [me] from finding Judge Field and horsewhipping him." When his listener said "this would be a dangerous thing to do, and that Judge Field would resent it," Terry's portentous reply, to be endlessly recalled in the dread days to come was, "If Judge Field resents it, I will kill him!" Sarah Althea threw her own senseless faggot on the mounting pyre. She told a reporter that she "expected to kill Judge Field some day." In one communion with the press, Terry blustered that the federal judges and marshals were "all a lot of cowardly curs" and he would "see some of them in their graves yet."

A jailhouse interview that would become significant in the light of later events was between Terry and Thomas T. Williams, a San Francisco editor. Terry asked Williams to call on him in the Oakland jail. Williams reported:

> *In speaking of the occurrences in the court, he said that Justice Field had put a lie in the record about him, and when he met Field he would have to take that back, "and if he did not take it back and apologize for having lied about him, he would slap his face or pull his nose."*
>
> *I said to him, "Judge Terry, would not that be a dangerous thing to do? Justice Field is not a man who would permit anyone to put a deadly insult upon him like that." He said, "Oh Field won't fight." I said, "Well, Judge, I have found nearly all men will fight; nearly every man will fight when there is occasion for it, and Judge Field has had a character in this State of having the courage of his convictions, and being a brave man." At the conclusion of that branch of the conversation, I said to him, "Well, Judge Field is not your physical equal, and if any trouble should occur he would be very likely to use a weapon." He said, "Well, that's as good a thing as I want to get." The whole impression conveyed to me by this conversation was, that he felt he had some cause of grievance against Judge Field; that he hoped they might meet, that he might have an opportunity to force a quarrel upon him, and he would get him into a fight.*

In the confused uproar that followed Terry's death, Williams recalled that after Field's return to California in the spring of 1889, he "had another conversation with Terry, in which the same vindictive feelings of hatred were manifested and expressed by him."

From the jail, Terry declared private war not only on Field, but on all the federal authorities. His foolish bitterness led to excesses on both sides of the quarrel. Under the law, Terry could have been released before the expiration of his six-month sentence "for good behavior," and the sheriff of Alameda County was planning to release him at the end of the fourth month.

His purpose came to the notice of the United States attorney in San Francisco, who applied to the court for an order directing the sheriff to hold Terry to the end of the six months. On February 1, 1889, Judges Sawyer and Sabin ruled that the "commutation" principle did not apply to punishment for contempt. They may have been correct as a matter of law, but it was certainly in their discretionary power to release the aged lion. Even Terry's foes felt the judges were acting vindictively when it was learned that Field had personally intervened to prevent an early release. He had written the two judges from Washington urging that the sentence should not be shortened. The San Francisco press lost no chances to heat up the quarrel: it published the report that Field had descended to this level of petty vengeance.

Terry spent his last weeks in prison letting off steam. He composed a diatribe against Field. *The Character and Career of Stephen J. Field* is a venomous screed put together from letters Terry sent to the San Francisco *Political Record,* whose editor was friendly to Terry, hostile to Field, and receptive to anything that would inflame the feud and increase his circulation. The pamphlet is carelessly researched and hastily written. Terry's rancor against the man who had become his chief oppressor divests it of much objective or historical value. He recounts at length the young Field's feud with Judge Turner so as to make Field out a loud-mouthed braggart and poltroon. He repeats the gossip that Field was addicted to gambling, and that while serving on the state supreme court he had taken bribes for decisions (the old "Gold Key" insinuations). He charges Field (justifiably, but carelessly) with being a tool of "the corporations," the California "Octopus," with being the corrupt hireling of the Central Pacific Railroad and its creators, Stanford, Huntington, Crocker, et al.:

> *Field is an intellectual phenomenon. He can give the most plausible reasons for a wrong decision of any person I ever knew. He was never known to decide a case against a corporation. He has always been a corporation lawyer and a corporation judge, and as such no man can be honest.*

It is an interesting speculation whether the Terry who wrote these words recalled the language that thirty years earlier had led to the Broderick duel.

Terry had some professional tasks to discharge in his improvised law office in Alameda County jail. In January 1888, the state supreme court had finally reversed Judge Sullivan's yuletide oblation to Sarah Althea; it ordered a new trial in *Sharon* v. *Sharon.* This was the final blow to Sarah Althea's hopes. Now, both state and federal courts had given the *quietus* to her quest for Sharon's gold. Terry composed a brief of almost two hundred pages in support of a motion to re-argue the court's decision. Terry was in court when the decision to reverse Sullivan's opinion was announced orally from the bench. He had a paroxysm of rage and indignation, fortunately outside the courtroom. It is related that as he left the court, he encountered a friend (identified only as "S ——"):

> Terry: *Well, S ——, they have salted me.*
> S ——: *What do you mean, Judge?*
> Terry: *The Supreme Court has reversed its own decision in the Sharon case and made my wife out a strumpet.*
> S ——: *What are you going to do about it, Judge?*

Terry: *What can a person do in the face of Sharon's millions? It is infamous! What is the world, anyway? . . . The corporations and capitalists are centralizing their power in all departments of the Government, both State and Federal. Justice has a dark outlook.*

On the subject of this reversal, Terry was out of control; he screamed that the decision was "fixed," that two of the judges who ruled against Sarah Althea "were placed on the Supreme Bench by the Sharon crowd!" He charged that Judges Searls and Sullivan, friendly to the Terry cause, were defeated "by Newlands and the Sharon crowd."

Much of Terry's time in the Alameda County jail was spent in preparing for re-argument of this galling defeat. But time was running out for Terry after he was released from the Oakland jail in April 1889. Field's decision was on its way to the United States Supreme Court, in Terry's own words, "the only tribunal in this country which can control the controversy." The Terrys were sustained by the feeble hope that the ultimate tribunal would reverse Field and Sawyer. Terry returned to his new home in Fresno, where life must have seemed dull after the theatrics of Alameda. But the monotony of their lives was broken in May 1889, when, shortly after Terry's release, the United States Supreme Court (*sans* Field) unanimously affirmed the decision of the circuit court of September 3, 1888, the opinion which had precipitated the ugly courtroom scene and the imprisonment of the Terrys for contempt. There was nothing new or noteworthy in the opinion. Mr. Justice Miller spoke for the Court, which simply agreed with Field and his colleagues. For Sarah Althea, it was the end of the legal road. For Terry, it was the end of everything. He sank into a deadly fury, relieved occasionally with public threats against his archenemy Field. His vaporings were duly communicated to Field back in Washington.

It was widely known that Field would follow his usual practice, and return to California in the summer of 1889 to perform his duties as circuit judge. The press made much of Terry's threats against the judge, and some of his friends tried to dissuade him from returning. Not Field. He said:

I cannot and will not allow threats of personal violence to deter me from the regular performance of my judicial duties at the times and places fixed by law. As a judge of the highest court of the country, I should be ashamed to look any man in the face if I allowed a ruffian, by threats against my person, to keep me from holding the regular courts in my circuit.

Since the Terrys were both under indictment in the federal court in San Francisco for criminal contempt, there was some apprehension that their trial would trigger a repetition of the violent scenes of September 1888. But the chief concern was for the personal safety of Field. On April 27, 1889, United States Attorney General W. H. Miller wrote Marshal Franks in San Francisco:

It is due to the dignity and independence of the court and the character of the Judges that no effort on the part of the government shall be spared to make them feel entirely safe and free from anxiety in the discharge of their duties.

One of Franks's efforts would be to appoint as a deputy marshal one David Neagle, specifically designated "to protect the person of Stephen J. Field."

Deputy Marshal David Neagle

XXXIII

DAVID NEAGLE

An honourable murderer, if you will,
For nought did I in hate, but all in honour.

William Shakespeare, *Othello*

After the events described in the next chapter, David Neagle's name was on the lips of millions of Americans. Men quarreled over the character and motives of this hitherto obscure man, as they did over the character and motives of the great and famous. During a single night, Dave Neagle was lifted from total obscurity into the spotlight of celebrity. To Field's host of friends and supporters — and they were in the overwhelming majority — he became a brave and devoted public servant. To Terry's handful of sympathizers he was a "hired killer," a "paid assassin." There would be a wild scramble by reporters to dig up his history, to establish his identity. There was no mystery about him.

Neagle was born in 1854 on Telegraph Hill in San Francisco. He lived in the frontier atmosphere of the growing city until he was seventeen years old, when he left to work for a mining contractor in Arizona. Business was bad and he was forced to take employment first as a bartender and then as a saloonkeeper in Tombstone, Arizona. These occupations developed quick reflexes. Young David proved so adept at dealing with the armed roughnecks in his saloon, that his fellow citizens elected him town marshal, a position that normally had a dim future. But he survived.

In 1889, he was thirty-five years old, a short man — only five feet four inches in height. He weighed only about one hundred fifty pounds. But he was noted for exceptional physical strength. He was left-handed and "quick with a gun" — a quality much admired in the Wild West, especially in Tombstone, later immortalized in western movies as the Toughest Town in the West. At one time Neagle worked as a payroll guard in Butte, Montana. He tried his hand at mining in Nevada and Arizona, but law enforcement was his métier. There was a certain aura to Neagle, because he had been a peace officer in Tombstone at the time of the legendary shoot-out at the O-K Corral, when Wyatt and Virgil Earp, Doc Holliday and other famous gunslingers did some of their fanciest shooting. Even the burly fellows who towered over him treated him with respect. In his "Introduction" to the reprint of Wagstaff, Eleazar Lipsky, the New York lawyer, champion of the theory that Terry was the victim of a murder plot, writes: "It seems the fact that Neagle in truth was a friend and crony of the Earps in Tombstone." *Noscitur a sociis.* Presumably, this is intended to signify that Neagle, judged by his associates, was a hired killer, which somehow bolsters the theory that he was employed to murder Terry. Lipsky also hints at some sinister connection between Neagle and "the Sharon interests." It is true that Ben Ali Haggin, one of the western mining overlords, was a brother-in-law of Lloyd Tevis, president of the Wells Fargo Express Company, whose daughter married Fred Sharon. Tevis was so close to Field that he traveled to the Democratic Convention in Cincinnati in 1880 to be one of Field's floor managers. Lipsky suggests that Neagle was "well known to Sharon's and Field's friends" and that they may have been the "responsible parties" who recommended him to Marshal Franks. A bodyguard was needed and it was entirely appropriate to select a man who had survived the vicissitudes of places like Tombstone. If he was known to some of Field's friends as reliable and temperate, so much the better! One thing is certain: Neagle was present at the imbroglio outside the courtroom on September 3, 1888. He was later identified as the "citizen" who helped to wrest the knife from Terry's hand. Neagle may have been an old-fashioned gunslinger, but that does not necessarily fortify the theory that Terry was "assassinated." What other type of man would Franks have hired to protect the old judge from one of Terry's reputation for quick violence?

Neagle came back to San Francisco in 1883, where he became a deputy sheriff and made a name for coolness and bravery in discharging the most dangerous duties of that office. He was working in the municipal license office when Franks appointed him Field's bodyguard, with the title of "Special Deputy United States Marshal." Neagle's assignment to guard Field grew out of the apprehension with which the federal officials in San Francisco regarded the Terrys. By their silly hectoring, their extravagant threats, the Terrys had fanned the flicker of concern into a flame of fear. On May 6, 1889, Franks responded to a letter of concern from the attorney general assuring that official of his vigilance.

> You can rest assured that when Justice Field arrives he, as well as all the federal judges, will be protected from insults, and where an order is made it will be executed without fear as to consequences. . . . The opinion among the better class of citizens here is very bitter against the Terrys, though, of course, they have their friends, and, unfortunately, among that class it is necessary to watch.

On May 7, the United States attorney added his voice to the demand for protection for Field against the Terrys. He wrote the attorney general of his "pleasure" that the head of the Justice Department was "in full sympathy with the efforts being made to protect the judges and vindicate the dignity of our courts." He added:

> I write merely to suggest that there is just reason, in the light of the past and threats made by Judge and Mrs. Terry against Justice Field and Judge Sawyer, to apprehend personal violence at any moment and at any place, as well in court as out of court. . . . Mr. Franks is a prudent, cool and courageous officer, who will not abuse any authority granted him. I would therefore suggest that he be authorized in his discretion to retain one or more deputies, at such times as he

may deem necessary, for the purposes suggested. That publicity may not be given to the matter it is important that the deputies whom he may select be not known as such, and that efficient service may be assured for the purposes indicated it seems to me that they should be strangers to the Terrys.

On May 27, the attorney general gave Franks written authorization to employ "certain special deputies" at a per diem of five dollars. Under this authority, Franks deputized Neagle to guard Field.

Field and his wife returned to the West in July 1889; Neagle met them at the railroad station in Reno and rode the train with them to San Francisco. There, friends suggested that Field carry a pistol for self-protection. He refused, saying,

When . . . the judges of our courts are compelled to arm themselves against assaults in consequence of their judicial action, it will be time to dissolve the courts, consider government a failure, and let society lapse into barbarism.

On August 8, Field, accompanied by Neagle, went to Los Angeles to hold court. On August 13, the two men left Los Angeles to return to San Francisco where, it was known, the Terrys were due to appear in court the next morning. It was also known that the night train would pass through Fresno, where they lived. Neagle, therefore, asked the porter on the sleeping-car to awaken him before the train reached Fresno. Thus it was that when the train stopped at Fresno in the night, Neagle was awake and recognized the Terrys as they boarded the train.

Of course, Neagle had not only been warned by Franks, but he had heard the general expectations voiced in the California press that when Field and Terry met, the clash would be violent. He knew of the "wooling" incident in the previous summer. He was a witness to the courtroom scenes of last September. He had been thoroughly briefed on Terry's past — the knifing of Hopkins, the Broderick duel, etc. In plain, he was conditioned to be alert, to be quick, to be fearful. The public concern that the Terrys would attack Field was so wide that it reached the ears of Rudyard Kipling, who arrived in San Francisco, in July 1889, laden with his normal cargo of phobias and prejudices against America and the Americans. He read the newspaper reports of the Terrys' threats against Field. Prophetically, he wrote in his journal of the events of his trip:

Just at present an ex-judge who was sent to jail by another judge (upon my word, I cannot tell whether these titles mean anything) is breathing red-hot vengeance against his enemy. The papers have interviewed both parties and confidently expect a fatal issue.

The Lathrop Station, where Neagle shot Terry to death

XXXIV

LATHROP, CALIFORNIA, AUGUST 14, 1889

*I will follow you in death, and men shall say that I was
the most wretched cause and comrade of your fate.*

Ovid, *Metamorphoses*

It was totally dark at 3:00 a.m. on Wednesday, August 14, as the Southern Pacific's overnight train from Los Angeles to San Francisco made its scheduled stop at Fresno. It would be recalled later that as the train slowed to a stop, a short stocky man, a slouch hat pulled down over his face, swung to the platform and in the dim light of the kerosene lamps, carefully scanned the faces of the only two passengers who came aboard. It was David Neagle, doing his job of guarding Field. In the dim half-light he recognized the new passengers as Terry and Sarah Althea. He expected them; he knew they were due to appear in federal court in San Francisco next morning in connection with their indictment for contempt of court. The pair carried no baggage, but Sarah Althea clutched to her side a small "reticule," the same satchel from which Neagle had seen her take a loaded pistol a year earlier in the Appraisers' Building.

When he had identified the two passengers, Neagle became so alarmed that he rushed through the train seeking the conductor, a Mr. Woodward. The train was halfway to its next stop at Merced, about fifty miles north of Fresno, when he found him. Conductor Woodward already knew that Neagle was a United States marshal, acting as bodyguard to Judge Field; he had himself recognized the two passengers who boarded at Fresno as Terry and his wife. He knew enough about them to be "apprehensive that when the train arrived at Lathrop there would be trouble between those parties."

Woodward told Neagle that there was a "constable" regularly stationed at the Lathrop depot, the train's next stop. From Merced he telegraphed to Lathrop a warning that the constable be on hand when the train arrived. He also wired the sheriff of San Joaquin County "to secure assistance for Neagle, should it be required." The train arrived at Lathrop about 7:30 a.m. in full daylight, for a scheduled stop of about thirty minutes, to take on fuel and water for the engine, and give the passengers a quick breakfast in the dining room. Before the train arrived at Lathrop, Neagle woke Field to inform him that the Terrys were on the train. "I hope they have a good sleep," said the doughty judge. Neagle suggested that, to avoid trouble, the judge remain on the train and take his breakfast in the buffet car, but the judge refused, saying that this would show "cowardice." "I have had good breakfasts in the dining room," said Field, "and I prefer to eat there." He and Neagle were among the first to enter the depot dining room.

Neagle later explained that from the moment the Terrys boarded the train, he was fearful of a bloody clash. He knew that the man he was guarding was then in his seventy-third year, a slight, trimly-built man who had taken to the use of a walking stick because of a recently-suffered knee injury. He was no match for the formidable Terry, six feet three inches and two hundred and fifty pounds, whose physical strength was as legendary as his ungovernable rages. Neagle knew that for fifty years, Terry's Bowie knife had sat loosely in its scabbard; that its blade had flashed in courtrooms, saloons and street brawls. He had seen and heard enough of Sarah Althea to know that she was hardly a demure Victorian lady; she had her own well-merited reputation for high-handed violence. Neagle knew of her proclivity to brandish a loaded revolver in public places, and even in courtrooms on at least two celebrated occasions. Perhaps the single event that most excited Neagle's imagination had occurred exactly one year before, when Terry and his wife insulted and attacked Judge Sawyer on the same train. To Neagle that incident foretold that their presence on the train presented the danger of an attack on Field.

All the acts of violence by the Terrys, all their threats were known to the deputy marshal, as he and Field seated themselves at a table in the middle of the depot dining room. If Neagle was "trigger-happy," as would later be charged, the Terrys had made many contributions to his state of mind. The customs of that time and place dictated that Field and Neagle pretend to ignore the danger and act with studied virile calmness. As he ordered his breakfast, Neagle's eyes darted from side to side, his hand on his revolver. The trouble he had been schooled to fear was not long in coming. The Terrys entered the dining room and marched up and down the aisles as if searching for somebody. They spotted Field, and Sarah Althea hastily left the dining room. The dining room manager, Mr. Stackpole, who was acquainted with Terry, showed him to a table in the corner of the room, as far as possible from Field and Neagle. He asked Terry bluntly if Sarah Althea "planned anything desperate." "Why?" asked Terry, "Who is here?" The manager gestured toward Field. "Well," said Terry, "you had better go and watch her." As the manager made for the door, Terry rose "with deliberation" and moved toward Field. He walked up and down immediately behind the judge, glaring at the back of his head. We can only assume that the sight of his enemy kindled in Terry a raging passion that consumed any sense of self-control. For when he was directly behind the judge, he suddenly turned and struck the old man twice, one blow in the face and the other on the back of his head.

The description of the events that ensued is abridged from the sworn testimony of Field and other witnesses. Field later testified:

Coming so immediately together, the two blows seemed like one assault. Of course, I was for a moment dazed by the blows. I turned my head round, and I saw that great form of Terry's, with his arm raised, and his fists clenched to strike me. I felt that a terrific blow was coming, and his arm was descending in a curved way, as though to strike

Terry, shortly before his death

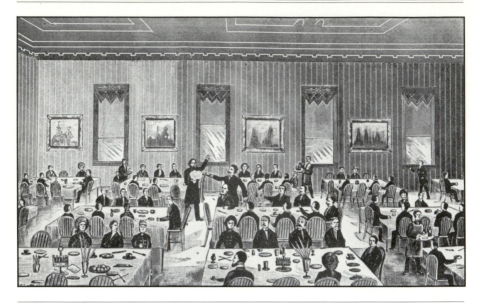

An artist's rendition of Neagle killing Terry

the side of my temple, when I heard Neagle cry out, "Stop! Stop! I am an officer."

As Terry struck his first blow, Neagle's pistol was drawn; at the second blow, he shot Terry twice; his pistol was only inches from Terry's chest as the first shot was fired. The bullet passed through Terry's chest and struck his spine — a fatal shot! As Terry staggered and fell, Neagle fired a second shot at Terry's head. The second bullet caught the lower part of Terry's ear and caused a cascade of blood. Bystanders related that as Terry fell to the floor dying, Field impassively rose from his chair, glanced at the body of his enemy, and walked to another part of the room. Field goes on:

> *Great excitement followed. A gentleman came to me whom I did not know . . . and said: "What is this?" I said: "I am a justice of the Supreme Court of the United States. My name is Judge Field. Judge Terry threatened my life, and attacked me, and the deputy-marshal has shot him."*

According to other witnesses, Neagle appeared to be "perfectly cool and collected." He turned to the horrified bystanders and said: "My name is David Neagle. I am a deputy-marshal, and I have shot him to protect the life of Judge Field."

Within seconds after Neagle fired his two shots, Sarah Althea came through the dining room door, clutching the satchel she had gone to fetch. She saw the hated Field; she saw the marshal, pistol still in hand; she saw her husband lying on the dining room floor as the last signs of life oozed from him. A bystander reached down to straighten Terry's leg which was awkwardly bent under his body. Sarah Althea screamed and raged. She tore open her satchel and drew a large pistol. But before she could use it on Field or Neagle, her arms were pinioned to her sides by the dining room manager and other bystanders. Another bystander took the pistol from her hand. At this point,

Neagle said to Field: "Judge, I think you had better go to the car." One Lidgerwood accompanied Field to the train, but at the judge's request returned to the dining room to reclaim his hat and walking stick.

After Sarah Althea was disarmed, she wrenched herself from the hands of the manager and threw herself on her husband's corpse, screaming that "they" had killed "her only friend." A contemporary newspaper account describes Sarah Althea's "terrific passion of rage and grief," how in a voice "made hoarse by agony of soul, she called down the judgment of heaven on her husband's slayer." She implored the witnesses to search her husband's body to prove that "they" had killed an unarmed man. She said:

> I took his arms from him in the car, because I didn't want him to shoot Judge Field! I wouldn't have minded if he had beaten him up with his fists.

Neagle later testified to his belief that Terry was reaching for his Bowie knife after he struck Field. He said:

> I believed if I waited two seconds I should have been cut to pieces.

He was then asked:

> What did the motion that Judge Terry made with his right hand indicate to you?

His response was:

> That he would have had that knife out there within another second and a half, and trying to cut my head off.

G. C. Gorham, one of Field's biographers, unabashedly avers that "the testimony subsequently taken left no room to doubt that Terry had his deadly knife in its place in his breast at the time he made the attack on Justice Field." In truth, no arms were found on Terry's body, although Field's partisans later contended that as Sarah Althea threw herself on Terry's corpse, she stealthily abstracted the Bowie knife he habitually carried, and secreted it in her bodice. Field's friends insisted that

> this woman, who had been to the car for her pistol and returned with it to join, if necessary, in the murderous work, had all the time and opportunity necessary for taking the knife from its resting place under his vest. . . . The idea uppermost in her mind was to then and there manufacture testimony that he had not been armed at all.

Terry normally carried his Bowie knife in a leather sheath, and no sheath was found on Terry's body. Sarah Althea cradled her husband's head in her lap. His blood stained her clothes as she kissed his face. "Oh my darling, my sweetheart," she moaned. She looked up at the shocked faces around her and moaned:

> Why don't they hang the man? The cowardly murderer! He was too cowardly to be given a trial so he hired an assassin! They shot him down like a dog in the road. He was the soul of honor.

Now the crazed woman stood up and screamed that the bystanders should lynch her husband's murderer. She cried out:

> If my husband had killed Justice Field, the crowd would have lynched him! Will you not help me punish the murderers of my husband?

The shocked onlookers were mystified when she asked, "Are there any Masons among you?" Then she said that her own father was a Mason and she implored any Masons in the white-faced crowd to join her in lynching

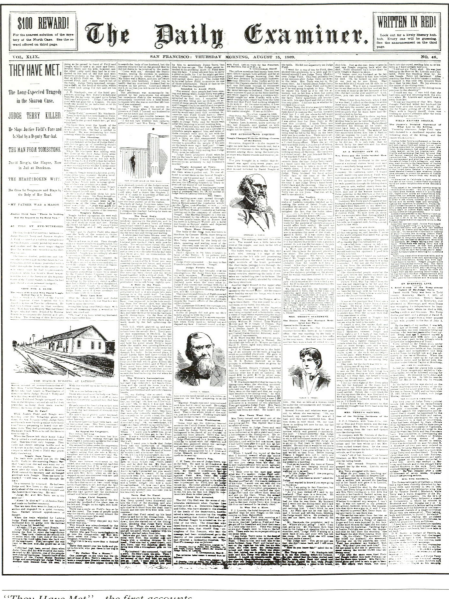

Field and Neagle. There were no volunteers. As Terry's body was being carried to a barber shop adjoining the restaurant, Sarah Althea ran to the train and tried to force herself into the car where Neagle was now attending to the bruise on Field's face. "Keep her out," shouted Neagle, "or I'll kill her too!"

Sarah Althea in mourning

XXXV

THE ARREST OF FIELD AND NEAGLE

You may charge me with murder — or want of sense —
(We are all of us weak at times):
But the slightest approach to a false pretence
Was never among my crimes!

Lewis Carroll, *The Hunting of the Snark*

By chance, R. B. Purvis, the sheriff of Stanislaus County, was en route to San Francisco on official business on the night of August 14. He boarded the northbound train at Modesto. He did not witness the shooting, but rushed into the dining room at the sound of shots. He was one of those who restrained Sarah Althea from violence. At first he refused to take any action, but he finally yielded to the wild importunities of Sarah Althea, who was being treated for shock and hysteria in the station waiting room. He came aboard the train, arrested Neagle, and relieved him of his revolver. Over Field's protest, Neagle and the sheriff left the train at Tracy, where Purvis turned Neagle over to the custody of one of his deputies who hired a horse and carriage and drove Neagle by back roads to the county jail at Stockton. The jailer received from the deputy Neagle's heavy forty-four-caliber Colt revolver, with its two empty chambers. By the time Neagle was locked up in Stockton's local jail, the news of the incident at Lathrop had been carried by telegraph to the state and nation. Some of the town toughs gathered outside the jail and talked loudly about a lynching. Sarah Althea rode to Stockton with Terry's body in the baggage car of a later train.

At the Stockton depot, Terry's body was lifted from the train to a wagon to be borne to the morgue. Sarah Althea climbed on the wagon and, as it made its way through the streets, it was followed by a cortege on foot of Terry's friends and sympathizers. For several hours Sarah Althea held court at the morgue, playing to the hilt the role of the bereaved widow. Ladies who had passed her in the street without a nod now looked in to pay their condolences; men who had shunned the Terrys in society and business joined in urging vengeance for foul murder. Newspaper reports to San Francisco were that "public opinion" was largely in favor of Sarah Althea and "many are the emphatic avowals that the affair was a brutal murder."

Early in the afternoon, Sarah Althea marched down the street to the office of Thomas Cunningham, sheriff of San Joaquin County, a close friend of Terry's. Flanked by some indignant Stocktonians she swore out a complaint for murder against Stephen J. Field. Sheriff Cunningham issued a warrant and telegraphed to San Francisco to have a detective meet Field at the Oakland depot, arrest him and bring him to Stockton. When the train from Los Angeles arrived at Oakland, a city detective was indeed waiting for Field to arrive, to execute the telegraphic warrant from Sheriff Cunningham. But Marshal Franks had been forewarned, and he was also on hand. He threatened to arrest the detective if he did not leave Field alone. The intimidated detective took no action, and Field crossed on the ferry with Franks. Field was met at the San Francisco ferry terminal by a group of his friends and advisers who "escorted him triumphantly to his quarters at the Palace Hotel."

Back in Stockton, Sarah Althea was no longer a social outcast; she found herself established in the role of tragic heroine, surrounded by grieving friends. She needed little encouragement to take vengeful action, but she was deluged with it. By afternoon, stimulated and abetted by sympathizers, she appeared before a local justice of the peace, and swore to a new complaint against both Field and Neagle, charging them with the murder of Terry. New warrants were issued; Neagle was brought before a local justice of the peace and held without bail for a hearing on August 21. That meant he would have to return to the local jail, to remain for six days, while an unruly mob surrounded the building, working up the courage for a lynching. On the night of August 15, Sheriff Thomas Cunningham entrained for San Francisco with the warrant directing him to arrest Field and bring him to Stockton.

Cunningham reached San Francisco at about 8:45 p.m. He registered at a local hotel and proceeded to police headquarters to obtain local assistance in executing his warrant for the arrest of Field. There, he was informed that Police Chief Crowley wanted to see him at the Palace Hotel, where he was met by Marshal Franks and Crowley. An *ad hoc* council was convened to ponder the mechanics of serving a murder warrant on a justice of the United States Supreme Court. Obviously, there were no useful precedents. It was decided to have the warrant served at one o'clock the next day at Field's private chambers in the federal court in the Appraisers' Building.

Next day at the agreed time, Cunningham came to the courthouse where Field awaited him, literally enthroned in his chambers amidst a group of other judges and the cream of the San Francisco bar. Field's attitude was friendly, even benign; he beamed a smile upon the agitated sheriff: "Proceed with your duty sir, I am ready. An officer should always do his duty." The sheriff showed an understandable diffidence; his duties as sheriff provided no previous experience in arresting justices of the Supreme Court for murder. He handed his warrant to Field, who adjusted his spectacles, examined the document and announced: "I recognize your authority, sir, and submit to the arrest; I am, sir, in your custody."

Poor Cunningham was overwhelmed by the majestic appearance and courtly manners of his eminent prisoner. He muttered some vague apology about causing the great man such inconvenience. "Not so, not so," said the great man. "You are but doing your plain duty, and I mine in submitting to arrest. It is the first duty of judges to obey the law."

If Cunningham thought Field was addressing him he was wrong; it took more than a county sheriff's sophistication to understand that Field's piety was directed to the press of the entire country. Field also needed a little time to work out his own scenario. With great ceremony, he invited the discomfited Cunningham to make himself comfortable while the jurist discharged a few exigent judicial chores. When he was finished, he arose. "Let me walk with you," said Field, and took the sheriff's arm.

Cunningham did not know that during the morning the United States attorney had prepared a petition on Field's behalf for a writ of *habeas corpus* charging:

> *The whole object of the proceeding is to subject your petitioner to the humiliation of arrest and confinement at Stockton, where the said Sarah Althea Terry may be able, by the aid of partisans of hers, to carry out her long-continued threats of personal violence upon your petitioner, and to prevent your petitioner from discharging the duties of his office in cases pending against her in the Federal court in San Francisco.*

While the little charade of "arresting" Field was being played out, this petition was presented to Judge Sawyer, awaiting it in his own chambers adjoining those of Field. Sawyer ordered the writ to issue, returnable forthwith. Thereupon the entire company, "prisoner," sheriff, marshal, lawyers and press moved to Sawyer's chambers where Cunningham presented a formal "return," conveniently furnished for his use by the helpful staff of the United States attorney. Sawyer directed Field's release on his own recognizance, and adjourned the hearing to August 22.

Now the little group in Sawyer's chambers turned to the next exigent piece of business: to snatch Neagle from his precarious plight in the Stockton jail. United States Attorney Carey had his staff prepare a *habeas corpus* petition for Neagle. Sawyer granted this writ, and it was served upon Cunningham. It directed him to produce Neagle in San Francisco on August 18. Cunningham returned to Stockton and on the afternoon of August 17, he brought Neagle by train to San Francisco, where the prisoner was delivered into Marshal Frank's tender custody, pending a hearing on August 22. Now, both Field and Neagle were safe from any local lynch mob in Stockton.

Terry's funeral procession

XXXVI

FIELD GOES FREE

*Unlimited power is apt to corrupt the minds of those who
possess it.*

William Pitt, Earl of Chatham, from an address
to the House of Lords, January 9, 1770

The telegraph had clicked out all over the country the report of Terry's death at Lathrop. Of course it created in California the highest sensation, but even in the East the news stirred tremendous excitement. Field's enemies — and there were many — now raked up old insinuations about his venality as a state court judge, his subservience to the railroad and industrial interests. He was damned as an intimate and ally of the men who had created the Octopus, and was derided for his associations by liberals and populists. Stephen M. White, one of the state's most respected lawyers, who later became a United States senator from California, had long despised Field for his conservative, anti-populist philosophy and he was offended by the general sentiment that Neagle's pistol had preserved a great popular hero from assassination at Lathrop. He wrote:

> *To be candid, it makes me tired to listen to the flunkey talk that is going on at this time about a man who, in my judgement, is one of the most dishonest characters that has ever discharged the functions of a judicial office.*

On the whole, press and public were hostile to the Terrys and sympathetic to Field. The San Francisco *Argonaut* revived stories about the threats made by Terry and Sarah Althea against Field, concluded that since they were engaged in a plot to kill the judge, there was "in [Neagle's] action . . . nothing to criticize."

The Sacramento *Themis* saw the tragedy as the inevitable consequence of Terry's marriage to the "raffish, demented Sarah Althea." An influential eastern magazine, *The Nation,* described Terry as "a desperado of thirty years' standing, who during all that period carried his life in his hand, and lived among other desperados as bad as himself." It snarled that "somebody ought to have killed Terry a quarter of a century ago." According to *The Nation,* Terry was "a regular antebellum blackguard, as out of place in our modern industrial and busy communities as a tiger in a barnyard."

One Sacramento paper not only denounced Terry, but quoted New York papers who thought there was no occasion to mourn "the fate of the fire-eating blood-drinking Terry." A partisan newspaper in the California hinterland, the Placerville *Observer,* termed Terry a "border ruffian of the 'fire-eating' type . . . a bully and blackguard"; its editor saw his killing as "an act of consummate skill." Neagle's pistol, it said, "closed a criminal career distinguished by shameless infamies. . . . In the cold-blooded and vindictive conspiracy to hunt down and kill the gallant Broderick, he sported a 'shield blazoned with the name of chivalry to cover the crime of murder.'" Nor did the press spare the character of Sarah Althea. The Placerville paper referred to Terry's "prurient marriage to an adventuress." The Chicago *Mail* of August 15, 1889, said:

> *When the story of the life of Sarah Althea Hill-Sharon-Terry is written . . . it will be the history of a trouble-maker. That woman — one of those fierce natures that are frequently found in the southern countries of Europe, but rarely in America — continued the struggle with [Sharon's] heirs. Into her net she drew Judge Terry, her counsel, and they were married. He was just the ally she wanted — a typical Western fire-eater, as hot-blooded as herself, as vengeful, as unrelenting in his hatred, and, withal, a duellist who had killed his man.*

One account asserted that "Terry lost his own life in his desperate attempt [to assassinate Field], by the alertness and courage of [Neagle] who had been deputized by his principal [Franks] to protect Justice Field from the assassin, who had, for nearly a year, boldly and without concealment, proclaimed his murderous purpose."

Congratulatory letters and telegrams came to Field from sympathizers and admirers all over the country. The judge kept them all in a special file which he later turned over to his fiercely partisan biographer, Gorham, who recorded many of them in his account of the "attempted assassination." T. F. Bayard, ex-secretary of state, wrote "Dear Brother Field," congratulating him on his escape "from the infamous assault of the Terrys — husband and wife — upon you," and on his "escape from the designs of this madman and of the shameless creature who was his wife and accomplice." E. J. Phelps, former minister to England, extolled Field's "coolness and carriage in confronting this danger in the discharge of your duty," gushing that it "must be universally admired, and will shed an additional lustre on a judicial career which was distinguished enough without it." The legendary Senator George F. Hoar of Massachusetts intoned a prayer that Field would "long be spared to the public service."

Governor Knott of Kentucky congratulated Field on his "fortunate escape from the fiendish assassination with which you were so imminently threatened." University presidents, bishops, judges, state and federal, competed in expressing joy and gratitude over Field's escape from the hands of a vengeful assassin. Terry's life, wrote one of them, has long been forfeited "to law, to decency and to morals." Another fervently felt that "it was meet that you should have been defended by an executive officer of the court assailed in your person. For doubtless Terry, and the hag who was on the hunt with him, were minded to murder you."

Indeed, newspapers and periodicals all over the country joined in the national *Te Deum* for the escape of Field. In an editorial which congratulated all Americans that "the person of one of the very highest American judges was preserved unharmed," the New Orleans *Times-Democrat* concluded with the pious thanks that "death palsied the murderous hand that had sworn to take his life." To the New York *Herald,* Field's "traits of judicial heroism" were "worthy of the admiration of the world." The Albany *Evening Union* praised his courage; the New York *World* referred to Sarah Althea as "the demented widow of the dead desperado." The Kansas City *Times,* the *Army and Navy Journal,* the Philadelphia *Inquirer,* the San Francisco *Argonaut* and countless other newspapers and periodicals spoke up for the valiant judge and his equally valiant bodyguard. Who spoke up for Terry?

Not the press of San Francisco. It was unanimously hostile to the dead man. Terry's defenders were mostly found in the neighborhood of Stockton and Fresno. On the day of Terry's funeral, a dispatch from Stockton to the San Francisco *Alta* described Sarah Althea's display of grief and reported:

Public opinion is in her favor, and many are the emphatic avowals that the affair was a brutal murder and that duty was too literally performed.

The Stockton *Mail* deplored the editorial support of Field; it carried a story that "newspapers that haven't been fixed invariably condemn [the shooting of Terry] as cowardly and brutal." It quoted another local gazette, the *Mountain Echo,* which wrote:

A judge who is under the necessity of hiring a bodyguard to protect him in his judicial rounds is a coward, and very likely to be corrupt!

Terry was buried on August 16 in the family plot at Stockton, between the graves of Cornelia and their son Samuel. Clinton, Terry's fourth son, attended the funeral but showed little friendliness or sympathy toward Sarah Althea. From under her heavy black veil came deep sobs and imprecations against the murderers of her beloved husband. The pallbearers included some of Terry's colleagues at the bar, a few friends, and a pathetic little knot of surviving Confederate veterans. Many prominent citizens were pointedly absent. The Supreme Court of California, in session on the day of the obsequies, failed for the first time in its history to adjourn "in respect" for the passing of a former member. When the omission was remarked upon, Chief Justice Beatty observed:

The circumstances of Judge Terry's death are notorious, and under these circumstances, this Court has determined that it would be better to pass this matter in silence and not to take any action upon it.

But the local bar of San Joaquin County adopted formal resolutions of grief and respect. The Fresno Bar Association met and, despite lively opposition, adopted resolutions that were generally respectful but included the comment that Terry was "bold to rashness; of generous impulses and an acute sense of personal honor, he naturally made many enemies and maybe some mistakes."

Against Field, the charge of "murder" proved short-lived. Sawyer had set the warrant proceeding for hearing on August 22. On that date, United States Attorney Carey supported by several leading San Francisco lawyers appeared in support of the writ of *habeas corpus.* Sawyer gave the state officials five days to file a brief in support of the warrant issued in Stockton and in opposition to the writ. In the interim, R. W. Waterman, governor of California, wrote state Attorney General G. A. Johnson, characterizing the arrest

The Terry monument, Rural Cemetery, Stockton, California

of Field "on the unsupported oath of a woman who on the very day the oath was taken and often before threatened his life" as "a burning disgrace to the state." He directed his attorney general to "disavow" the action and instruct the district attorney of San Joaquin County to dismiss the charge of murder against Field. "The unprecedented indignity on Justice Field does not admit of argument."

Terry's friends howled that the governor was under the influence of Field's powerful friends in the industrial and railroad establishment. But the pressures prevailed, and on August 26, the justice of the peace who had issued the warrant *sua sponte* vacated the warrant and dismissed the charge. Next day, Judge Sawyer issued an opinion in which he announced his gratification that the governor's action had terminated this "shameless proceeding" and that "the stigma cast upon the State of California by this hasty and, to call it by no harsher term, ill-advised arrest, will not be intensified by further prosecution."

So much for the arrest of Mr. Justice Field.

Neagle receiving his friends in jail

XXXVII

NEAGLE GOES FREE

When your Majesty says, "Let a thing be done," it's as good as done — practically it is done — because your Majesty's word is law.

W. S. Gilbert, *The Mikado*

B ut David Neagle was still in danger. True, he was back in San Francisco, no longer at the mercy of a mob of Terry's vengeful friends in the valley. Still, the state's criminal proceedings against him remained outstanding, as yet unaffected by the proceedings before Sawyer. While there was a popular revulsion against the arrest and prosecution of Field, the feeling toward Neagle was mixed; it ranged from the extreme view that the shooting of Terry was a conspiratorial murder in which Neagle played the guilty role of triggerman, to the position that he was a hero who had foiled the assassination of the great Field. Between these extremes there were many who felt that Neagle had over-reacted, that he could have carried out his assignment without bloodshed. Of course, Terry's friends saw Neagle as a cold-blooded murderer, and shouted that if they could force him to trial in San Joaquin County, he would be in desperate jeopardy, either from a local jury or from a lynch mob.

Even Terry's most devoted partisan, Wagstaff, acknowledges that by the circumstances of his death and his unfortunate marriage, Terry had probably forfeited the respect and friendship of the more respectable elements in the Stockton area. Doctors, lawyers, merchants and judges understood that the dead man was a victim of his own uncontrollable rage, his history of violence and his intemperate threats against Field. The most prominent men of the valley area made no particular demonstrations and exhibited no sign of a spirit of revenge over Terry's death. But to the "country people," the ranchers and the stockmen, Terry had been a friend and champion, and they "were loud in their denunciation of the authorities and of the man who had committed the deed."

Terry's funeral brought many farmers and ranchers into Stockton and much talk in the streets and saloons of lynching Neagle. On August 16, an Associated Press stringer in Stockton filed with the eastern papers a story which squeezed every bit of excitement out of the situation:

There is every prospect of a lively row at the Terry funeral this afternoon, and violence afterward. One of Terry's friends, Judge Porter of Arizona, proposes to deliver the funeral oration. He says he will go for Field, and denounce Terry's shooting as foul murder. . . . Feeling runs very high in the town. Last night groups of men discussed the case for and against the Terrys. The ranchers and farmers from the interior came into town and mingled with the Stockton people. . . . In many cases the killing of Terry was pronounced cold-blooded murder.

In consequence of talk upon the streets some alarm is felt at the county jail where Neagle is confined. . . . During the night a small number of Terry followers, all rather desperate in character, gathered near the jail and made a careful inspection of the old trap. No threats were made, but one of the number quietly remarked later that it would be child's play to storm that "paper box" and pull Neagle out for introduction to Judge Lynch.

This morning the situation is ominous. No loud professions of a programme are made by Terry men, but they are holding whispered conferences at street corners, and evidently intend to carry out some desperate plot at the funeral this afternoon. There is great alarm in all the country around Stockton, and citizens have ordered the women and children to remain indoors till the threatened trouble is over.

Judge Porter prudently declined to be Mark Antony to Terry's Caesar, and there was no inflammatory funeral oration, no lynching. Neagle was kept safe from the mob until he came to his sanctuary in San Francisco. But he was not yet safe from the full reach of California law. In the letter to the attorney general instructing him to obtain dismissal of the proceedings against Field, Governor Waterman made it clear that there would be no such protection for the bodyguard. While "the unprecedented indignity on Judge Field does not admit of argument," wrote the governor to his attorney general, "the question of the jurisdiction of the state courts in the case of the duty of United States Marshal, Neagle, is one for argument." Indeed it was, and much argument was to come. If Neagle was to be plucked from the vengeance of a Stockton-San Joaquin County jury, it would not be by the State of California. His rescue would have to be effected by the federal authorities, led by Mr. Justice Field. Field took command of the relief expedition with his usual vigor and enthusiasm.

Many Californians resented the "interference" of the federal authorities in what they perceived as a local matter, governed by state law as interpreted by state courts. While he may have been influenced by his deep personal antagonism to Field, Stephen M. White, one of the leading lawyers in the state whose views were heard with respect, undoubtedly epitomized a broad attitude among Californians when, shortly after Terry's death, he wrote a Washington friend:

That Terry-Field episode was a most unfortunate affair. I think it is a grave mistake to assert federal control of the case. The United States judges are personally bitterly hostile to the Terry side and I believe they will take jurisdiction and discharge Neagle without a trial. The case is practically being tried by Field though he is behind the scenes. When Field "hates" he hates "for keeps" and will do anything to win.

White urged Attorney General Johnson that Neagle "certainly ought to be tried and fully prosecuted. He has committed a homicide and if he can show he acted in self-defense, all right, but he should be made to show it." White was not some reckless firebrand. The attorney general responded by offering to name him as special prosecutor, to take command of all proceedings against Neagle. White declined the appointment because he said his presence would prejudice the state's case. He told the attorney general that if he were to appear for the state, "Field would use his very great influence on Sawyer whom he controls and upon Deady or Brewer or whoever might sit in the matter to prejudice them against me."

Many sober and respected Californians shared White's attitude that Terry may well have been the victim of a deliberate plot to kill him. Many felt that Field and his establishment friends, including the hated bosses of the Central Pacific Railroad, the Octopus, were now engaged in a second conspiracy to protect the murderer. The cynicism of many Californians is exemplified in a satirical piece in the Stockton *Mail,* which was widely copied throughout the state:

Terry had a bowie knife all the way from a foot to eighteen inches long, with the blood of his last victim still upon the blade. He stood picking his teeth with it when the Rev. Mr. Nagle [sic] *a distinguished prelate from Arizona entered the room upon the arm of Stephen J. Field, a sacred personage descended from Heaven to execute the will of God upon earth. (It is unusual for a person to pick his teeth before eating, but any person hesitating upon this point will be in contempt of the Federal Circuit Court and may be shot at any time convenient to the shooter.)*

It is the author's conclusion that there was no wilful homicide — just a tragic accident. Despite all the talk by Terry's friends about dark plots and conspiracies to assassinate the bedeviled old man, in all probability Terry died because he broke the "rules." He had lived and suffered for adherence to an imbecile code, and he died because he violated another equally imbecile code: the Code of the West. If he had stood before Field and reviled him with words of scorn and contempt, even if he had repeated some of the threats he uttered in Alameda and in his undisciplined screeds, Neagle would probably have pushed the judge aside; there would have been the classic western confrontation, the gunfighter's invitation to "draw," in the high noon tradition, and since Terry had nothing to draw, there might have been a scene or a scuffle, but no shooting. But Terry struck Field reflexively, in fury and passion. Neagle, schooled in the saloons and dusty streets of Tombstone and the mining camps, reacted just as reflexively. When Terry struck his blows at Field, instead of speaking, Neagle fired the two shots as he would have reached for a handkerchief to stifle a sneeze! Had Terry "drawn," if he had had anything to "draw," and Neagle had then shot him, there would have been a clear case of self-defense, and the Code of the West would have been satisfied.

The comedy of Neagle's rescue from California justice was played out by Field's script. On the morning of Saturday, August 17, Sheriff Cunningham brought Neagle from Stockton to San Francisco. When Sarah Althea and her lawyer, Maguire, learned that Neagle was being moved to San Francisco, they rushed to board the same train. Despite the lady's penchant for melodrama on the rails, the journey was uneventful.

On August 22, Neagle was released on $5,000 bail by Judge Sawyer pending a hearing on the writ of *habeas corpus,* to be held on September 3 before Judges Sawyer and Sabin. On that date the United States attorney in San Francisco and seven private lawyers, all distinguished San Francisco *bâtonniers* specially recruited for the task by Field, appeared for Neagle. Down the hall in his chambers, his formidable presence unseen but felt, sat the Commander of the Neagle Relief Force, Mr. Justice Field. His troops were numerous and overwhelmingly strong.

Indeed, as soon as the import of the Lathrop tragedy was understood, Carey had telegraphed Attorney General Miller in Washington:

Deputy US Marshal Nagle [sic] *who killed Terry is under arrest by state authorities. I have after careful research been able to find an unquestionable way for the federal courts to interfere for his release. He is in jail charged with murder. I deem it important that his defense be supported actively by the Government. Shall I in my official capacity take an active part in his defense?*

Washington gave its vigorous affirmative, coupled with the authorization to hire special counsel to assist Carey in the case. Carey's helpers included six prestigious San Francisco lawyers, among them William F. Herrin, Richard S. Mesick, and Samuel M. Wilson, all lawyers for the Central Pacific Railroad controlled by Field's crony, Huntington. Herrin was also the law partner of Senator William Stewart, listed as chief counsel for Sharon's estate in *Sharon* v. *Hill,* the action in which Field slammed the door on Sarah Althea's hopes on September 3, 1888. Stewart, too, was an intimate friend of Field. Samuel M. Wilson is listed as counsel for the Sharon estate in *Terry* v. *Sharon,* the motion by the estate to dismiss Sarah Althea's appeal from Field's judgment.

To Terry's friends and Field's enemies, the composition of government counsel was virtually an announcement of the community of purpose among Field, Newlands, the Sharon heirs, the railroad interests and the defense of Neagle. They saw the defense as an extension of the original sinister purpose: to encompass the death of Terry, and thus put the *quietus* on the Sharon-Hill litigation.

The thrust of the argument for Neagle was simple:

An officer of the United States, specially charged with a particular duty, that of protecting one of the justices of the supreme court of the United States while engaged in the performance of his duty, cannot, for an act constituting the very performance of that duty, be taken from the further discharge of his duty, and imprisoned by the state authorities; and that when an officer of the United States, in the discharge of his duties, is charged with an offense consisting in the performance of those duties, and is sought to be arrested, and taken from the further performance of them, he can be brought before the tribunals of the nation of which he is an officer, and the fact there inquired into. And if it be found that the act complained of was in the performance of his duties, he could not be tried and punished by the State.

In short, Neagle must go free!

The interests of the State of California were presented by G. A. Johnson, the attorney general, assisted by Avery C. White, the youthful district attorney of San Joaquin County. Their position was equally simple: a homicide had been committed in the state and only the officers and courts of the state had the legal authority to deal with it and to punish the malefactor. In brief, they said, Neagle's fate should be decided by a court and jury in the San Joaquin Valley.

In our time, judges are more fastidious about acting when they are themselves intimately connected with the events leading up to an offense. Today, the chief actors would have "recused" themselves and turned the task of judging over to the hands of jurists whose dispassion and objectivity were not open to question. But Sawyer and Sabin never flinched from their "duty" — undoubtedly delineated for them by Field. Apparently, counsel for the state shrank from the embarrassment of even suggesting to the two federal judges that their connection with the facts and parties should disqualify them. The unpleasant subject was never mentioned.

The argument on the "writ" (i.e., for the release of Neagle) was reported throughout the country. The New York *Tribune* commented editorially that the case would "pit the federal and state district attorneys against each other, if Neagle be put on trial for murder, and will bring up many questions of national and state jurisdiction and authority for which no precedents have been established." This is a fair statement of the issue. The government presented an elaborate evidentiary case including every violent expression, every angry outburst of Sarah Althea and Terry against Field and the federal judges, including Sawyer. The plain thrust was to convince the court (as if it needed convincing) that from the moment the Terrys left the jail at Alameda they were intent on killing Field. They argued that Neagle was justifiably apprehensive that Terry's blows to Field's head in the station dining room were preliminary to the appearance of the well-publicized Bowie knife, and that in shooting Terry, Neagle had taken the only possible step to protect Field's life.

The circuit court accepted all the government's arguments in support of Neagle's justification in shooting Terry. In effect, the court tried Neagle for homicide and acquitted him — a process which understandably drew the fire of Terry's supporters. While the issue before the court seemed purely a question of law, Sawyer saw fit to enliven his opinion with a full and colorful rehearsal of the Sharon-Hill litigation, the courtroom misbehavior of the Terrys and the characters of both Sarah Althea and Terry. Before he addressed the issue of law, Sawyer gave a point-by-point description of the litigation history of *Sharon* v. *Hill;* next came a blow-by-blow description of the courtroom scene on September 3, 1888, and the sentences imposed on Terry and Sarah Althea. Sawyer placed the *imprimatur* of a federal court on Neagle's deed:

> *In our judgment [Neagle] acted, under the trying circumstances surrounding him, in good faith and with consummate courage, judgment and discretion. The homicide was, in our opinion, clearly justifiable in law, and in the forum of sound, practical common sense — commendable.*

As a matter of logic, it can be argued with force that whether Neagle's act was "justifiable" has nothing to do with whether he was a federal agent, acting in the discharge of his designated duties and therefore not amenable to the state's legal processes. Sawyer himself stated it well:

> It is therefore, only necessary to dispose of the case to inquire and ascertain, whether the petitioner is in custody for an act done in pursuance of a law of the United States.

But after this lip-service to the legal principle, the opinion is an apology for the act on an evidentiary basis. To what useful end, asked the court, would Neagle be sent back to be tried in the state court? He would still be discharged by the national courts because the act was "performed in pursuance of a law of the United States." Sawyer even expressed a pious concern over exposing the state of California "to such great useless expense."

Sawyer concluded his opinion with an exposition of the Lathrop events in language so dramatic as to be more appropriate to the local journals than to a judicial opinion. He has Terry walking "stealthily" in the rear of Field, and dealing "the unsuspecting jurist two preliminary blows doubtless by way of reminding him that *the time for vengeance* [italics in the original] had at last come." He described how Field "in a dazed condition" from Terry's blows "awoke to the reality of the situation, and saw the stalwart form of the deceased with arm drawn back for a final mortal blow." Now Neagle observed "the powerful arm of the deceased drawn back for the final deadly stroke, instantly change its direction to his left breast, apparently seeking his favorite weapon, the Knife." Thus, since the evidence left no doubt whatever that the homicide was fully justified by the circumstances, Neagle was discharged.

Sawyer's opinion was so transparently devised, his translation of subjective emotions into substantive evidentiary facts so repugnant to reasonable standards of judicial objectivity, that one must speculate on the part played by the shrewd old fox sitting in his lair down the hall. Reynard knew from the shouts of exultation that came down the corridor that Neagle was free. Flanked by his victorious lawyers, the press and his partisans, Neagle came in triumph to Field's chambers. The judge invited all into his chambers where he made a little speech of gratitude to Neagle and presented him with a gold watch and chain. Field must have had great confidence in the outcome of the "trial," for the watch already bore an engraved dedication:

> *Stephen J. Field to David Neagle, as a token of appreciation of his courage and fidelity to duty under circumstances of great peril at Lathrop, Cal. on the fourteenth day of August, 1889.*

Sawyer's decision releasing Neagle roused Terry's partisans to new heights of fury against Field, Neagle, the federal judiciary and the economic establishment of California. On September 14 Sarah Althea threw the first rotten egg in a letter to United States Attorney General Miller. She attacked federal District Attorney Carey as a man that "his wives have secured divorces from him for cruelty and wife-beating . . . he belongs to the Newlands and Sharon crowd — and they have spared no money to clear one of my husband's murderers." Some "Anonymous Friends" of Terry printed in Fresno a pamphlet entitled *Stephen J. Field — Arrested for Conspiracy and Murder of the Hon. David S. Terry* to place "the facts" before the public,

STEPHEN J. FIELD

ARRESTED

FOR

CONSPIRACY AND MURDER

OF THE

HON. DAVID S. TERRY.

Some of the reasons why he did not dare stand an investigation, but attempted to stigmatize the Judge's wife in an application to Governor Waterman of California begging to be released.

FRESNO, CALIFORNIA:

1889.

The title page of the pamphlet prepared by Sarah Althea

in order that a more just and impartial view may be taken of that affair and to show, as they abundantly warrant, that it was the result of a deliberate conspiracy to assassinate him.

The pamphlet included the letters which passed among Franks, Carey and the attorney general leading to the appointment of Neagle. It argued that if the full correspondence were released,

the public could and would see conclusively that the assassination of Judge Terry was merely a cold conspiracy on the part of Field, Carey, Franks and the Sharon attorneys. It is now believed, and justly, that it was not only the intention to assassinate Judge Terry, but Mrs. Terry also.

Next the "anonymous writers" pointed out that it was Senator Stewart, "known as a tool of the Sharon interests," who advised the attorney general "to give the necessary direction to the Marshal to see that not only [Field], but Sawyer should be protected."

The writer refers to the employment of a detective to shadow the Terrys. That much, at least, is true. In June 1889, one Henry Fenton, of Finegas's Detective Service in San Francisco, called on John A. Barker, city marshal and chief of police of Fresno, to advise that he "had been hired by Justice Field and Marshal Franks to watch Judge and Mrs. Terry." It has never become known who actually employed Fenton, but there was such a man and his task was no secret in Fresno. He was there to watch the Terrys. Fenton made his headquarters in the bar of Fresno's Grand Central Hotel, from which he watched the Terry house; he also trailed the pair on trains. He was heard to boast that if Terry made any violent moves, he would be shot. On the night of Lathrop, Fenton missed the Terrys at the Fresno depot only because he was in the station bar, too drunk to see them board the train. Terry's anonymous defenders said that Fenton advised Field and Neagle of "every move the Terrys made." They charged that there was an earlier conspiracy to kill Terry on the night of August 8 on the San Francisco-Oakland Ferry, but it aborted when the Terrys accidently arrived at the ferry terminal after the boat had departed; that on the night of August 13, Field received a telegram from Fenton at Tehachapi advising that the Terrys would be on the night train from Los Angeles to San Francisco.

The anonymous apologue was widely distributed and read in California in the weeks after Terry's death. Many accepted it as true. While it bore the name of no author, a comparison of the prose with the Hill-Sharon letters leads one to believe that Sarah Althea had a large hand in its composition. She must have had editorial assistance with the syntax and style, but the rhetoric is unmistakable. Speaking of Field's reference to Sarah Althea as "an abandoned woman and one without character," the pamphleteers regale us with this:

A woman without character! Is there no defense for the women of the country from such vile and contemptible slanderers? Can a man, even a Justice of the Supreme Court of the United States, traduce the characters of the wives and widows of true and honorable men for the sole purpose of venting a spite and malignity which a devil would be ashamed to own thus with impunity? If memory fails not and the records have been correctly read the hired minions and emissaries of

William Sharon, backed by his millions of wealth and the influence with which they naturally endowed him, failed to bring one word of credible proof against her or to imprint one stain upon her name as a wife throughout the tedious years of litigation she had with him.

The Supreme Court that decided In re Neagle

XXXVIII

IN RE NEAGLE

A lawyer has no business with the justice or injustice of the cause he undertakes. . . . The justice or injustice of the cause is to be decided by the judge.

Samuel Johnson, quoted in Boswell's *Journey to the Hebrides*

The State of California appealed to the highest Court in the land from the judgment of Sawyer and his colleagues, and it became the task of Field's own Court, the Supreme Court of the United States, to pass on the elemental question: should Neagle's deed be weighed by the state authorities and a jury of San Joaquin Valley citizens, or was he as a federal officer entitled to the full immunity vested in him by Sawyer's opinion? The gravity of the question moved the justices to grant two full days for argument, March 4 and 5, 1890.

Field's influence had already provided Neagle with eminent local counsel in the circuit court in San Francisco. Now, in the final test in the Supreme Court, the old fox outdid himself in enlisting support for his imperiled protector. Field bespoke Joseph H. Choate of New York, probably the leading advocate of his time. Writing at the end of the nineteenth century, Francis L. Wellman called Choate "the idol of all court lawyers of recent years." The great lawyer gave his assistance (without fee) to W. H. H. Miller, the United States attorney general. He argued in support of Neagle. For California, Attorney General G. A. Johnson appeared.

Despite the gravity of the issue, the length of the argument, what the Court itself called "the elaborate character" of the briefs, the Court needed only five weeks for a decision. On April 14, 1890, Mr. Justice Miller delivered the majority opinion, two justices dissenting. He noted that "Mr. Justice Field did not sit at the hearing of this case and took no part in its decision."

Mr. Justice Miller was then in his seventy-fourth year. He had come to the Court from Iowa a year before Field. There was an intellectual affinity and personal comradeship between the two men. It showed in Miller's opinion. The majority opinion merits the same criticism as does Sawyer's: for them the issue is one of law, but the author went on for page after page rehearsing "the facts." There is a full recital of the history of the incidents "which led to the tragic event of the killing of Terry by the prisoner, Neagle." We are told about the Sharon-Hill lawsuits, and about the opinions of Judges

Deady and Sawyer, with their charges of fraud, perjury and forgery; the hair-pulling incident in the train on August 14, 1888; the scene in the courtroom on September 3, 1888 — of Sarah Althea's outburst, of Terry's passionate eruption, and the sentence of contempt. "From that time until his death, the denunciations by Terry and his wife of Mr. Justice Field were open, frequent and of the most malevolent character." After a catalogue of the Terrys' threats against Field and the precautionary steps taken by the government, Miller concluded:

> Without a more minute discussion of this testimony, it produces upon us the conviction of a settled purpose on the part of Terry and his wife, amounting to a conspiracy, to murder Justice Field. And we are quite sure that if Neagle had been merely a brother or a friend of Judge Field, traveling with him, and aware of all the previous relations of Terry to the judge — as he was — of his bitter animosity, his declared purpose to have revenge even to the point of killing him, he would have been justified in what he did in defense of Mr. Justice Field's life and possibly his own.

When Mr. Justice Miller had concluded his description of the facts, the guilt of Sarah Althea, Terry's murderous rage and Neagle's heroism were there for all America to see, narrated in language adopted and approved by five justices of the United States Supreme Court, and eternally encapsulated for history. However irrelevant this may have been to the basic question before the Court, this description of the facts served an important historical purpose. From that moment, in the public mind, Terry was a bloodthirsty bully; Sarah Althea, a whore, a perjurer and a forger. The two had planned to murder the stalwart Judge Field in vengeance for his judicial revelation of their characters, and their purpose was thwarted only by the heroic act of a selfless and dedicated peace officer carrying out duties assigned him by the highest authority in the land. These flies were forever fixed in the amber of history.

When the majority opinion finally turned to the law applicable to the case, it echoed Sawyer, and concluded:

> The result at which we have arrived upon this examination is that in the protection of the person and life of Mr. Justice Field while in the discharge of his official duties, Neagle was authorized to resist the attack of Terry upon him; that Neagle was correct in the belief that without prompt action on his part the assault of Terry upon the judge would have ended in the death of the latter; that such being his well-founded belief, he was justified in taking the life of Terry, as the only means of preventing the death of the man who was intended to be his victim; that in taking the life of Terry, under the circumstances, he was acting under the authority of the law of the United States, and was justified in so doing; and that he is not liable to answer in the courts of California on account of his part in that transaction.

In reaching this end, the Court relied on cases where army recruiting officers were attacked, election officials assaulted, the mails imperiled and officials protecting timberlands from depredation were shot down. A leading constitutional scholar has said that the Court's sanction of Neagle's deed "was the broadest interpretation yet given to the implied powers of the National Government under the Constitution."

But this result, so crystal-clear, so seemingly just, so appropriate, to the majority, was not satisfactory to Chief Justice Fuller or to Mr. Justice Lamar. The dissent of Lucius Quintus Cincinnatus Lamar should have been no surprise. He was a Mississippian who had left a seat in Congress to join the Confederate Army. He rose to a colonelcy, but resigned to become Jefferson Davis's special emissary to Russia. After the war, he served in Congress, became United States senator from Mississippi and Cleveland's secretary of the interior until he went to the high Court in 1888. It has been said that "[p]lacing Lucius Quintus Cincinnatus Lamar on the Supreme Court in 1888 must have been as politically unlikely in 1868 as nominating Thurgood Marshall for the Court would have seemed in 1947." He was a States-Rights man to the end, and his dissent in *Neagle* is regarded by scholars of constitutional law as the classic, if valedictory, denial that powers belonging to Congress, but not exercised, were by implicaton vested in the executive branch of the federal system. To Lamar, such powers belonged to the states.

Fuller's vote was a surprise. Like Lamar, he was new to the bench, although he was chief justice. He was a Down-Easter from Maine, who had made a notable professional career in Chicago. When Cleveland made him chief justice in 1888, many felt the post should have gone to Field, despite his age. The same people muttered when Fuller joined the rebel Lamar in dissent, that his vote was based not so much on deep constitutional convictions, as on his resentment against Field, who is said to have received him in the Court with a show of condescension.

The dissenters took no view of the guilt or innocence of Neagle or of the characters of Terry or Sarah Althea, holding those things immaterial to the critical issue of law, and urging that for the exercise of his clear right and duty to protect the person of Field, Neagle was "answerable to the courts of California, and to them alone." On constitutional grounds they argued there was no authority in the federal court to exonerate Neagle.

> *The gravamen of this case is in the assertion that Neagle slew Terry in pursuance of a law of the United States. He who claims to have committed a homicide by authority must show the authority. If he claims the authority of law, then what law? And if a law, how came it to be a law? Somehow and somewhere it must have had an origin. Is it a law because of the existence of a special and private authority issued from one of the executive departments? So in almost these words it is claimed in this case. Is it a law because of some constitutional investiture of sovereignty in the persons of judges who carry that sovereignty with them wherever they may go? Because of some power inherent in the judiciary to create for others a rule or law of conduct outside of legislation which shall extend to the death penalty? So also, in this case,* in totidem verbis, *it is claimed. We dissent from both these claims. There can be no such law from either of those sources. The right claimed must be traced to legislation of Congress, else it cannot exist.*

The two dissenters concluded that Neagle should be turned over to the authorities of

> *San Joaquin County, California; and we are the less reluctant to express this conclusion, because we cannot permit ourselves to doubt*

that the authorities of the State of California are competent and will-
ing to do justice; and that even if the appellee had been indicted, and
had gone to trial upon this record, God and his country would have
given him a good deliverance.

With these stirring words the Sharon-Hill-Terry-Neagle litigation ground
to its final end. For Field, there was grim satisfaction and not, let us hope,
revenge. For Neagle, freedom. For Terry and Sharon, no man can know. But
for the pathetic figure of Sarah Althea, the road still led down, down to new
humiliation, poverty and finally, madness.

In re *Neagle* is regarded as a monument in constitutional law. It affirms
the critical proposition that an officer of the United States acting under federal law cannot be prosecuted under state law for a state crime committed
in the course of his duty. Equally important — and novel — was the majority's conclusion that the operative federal "law" under which the accused
federal agent acts, need not be a valid congressional enactment; an act done
in obedience to a federal regulation, or even to a directive from the head of
a govenment department (e.g., the attorney general) is still immunized from
state jurisdiction.

Whether the Court would have reached this conclusion if Field's interest, honor and reputation were not involved is an interesting speculation,
which is left for the professional exegetes — the judges and law professors
who have drenched the subject with torrents of judicial and scholarly ink,
poured over cases involving game wardens, revenue agents, customs officers, United States marshals, army privates, etc. — all seeking safety from
state law by invoking the name of Neagle.

When the Supreme Court had spoken, the controversy ended for all
but the noisy little band of diehard Terry partisans in California. Everybody
else was tired of Sarah Althea and Terry and Sharon. Even the press was happy to see the affair laid to rest. Terry and Sarah Althea had been covered with
final obloquy; their guilt bore the *imprimatur* of the noblest of American institutions, what de Tocqueville had rightly called "the head of all known tribunals."

History, Carlyle tells us, is "a distillation of rumor." As late as 1912,
two of the most eminent historians of California repeated as "history" some
of the persistent nonsense that clouds the shooting of Terry. Elijah R. Kennedy, the respected author of *The Contest for California in 1861,* writes that
Terry "was shot to death by Special Officer Nagle *[sic]* who had been detailed
to guard Justice Field of the United States Supreme Court and who saw Terry
approaching the Justice with the evident and undoubted purpose of shooting
him." Bancroft, revered by so many as the leading historian of the West, writing in 1912 on the same point, says:

A judge of the United States Supreme Court, Stephen J. Field, sitting
in San Francisco and Los Angeles, feared assault from a former
judge of the Supreme Court of California, David S. Terry, employed
not the law but an attache of the court to attend and protect him.
Traveling up from the south on one occasion, it happened that the
two judges found themselves on the same train. Stopping to dine,
Terry finished, and was passing out by where Field was seated with
his man. Terry flipped his glove in Field's face. Whereupon Field's

man rose in his seat and shot Terry dead. The slayer, some would say murderer, was arrested, and after a form of trial was, of course, acquitted.

The truth, according to Oscar Wilde, is never pure and seldom simple. Terry's "evident and undoubted purpose," as seen by Kennedy and Bancroft's "flip of the glove," are foam-balls on Matthew Arnold's "vast Mississippi of falsehood called history."

Sarah Althea's grave

XXXIX

HOW SARAH ALTHEA
WENT MAD AND DIED

Alas! I have no hope nor health,
Nor peace within, nor calm around.
Percy Bysshe Shelley, "Stanzas Written in Dejection, Near Naples"

Wagstaff wrote his "authorized" *Life of David S. Terry* in 1892, too early to record the dismal story of Sarah Althea's decline into final madness. Had he waited a year or two, the biographer could have turned his lens on the most pathetic of the personalities in the drama of Terry's life, a creature dissolving in misery and madness.

After Terry's death, Sarah Althea lived on in Fresno. By now, litigation had become a way of life for her. Son Clinton saw in Sarah Althea the instrument of his father's humiliation and death; he openly despised her and refused her money. She quarreled with him with her usual acerbity over the proceeds of Terry's insurance. As a matter of course, she sued him in the local courts. Next, she attacked C. G. Sayle, the administrator of Terry's estate, for his refusal to give her money. In her pursuit of Terry's meager assets, she employed a Fresno lawyer, N. C. Caldwell, but soon she was in an imbroglio with him and slapped his face in a courtroom. To the newspapermen, delighted with the reappearance of their favorite courthouse wildcat, she announced that Caldwell had made improper advances to her. Then she assaulted Caldwell in his office and the lawyer had her forcibly ejected. Of course, she charged him with assault. He was acquitted.

After this, her life became a frantic and senseless running back and forth between Fresno and San Francisco, on the pretense of important legal business. She would appear at the homes of former friends at strange and unconventional times, dunning them for money, embarrassing them with fanciful stories, relating imaginary conversations with her martyred husband. She filed a complaint with the San Francisco police that her room in a boardinghouse on Sutter Street had been burglarized and jewels "of great value" taken. She unceasingly harassed the constabulary over their reluctance to investigate the theft, to capture the thieves. The police officers treated her with special patience; they felt that the poor woman suffered from "hallucinations."

By February 1892, the consensus was that Sarah Althea was "dangerously unbalanced." A local newspaper reported that "it now seems probable that the plaintiff in the famous Sharon-Hill litigation will end her days in an asylum for the insane. . . . Her mental disorder shows itself at times by a mark-ed aversion to her known friends. In addition to this, her thoughts seem con-centrated upon the single idea that she is constantly attended by hosts of spirits." Friends who sheltered her in a house on McAllister Street had to lock her in a room to keep her from prowling the streets. Her appearance was deteriorating. One could hardly recognize the *quondam* "famous Missouri beauty" in "this disheveled woman with care-lined features and unkempt hair streaked with gray." Grief, frustration, penury and want transformed the belle of Cape Girardeau, the auburn beauty who was the bright ornament of Mammy Pleasant's garden of pulchritude, into a furtive hag. In her lucid mo-ments she sought shelter with Mammy Pleasant in the Thomas Bell mansion.

The writers of *Bonanza Inn* describe how a reporter visited her as she was leaving the Bell house in company with Mammy for "a breath of air." After a ride in a cable car, the three sat down to rest on the steps of a residence. The reporter wrote:

> *There, in the pale light of the gas lamp on the corner, sat the woman whose name at one time was familiar to the whole civilized world, and who has had more sensational experiences in the short space of about eight years than perhaps any other woman alive.*

Mammy Pleasant remained faithful. She fed and housed her (at Tom Bell's expense), bought her new clothes, tried to restore her health. Vigilant newspapermen surprised Sarah Althea in some strange antics that made good copy. She stood in a downpour at Kearny and Post streets and waded knee-deep through the puddles. Next she was detected trying to get credit in a restaurant for a watch. Ambrose Bierce, San Francisco's angry man and town crier, noted in his column in the *Examiner:*

> *The male Californian — idolater of sex and proud of abasement at the feet of his own female — has now a fine example of the results entailed by his unnatural worship. Mrs. Terry, traipsing the streets, uncommonly civic, problematically harmless but indubitably daft, is all his own work, and he ought to be proud of her.*

At length, even the devoted Mammy Pleasant gave up on Sarah Althea. The black lady appeared before San Francisco's insanity commissioners and put her signature to a petition to have Sarah Althea Terry committed to an institution for the care of the insane. On March 9, 1892, a frightened and disheveled Sarah Althea appeared in court for a hearing. The *Morning Call* had its man in court, along with reporters from every other local paper, and a throng of spectators. The *Call* wrote:

> *As she appeared in the courtroom she was a picture of woe. Her rai-ment was in a wretchedly dilapidated condition, her hair unkempt and her eyes glassy and staring. Even the curious spectators, hard-ened to such scenes, were touched with the sadness of this one.*

The *Chronicle* wrote:

> *The poor woman, broken in spirit and mind had her hearing before Judge Levy, sitting in Judge Lawler's courtroom, his own being too small to accommodate the crowd that had gathered. . . . Mammy Pleas-ant appeared at once as complainant and friend, and of all the peo-ple present, male and female, was the only one who showed any sym-pathy for the demented creature.*

"Hush! Hush!" "Mammy" Pleasant and Sarah Althea at the competency hearing

Called to the stand in support of her application, Mammy Pleasant described the mental aberrations of her protégée, including imaginary conversations with spirits, especially with the shade of Judge Terry. A reporter-witness recounted Sarah Althea's strange and irrational behavior. A Scottish-trained psychiatrist (in the insensitve terminology of the time, a "commissioner of insanity") expressed the professional opinion that she was insane. But, even in her downtrodden state, under the sour cross she bore, the veteran courtroom warrior asserted herself. She demanded the right to cross-examine. When it was granted, she went at the doctor with the same panache with which she had enlivened so many courtrooms:

Sarah: *And do you think, doctor, I ought to be sent to an insane asylum?*

Doctor: *I do, most assuredly, Mrs. Terry.*

Sarah: *Well, doctor, don't you think that if you were examined pretty closely, some of these people would believe that you ought to be there?*

There was a murmur of approbation in the room, and on this note, her last forensic triumph, Sarah Althea was pronounced insane and committed to the Stockton State Hospital for the Insane. It is recorded that among those who witnessed Sarah Althea's humiliation was her old adversary, "General" Barnes. He explained to the press that he had come to observe "the last scene of the last act in the legal history of a case that has wrecked the lives and reputations of many people."

Faithful to the end, Mammy Pleasant accompanied Sarah Althea to the train. When the sad creature tried to address the people on the station platform, the black lady soothed her and led her to a seat in the train that conveyed her to her last refuge, out of the world that had lain in ruins about her since Lathrop.

STRUGGLE AGAINST GOING INTO THE CAR.

Sarah Althea on her way to Stockton Asylum

What was left of Sarah Althea lingered in the Stockton hospital until February 14, 1937. She survived all the other actors in the Sharon-Hill litigation. Field died in 1899, and Mammy Pleasant in 1904. She was completely forgotten, even by the San Francisco reporters who had once relished her outbursts. A year before her death, Evelyn Wells, a newspaper reporter, became her first visitor in twenty years. During the interview, Sarah Althea's mind moved in and out of focus with reality and the times. She asked after people long dead; she stated she had been married to Abraham Lincoln and General Grant; she described her life with Terry, and the precise details of his death; and she recounted the story of her "marriage contract" with Sharon. Yet, even at the end, Sarah Althea retained some of the airs and the mystery of decades ago. According to Wells,

> There still hung over her, even in those later years, a perfume of desireability, as of a withered rose pressed in a book.
>
> I tried in vain to get her true age from her. No one had ever found it out.
>
> "And how old were you," I would ask, "when you married Terry?"
>
> The withered cheeks of the Rose of Sharon would show ghosts of dimples.
>
> "Oh, I was old enough to get married," she would answer teasingly.
>
> I never did find out.

*The Female Department of Stockton State Hospital, where Sarah Althea lived for
45 years until her death in 1937*

She died in the Stockton hospital on February 14, 1937. By the charity
of Terry's granddaughter, Cornelia Terry McClure, and some local attorneys
in Stockton, who recalled with respect the memory of the unfortunate judge,
Sarah Althea was buried in the Terry family plot in the rural cemetery at
Stockton.

A BIBLIOGRAPHICAL SKETCH

WHEN I HAD FINISHED the manuscript of this book, it was so festooned with footnotes that some advance readers suggested that the footnotes hindered rather than helped the "general" readers. I concluded that they were right and that I had fallen into the common error of the lawyer-author, who (to paraphrase Kipling) wraps his work in footnotes "as a beggar would enfold himself in the purple of emperors." Since this book is aimed at the "general" reader who reads for pleasure and not at historians or Ph.D. candidates, the footnotes have come out. But I felt some need to furnish my readers with a guide to the literature of the five decades in California history that I have tried to portray, and from which I have drawn my facts.

As I have told you, the facts related in the narrative, however paradoxical, are the fully-authenticated truth. For those who would like to read more about the fascinating people in my story, I am identifying in this note my principal sources.

The events that happened in San Francisco in the period 1846–1906, from the American Annexation to the Great Earthquake, offer the researcher vast riches. Few cities have stimulated such literary effusion. From its earliest days to the present, the Bay City has inspired authors, poets and historians. For the early history of San Francisco, it is well to begin with Hubert Howe Bancroft's monumental *History of California* (San Francisco: The Bancroft Co., 1884–1890), especially volumes VI and VII. Bancroft himself was a virtual historical industry; he operated a massive historical publishing project employing dozens of researchers and assistants. By 1900, he had personally interviewed everybody of any consequence in California history. Herbert Asbury's *The Barbary Coast* (New York: Garden City Pub., 1933) is an engrossing study of the seamy underside of early San Francisco. Frank Soule's *Annals of San Francisco* (New York: Appleton, 1854), fortified with fascinating contemporary engravings, tries hard to convey the image of a city which had dragged itself out of the mud and imposed civilization on the Bay area in a mere five years. Of course, events proved him wrong. The best way to glean the quality of life and the concerns of the early San Franciscans is to study the day-to-day newspaper accounts, particularly of the *Alta California,* the *Call,* the *Bulletin,* and the *Examiner.*

There are at least two full-length biographies of David S. Terry, the chief anti-hero of our tale. First is A. E. Wagstaff's *Life of David S. Terry,* first printed in San Francisco in 1892; it is a typical nineteenth century *apologia* by an admiring friend trying his best to rub away the tarnish, and it must be read as a period piece by connoisseurs of literary rococo. Wagstaff's book was reprinted in 1971 (South Hackensack, N.J.: Rothman Reprints), with a piquant introduction by Eleazar Lipsky, a New York lawyer. Titled "Due Process for the Dead," it concludes with a slashing polemic judgment that Terry was foully done to death, with Field's complicity. The other treatment of Terry's career is A. Russell Buchanan's *Life of David S. Terry,* unhappily subtitled *Duelling Judge* (San Marino, Ca.: Huntington Library Publications, 1956). This is a serious and scholarly work, partly doctoral thesis, partly biographical essay. It smells slightly of the lamp and is not for the "general" reader.

The Bancroft Library collection of materials contains unpublished "Notes prepared for Mr. Klette," written by J. W. Terry, a nephew of David Terry, who had met his uncle in 1888, and who practiced law in Galveston until his death in 1936. The Bancroft collection also includes several autograph letters, among them Terry's memorable letter to the Vigilance Committee. The original duel letters are in the collection of The Society of California Pioneers. The best example of Terry's pompous literary style is found in his diatribe entitled *The Character and Career of Stephen J. Field.* Terry's more reasonable moods are reflected in his judicial opinions, reported in the early volumes of the *California Reports.* Ex parte *Newman* (9 Cal. 502, 1858) is especially interesting and prophetic, with Terry arguing the side of freedom and conscience, and his future enemy, Field, dissenting with a strict constructionist point of view.

David Broderick's career is provender for every history of California in the nineteenth century. Josiah Royce, Gertrude Atherton, and H. H. Bancroft, the leading chroniclers of the period in California history, all extol the virtues of the tempestuous Gael and bemoan his early death. There is also *A Senator of the Fifties* (San Francisco: A. M. Robertson, 1911), a full-length biography of Broderick, by one Jeremiah Lynch, an admiring contemporary. But Lynch's work is adulatory treacle, anti-critical and smothered by a prose style that went out with gaslight and the parlor stereopticon. Anyone seeking more light on Broderick's mottled history should examine James O'Meara's *Broderick and Gwin* (San Francisco: 1881). There is a description of the Terry-Broderick duel in Don C. Seitz's *Famous American Duels* (New York: Crowell, 1929) that is a masterly vignette, but concerned as it is with a single event in Terry's long, colorful and chaotic career, it does not come close to describing the lives of the two adversaries.

For those interested in the accomplishments of the Vigilance Committee, there is Alan Valentine's *Vigilante Justice* (New York: Reynal, 1956). Best of all, there are the contemporary accounts which convey a vivid sense of the desperation and urgency behind the popular support of the vigilance movement. The Bancroft Library at Berkeley has a superb collection of Vigilance Committee memorabilia, including the original subscription agreements and many of the original notes and letters generated by the committee itself. From them one senses not only the passions that ruled the actors but also the physical environment in which the drama was played out. Many photographs in Fardon's *San Francisco Album* (1856) were made during the actual operations of the committee.

A good introduction to the flavor of San Francisco in the 1880's is derived from Julia Altrocchi's *The Spectacular San Franciscans* (New York: Dutton, 1949) and from Oscar Lewis and Carroll D. Hall's *Bonanza Inn* (New York: Knopf, 1946). But the highest yield in understanding the character of the city during that period is from the city's daily and weekly newspapers. This is especially true on subjects relating to the Sharon divorce trial, which was given detailed front-page, day-to-day coverage for years.

There are available biographies of Senator Sharon, Sarah Althea and "Mammy" Pleasant. There are countless magazine articles and newspaper pieces on all the major events described in the book. Judge Robert H. Kroninger's *Sarah and the Senator* (Berkeley: Howell-North), published as recently as 1964, is a witty and charming portrayal of the demented trollop who finally destroyed Terry, but its compass is necessarily narrow. The full story needs more reach. A novelized account of Sarah Althea by Eleazar Lipsky, Terry's champion, *The Devil's Daughter* (New York: Meredith Press, 1969), is more television soap opera than a *roman à clef.*

Sarah and the Senator and *Bonanza Inn,* both mentioned above, afford good studies of William Sharon and of the divorce proceedings themselves. All the participants in the Sharon-Hill litigation are deliciously caricatured in a series of cartoons in Ambrose Bierce's *Wasp.* Helen Holdredge's *Mammy Pleasant* (New York: Putnam, 1953) is an amusing attempt to deal with one of the most mystifying of our central characters, and to sort out the facts from the fantasies.

Mr. Justice Field is the subject of a felicitous biography by a noted scholar in Carl B. Swisher's *Stephen J. Field: Craftsman of the Law* (Washington, D.C.: Brookings Institute, 1930). But this fine work, while a scholarly critique of the subject's judicial attainments, does not tell the whole story of this many-sided man. A campaign biography of Field concocted by his admirers in 1882 has all the vices of purchased eulogy. The interested reader can form his own view of Field's character from Field's *Personal Reminiscences of Early Days in California,* which he caused to be privately printed in 1893 (reprinted, New York: De Capo Press, 1968). That volume also contains George C. Gorham's "The Story of the Attempted Assassination of Justice Field by a Former Associate on the Supreme Bench of California," which is a typical example of the hero worship Field inspired after Terry's death. In my view, Field's true character has never been fully explored, particularly with respect to his relations with Leland Stanford and the other banditti who ran California's railroads. Field's *apologia* for his economic views is expressed in his opinion in the *Slaughter House* cases, (16 Wall 36, 1873).

Finally, anyone interested in reading the full story of the divorce proceedings should read *Sharon* v. *Sharon,* 67 Cal. 185, 7 Pac. 456 (the state court's initial appellate decision); 75 Cal. 1, 16 Pac. 345 (affirming the divorce decree but reducing the alimony and setting aside the award of attorney's fees); and 79 Cal. 633, 22 Pac. 26 (reversing Judge Sullivan's decision *in toto,* and remanding the case for retrial). At the decisive federal level, see *Sharon* v. *Hill,* 26 Fed 337 (decisions of Judges Deady and Sawyer declaring the marriage contract void), and 36 Fed. 337 (Field's decision, in essence, affirming and reviving the decree of the lower court, which triggered Sarah Althea's fatal outburst in the courtroom). Field's opinion on Terry's contempt, In re

Terry, 36 Fed. 419, was affirmed by the Supreme Court in 128 U.S. 289. In re *Neagle,* in which the Supreme Court tried to tell the whole story, is reported at 135 U.S. 1, the opinion that launched me in 1932 on the half-century journey that now ends.

Here is a further list of useful books on the period:

Atherton, Gertrude. *California, An Intimate History.* New York: Harper, 1914.

Bancroft, Hubert Howe. *Retrospection, Political* and *Personal.* New York: The Bancroft Co., 1912.

De Voto, Bernard. *The Year of Decision—1846.* Boston: Little Brown and Co., 1943.

Dobie, Charles Caldwell. *San Francisco, A Pageant.* New York: D. Appleton-Century, 1933.

Jackson, Joseph Henry, ed. *The Western Gate, a San Francisco Reader.* New York: Farrar Straus and Young, 1952.

Kennedy, Elijah R. *The Contest for California.* Boston: Houghton Mifflin, 1912.

Kipling, Rudyard. *From Sea to Sea: Letters of Travel.* New York: Charles Scribner's Sons, 1889.

Paul, Arnold N. "Lucius Quintus Cincinnatus Lamar," in *The Justices of the United States Supreme Court 1789–1969.* New York and London: Chelsea House Publishers in association with R. R. Bowker Company, 1969.

Royce, Josiah. *California from the Conquest in 1846 to the Second Vigilance Committee in San Francisco.* Boston: Houghton Mifflin, 1899.

Truman, Benjamin C. *The Field of Honor.* New York: Fords, Howard, and Hulbert, 1884.

As to newspapers, the best accounts of the vigilance movement, the Terry-Broderick duel, and the Sharon-Hill litigation and its terrible sequelae are in the contemporary accounts printed in the *Daily Alta California.*

ACKNOWLEDGMENTS

THE PREPARATION of this book would have been an almost futile endeavor without the assistance of Steven E. Levitsky. He searched out source materials, located and prepared the illustrations and made some valuable suggestions about the text.

I am indebted to my secretary, Roberta Bieber, who assiduously and efficiently discharged the task of translating my scribbling into a legible manuscript.

I am grateful for the editorial suggestions of Jean Bradford and Carol Bowers of Copley Books.

The late John Howell, San Francisco's legendary bibliophile, not only supplied many of the books, pictures and newspapers that I have used, but also gave me a number of useful points about the colorful past of the city.

Above all, I owe a boundless debt to my wife, Eleanor, whose patient forbearance and encouragement have made this work possible.

ILLUSTRATIONS AND
THEIR SOURCES

INDEX